KEEP THE ORDINANCES

ACTS THAT DIVIDE: PRACTICES THAT UNITE

JERALD L. MANLEY

Keep the Ordinances was written from the perspective of nearly six decades of study and interaction as a Baptist pastor with the practical impact of doctrinal beliefs on churches and in the lives of believers and non-believers. The innumerable articles and books that have been read over those decades undoubtedly have influenced my choices for wording, as have the uncountable conversations and discussions on this topic that have occurred over these years. A diligent effort was made to provide the proper and deserved credit for thoughts and quotes that are known to have originated with someone else. It is not my intention to claim originality for that labor which others have given.

The Authorized Version, commonly called the King James Version, is the source for all of my Biblical quotations.

Biblical references in citations from other authors are their choices and must be their responsibility.

Alas! and did my Savior bleed,
And did my Sovereign die?
Would He devote that sacred head
For such a worm as I?

Was it for crimes that I had done
He groaned upon the tree?
Amazing pity, grace unknown,
And love beyond degree!

Well might the sun in darkness hide
And shut his glories in
When God, the mighty Maker, died
For man the creature's sin.

Thus might I hide my blushing face
While His dear cross appears,
Dissolve my heart in thankfulness,
And melt mine eyes to tears.

But drops of grief can ne'er repay
The debt of love I owe;
Here, Lord, I give myself away,
'Tis all that I can do.

Isaac Watts, 1674–1748

DEDICATION

In 1999, the LORD of the harvest brought a young Texan to the church that I pastor. In the following years, he has become my fellowservant and co-laborer in the ministry. In ways unmistakable, the LORD of the harvest has confirmed that he would be the man to work with me and to succeed me when the LORD deems it time.

He is settled in the faith and in the doctrines and practices of Baptists. *Keep the Ordinances* is dedicated to Jody Alan Wolf.

Jerald L. Manley

CONTENTS

CONTENTS (continued)

PREFACE

Though the LORD Jesus intended the two ordinances that He designed for His church to be acts that would *unite* His followers, the departure from the Scriptural parameters for those two ordinances by professing followers has transformed baptism and Communion into acts that *divide* Christianity. Nearly every soteriological doctrinal division that affects Christians has a direct relationship either with baptism or Communion or with both ordinances.

The study of the Biblical doctrines of these ordinances must reference the errors that have entered Christianity with the resultant altering of the purpose, the timing, even the mode of baptism and with the intention of changing the purpose and the substance of the elements placed on the Table of the LORD. However, this consideration will concentrate primarily on the Scriptural declarations rather than engage in a detailed refutation of the errors. The presentation of the revealed truth of Scripture is the best defense against error.

Baptism and Communion are not human-ly derived rites; the Head of the church instituted them and, as He did so, He established the means, manner, method, and meaning of each ordinance. His purposes for the ordinances and their relationships to the church needs to be recognized.

The church (the local assembly of believers and not a denominational organization or a mystical, ethereal, unassembled body) that the LORD Jesus instituted exists in this world to bring glory to GOD the Father through GOD the Son by the ministry of GOD the Holy Spirit. That truth is particularly emphasized in the Epistle to the church at Ephesus. The assembled believers have the purpose of working together to bring glorify GOD.

> Ephesians 3:14 For this cause I bow my knees **unto the Father of our Lord Jesus Christ**, 15 Of whom the whole family in heaven and earth is named, 16 That he would grant you, according to the riches of his glory, to be **strengthened with might by his Spirit** in the inner man; 17 **That Christ may dwell in your hearts by faith**; that ye, being rooted and grounded in love, 18 May be able to comprehend with all saints what *is* the breadth, and length, and depth, and height; 19 And to know the love of Christ, which passeth knowledge, that ye might be filled with all the fulness of God. 20 **Now unto him that is able to do exceeding abundantly above all that we ask or think, according to the power that worketh in us,** 21 **Unto him** *be* **glory in the church by Christ Jesus throughout all ages, world without end. Amen.**

The individual believer brings glory to the

Father by being fruitful. The LORD Jesus explained, "Herein is my Father glorified, that ye bear much fruit; so shall ye be my disciples" (John 15:8). This declaration is the summation of His teaching the disciples as to the process by which the believer is brought to fruitfulness. The LORD began by revealing how essential it is that the believer bears fruit as He speaks of the unfruitful branch being removed.

> John 15:1 I am the true vine, and my Father is the husbandman. 2 Every branch in me that beareth not fruit he taketh away: and every *branch* that beareth fruit, he purgeth it, that it may bring forth more fruit. 3 **Now ye are clean through the word which I have spoken unto you.** 4 Abide in me, and I in you. As the branch cannot bear fruit of itself, except it abide in the vine; no more can ye, except ye abide in me. 5 I am the vine, ye *are* the branches: He that abideth in me, and I in him, the same bringeth forth much fruit: for without me ye can do nothing. 6 If a man abide not in me, he is cast forth as a branch, and is withered; and men gather them, and cast *them* into the fire, and they are burned. 7 If ye abide in me, **and my words abide in you,** ye shall ask what ye will, and it shall be done unto you.

Notice that the LORD Jesus taught that each believer is considered individually regarding his fruitfulness—"every branch in me that beareth not fruit ... every branch that beareth fruit ..." The apostle presented this truth as a warning, "Who art thou that judgest another man's servant? to his own master he standeth or falleth. Yea, he shall be holden up: for God is able to make him stand." (Romans 14:4)

The emphasis is that while the church operates *united and collectively*, the believer functions *separately and individually*. This does not suggest or justify intentional isolation by a believer. The Saviour never sent one of His disciples on a solitary journey.[1] Though the believer is to a member of and serve through his church, each believer will answer to his LORD for himself regarding his personal fruitfulness.[2]

It is not within the scope of this study to examine extensively either the purging or the removal of the believer. However, it is necessary that attention is called to the statement of the LORD Jesus that the method required for the purging to produce fruitfulness[3] in the believer is the application of His words, "ye are clean through the word which I have spoken unto you." The word of GOD read and applied brings that cleansing.[4] This was also the testimony of the psalmist.

> Psalms 119:9 Wherewithal shall a young man cleanse his way? by taking heed *thereto* according to thy word. 10 With my whole heart have I sought thee: O let me not wander from thy commandments. 11 Thy word have I hid in mine heart, that I might not sin against thee.

The settled foundation for the life of the believer is the word of GOD. Scripture is the only base that will provide stability for living that pleases GOD. From the day of the creation of Adam, the only authority for humanity has been the word of GOD. The first temptation Satan dangled before man was the insinuation that the words of GOD might not be authoritative. While Eve was deceived by the subtleness of the suggestion, Adam was not; however, Adam deliberately ignored the command of GOD and accepted the invitation of Eve to eat of the forbidden fruit. The tactic of Satan was so successful that he has continued using the same techniques through the present hour.

All propositions of philosophy or theology that are advanced for human consideration must be judged by the standard of the word of GOD. It would be foolish for any believer credulously to accept the *multitudinous marauding machinations* proposed by Satan through his human mercenaries that swirl among humanity with their beguiling pro-posals without testing them against the truths of Scripture. The believer is commanded to compare philosophical and spiritual teachings with Scriptural teachings and warned to avoid that which does not conform to the word of GOD.

> 1 Thessalonians 5:21 Prove all things; hold fast that which is good.
>
> 1 John 4:1 Beloved, believe not every spir-it, but try the spirits whether they are of God: because many false prophets are gone out into the world.
>
> Isaiah 8:20 To the law and to the testimo-ny: if they speak not according to this word, *it is* because *there is* no light in them.

We are not to attempt to find *something* good within a philosophy so that we might redeem it; instead, we are to recognize the precept that whatever conflicts with Scripture is without light. Those that set aside the word

of GOD and follow the words of other men or
the expressions of Satan are described as
those who are devoid of wisdom.

> Jeremiah 8:9 The wise *men* are ashamed,
> they are dismayed and taken: lo, they
> have rejected the word of the LORD; and
> what wisdom *is* in them?

Substituting the traditions and doctrines
originating in the hearts of men or insinuated
there by Satan for the commandments that
GOD has given is to elevate the human mind
above the mind of GOD.

> Mark 7:7 Howbeit in vain do they worship
> me, teaching *for* doctrines the command-
> ments of men. 8 For laying aside the
> commandment of God, ye hold the tradi-
> tion of men, *as* the washing of pots and
> cups: and many other such like things ye
> do. 9 And he said unto them, Full well ye
> reject the commandment of God, that ye
> may keep your own tradition. ... 13 Mak-
> ing the word of God of none effect through
> your tradition, which ye have delivered:
> and many such like things do ye.

The effect of favorably comparing the humanistic traditions with the word of GOD or of
substituting any of those traditions for the
place of Scripture is to make the Bible of *none
effect.* Following the traditions of men is not
considered obedience to the commands of
GOD. Instead of a blessing for agreement with
GOD, there will be judgment for the disagreement with the word of GOD.

Comingling humanistic traditions and
Biblical revelation is to create a concoction in
which truth is diluted with poison. The result
is that the words of GOD are presented in a
corrupted fashion.[5]

When either baptism or Communion is incorporated into salvation, instead of producing blessing, the ordinance is corrupted so that it brings the curse of damnation. To the extent that a person places faith in either baptism or Communion for the removal of sin, to that extent the person is not trusting in the LORD Jesus for salvation, but is trusting in either baptism or Communion.

Understanding the significance, the purpose, the method, and the consequence of baptism and Communion is essential. The authority that establishes these issues must be exclusively the word of GOD.

The plea of this study is that believers should anchor themselves into the word of GOD and set their anchor deeply and permanently in the Bible, the Holy Scriptures of GOD.

> Isaiah 26:3 Thou wilt keep *him* in perfect peace, *whose* mind *is* stayed *on thee*: because he trusteth in thee. 4 Trust ye in the LORD for ever: for in the LORD JEHOVAH *is* everlasting strength:

¹ Mark 6:7 And he called *unto him* the twelve, and began to send them forth by two and two; and gave them power over unclean spirits;
Luke 10:1 After these things the Lord appointed other seventy also, and sent them two and two before his face into every city and place, whither he himself would come.
The LORD Jesus sent His disciples two and two so that their testimony might be received. John 8:17 It is also written in your law, that the testimony of two men is true.

² Romans 14:10 ... for we shall all stand before the judgment seat of Christ. 11 For it is written, *As* I live, saith the Lord, every knee shall bow to me, and every tongue shall confess to God. 12 So then every one of us shall give account of himself to God.

³ Fruitfulness consists of individual personal spiritual growth on the part of the believer *and* of the sowing of the seed of the word of GOD and the reaping of the results of that sowing.
Colossians 1:9 For this cause we also, since the day we heard *it*, do not cease to pray for you, and to desire that ye might be filled with the knowledge of his will in all wisdom and spiritual understanding; 10 That ye might walk worthy of the Lord unto all pleasing, **being fruitful in every good work, and increasing in the knowledge of God;** 11 Strengthened with all might, according to his glorious power, unto all patience and longsuffering with joyfulness; 12 Giving thanks unto the Father, which hath made us meet to be partakers of the inheritance of the saints in light: 13 Who hath delivered us from the power of darkness, and hath translated *us* into the kingdom of his dear Son: 14 In whom we have redemption through his blood, *even* the forgiveness of sins: 15 Who is the image of the invisible God, the firstborn of every creature: 16 For by him were all things created, that are in heaven, and that are in earth, visible and invisible, whether *they be* thrones, or dominions, or principalities, or powers: all things were created by him, and for him: 17 And he is before all things, and by him all things consist. 18 And he is the head of the body, the church: who is the beginning, the firstborn from the dead; that in all *things* he might have

the preeminence. 19 For it pleased *the Father* that in him should all fulness dwell; 20 And, having made peace through the blood of his cross, by him to reconcile all things unto himself; by him, *I say,* whether *they be* things in earth, or things in heaven.

1 Corinthians 3:6 I have planted, Apollos watered; but God gave **the increase.** 7 So then neither is he that planteth any thing, neither he that watereth; but God that giveth **the increase.**

2 Corinthians 9:10 Now he that ministereth seed to the sower both minister bread for *your* food, and multiply your seed sown, and **increase the fruits of your righteousness;)**

Ephesians 4:16 From whom the whole body fitly joined together and compacted by that which every joint supplieth, according to the effectual working in the measure of every part, maketh **increase of the body** unto the edifying of itself in love.

Philippians 1:11 Being filled with **the fruits of righteousness,** which are by Jesus Christ, unto the glory and praise of God.

Colossians 2:19 And not holding the Head, from which all **the body** by joints and bands having nourishment ministered, and knit together, **increaseth with the increase of God.**

⁴ This truth is found elsewhere in Scripture. John 17:17 Sanctify them through thy truth: thy word is truth.

Ephesians 5:26 That he might sanctify and cleanse it with the washing of water by the word, 27 That he might present it to himself a glorious church, not having spot, or wrinkle, or any such thing; but that it should be holy and without blemish.

Psalms 119:9 Wherewithal shall a young man cleanse his way? by taking heed *thereto* according to thy word.

⁵ 2 Corinthians 2:17 For we are not as many, which corrupt the word of God: but as of sincerity, but as of God, in the sight of God speak we in Christ.

2 Peter 2:1 But there were false prophets also among the people, even as there shall be false teachers among you, who privily shall bring in damnable heresies, even denying the Lord that bought them, and bring upon themselves swift destruction. 2 And many shall follow their pernicious ways; by reason of whom the way of

truth shall be evil spoken of. 3 And through covetousness shall they with feigned words make merchandise
of you: whose judgment now of a long time lingereth
not, and their damnation slumbereth not.

2 John 1:7 For many deceivers are entered into the
world, who confess not that Jesus Christ is come in the
flesh. This is a deceiver and an antichrist. 8 Look to
yourselves, that we lose not those things which we have
wrought, but that we receive a full reward. 9 Whosoever
transgresseth, and abideth not in the doctrine of
Christ, hath not God. He that abideth in the doctrine of
Christ, he hath both the Father and the Son. 10 If
there come any unto you, and bring not this doctrine,
receive him not into *your* house, neither bid him God
speed: 11 For he that biddeth him God speed is
partaker of his evil deeds.

INTRODUCTION

In this blending era when distinctives in doctrine and practice are intentionally and carefully minimized or deliberately and routinely ignored by the majority of religious entities; and therefore, are unknown to the wider religious community and to the general public at large, the necessity for clarity in the proclamation of those particular practices and doctrines that identify Baptists has never been more needful. When I entered the ministry nearly six decades ago, the basic doctrines and practices that have identified Baptists for nearly two millennia were *common knowledge* equally among the religious, the irreligious, and the antireligious of this nation and the western world.

The years of the participation by Baptist people in the ecumenicity of Fundamentalism and in the inclusivity of Cooperative Evangelism have served to erase this knowledge. Individually or separately, but especially as a combination, fundamentalism and cooperative evangelism require the commingling of divergent doctrines. The harmonious amalgamation of those who are being consolidated for the accomplishment of what is promoted as the best human means to achieve the *greater purpose* of saving souls prohibits the propagation of differences and permits only the discussion of agreements. Advancement of the *cause of Christ* was fanatically intended and fervently promised, but the cumulative evidence provided by an entire century of participation by a wide range of Christians demonstratively reveals that the western world is measurably influenced less by *the cause of Christ* after this organized intermingling than it was before the efforts were made.

The two programs of activities had different purposes in their formation even though they had the same philosophy of methodology. The Fundamentalists sought to bring glory to GOD by defending the deity of Jesus of Nazareth and the integrity of the Scriptures. The Cooperative Evangelists sought to bring glory to GOD by leading lost souls to salvation in Christ Jesus. Both ideologies depended upon a contrived and artificial association that would supposedly accomplish the desired purposes by producing numbers though this manufactured unification that would impress and change minds.

The structuring foundations of Fundamentalism were laid in the late 1800s by men representing mainline denominations, primarily Presbyterian ministers, Episcopalian bishops, and Methodist evangelists.[1] A great cause was required to persuade such divergent theologies to converge and to cooperate. The catalyst that precipitated the formation of fundamentalism was the perceived need to organize to oppose the infiltration of *modernism,* imported Nineteenth Century German rationalism, in denominational seminaries and universities.[2]

Those institutions and the denominational structure that those Fundamentalists passionately desired to salvage rapidly fell to the fierceness of the forces of infidelity and became apostate in defiance of the unified opposition.[3]

The unintended consequence of Fundamentalism was the infection of Baptists with the philosophy of doctrinal compromise for the greater good. The differences were removed from discussion so that the infiltration of rationalism could be identified and eliminated from the seminaries.

When Baalism needed to be opposed in Israel, the apostatizing Northern Kingdom, Elijah did not yoke himself with Obadiah. The Obadiah of Elijah's day was the governor of the house of King Ahab. While Obadiah feared the LORD greatly, it is evident that he feared Ahab even more, because though he sheltered and fed one hundred prophets of the LORD, he continued to serve in the employment of Ahab.[4]

Fundamentalism sought to achieve a victory over modernism through a united front assembled on the premise of compromised beliefs. To accomplish numerical strength, the early Fundamentalists agreed to base fellowship and cooperation on only five cardinal truths, which they described as the necessary and essential doctrines of Christianity. These became known as the *Fundamentals.*

1. The inspiration and infallibility of the Scriptures [The term inerrancy did not become a battlefield until the middle of the twentieth century.]
2. The deity and virgin birth of Jesus
3. The vicarious substitutionary death of Jesus
4. The literal physical resurrection of Jesus
5. The return of Christ

While it might be inferred from the inclusion of the phrase "vicarious substitutionary death" that the doctrine within soteriology of fundamentalism is that salvation is by grace through faith, that doctrine is not among the *fundamentals* around which the *fundamentalists* gathered. This omission is only one of the unexpected doctrinal exclusions.

Creation by the direct act of GOD was not incorporated into the Fundamentalist Creed; consequently, among the early fundamentalists were some men that were favorable toward at least considering the accommodation of theistic evolution, such as Benjamin Breckinridge Warfield and George Frederick Wright (Christian Darwinist). While others, such as William Jennings Bryan, considered evolution the epitome of the work of Satan.

Even the agreed *essentials* were not defined with extensive detail or explanation. This provided wide latitude in the understanding or application of each of the five *essential* doctrines. Actually, considerable nebulousness would be required to facilitate the union among Calvinists and Armenians, dispensationalists and covenant theologians, Baptists and Episcopalians (Anglicans), and other conflicting views such as that of B. B. Warfield, who was Professor of Theology at Princeton Seminary and who wrote strongly to expose the errors of Charles G. Finney, and George Frederick Wright, who had studied under the tutelage of Finney and who was the Professor of theology at Oberlin College.

When the series known as *The Fundamentals* was published between 1909 through 1915 in twelve volumes of paperback books, Baptists had more of a token representation than strong participation among the seventy-five original authors and in the sixty-four writers that were retained in the combined four-volume reprint of 1917.[5]

Perhaps, most bewilderingly, among the writers included in *The Fundamentals* was Robert Speer.[6] Why this man would be included is a mystery. He had played a vital role in the formation of the Federal Council of Churches (later becoming identified as the National Council of Churches) in 1908. He was instrumental in the adoption of a progressive social agenda by the Presbyterian Church of America in 1910 that the conservatives in the denomination strongly resisted. He seems to be the epitome of those that the Fundamentalists opposed and exposed; even so, he was included in both the 1909 printings *and* the 1917 re-publication of *The Fundamentals*. Inclusivism creates some strange situations of toleration—always for the greater good, of course.

Though the movement did not begin with

Baptists and did not have strong Baptist involvement in the earliest days, men who identify themselves as Baptists have become so identified with fundamentalism and cooperative evangelism in the subsequent years that the impression has developed that these two movements are the essence of Baptistic thought. This impression is evident in the minds of both the public and religious communities. Sadly, this has become the accepted common understanding of the majority of Baptists at the beginning of the Twenty-first Century.

Fundamentalist Baptists William Bell Riley, T. T. Shields, Curtis Lee Laws, and J. Frank Norris (among others) brought their fellow Baptists into Fundamentalism in the 1920s. Their influence was such that by the middle of the Twentieth Century, Independent Baptists (in particular) predominately identified themselves as Fundamentalists. This alignment has naturally led to the de-emphasis of Baptist distinctives, because Fundamentalism is by its nature the emphasis on areas of agreement and the downgrading of areas of disagreement.

Fundamentalism led to the development of several non-denominational Bible schools and churches that devoted their existence to propagating the essentials and minimizing the non-essentials. The inherent danger in this philosophy is that Scripture does not grant the authority to any individual to determine which of the doctrines of Scripture are to be deemed *unimportant* and, therefore, safely ignored. On the contrary, it would seem that the LORD Jesus warned against this specific division of commandments.

> Matthew 5:19 Whosoever therefore shall break one of these least commandments, and shall teach men so, he shall be called the least in the kingdom of heaven: but whosoever shall do and teach *them*, the same shall be called great in the kingdom of heaven.

Is that not the essence of the warning that is found twice repeated in Deuteronomy?

> 4:2 Ye shall not add unto the word which I command you, neither shall ye diminish *ought* from it, that ye may keep the commandments of the LORD your God which I command you. ... 12:32 What thing soever I command you, observe to do it: thou shalt not add thereto, nor diminish from it.

David realized that not to obey all of the commands of GOD would lead to shame.

> Psalms 119:6 Then shall I not be ashamed, when I have respect unto all thy commandments.

While a given command or doctrine might not be essential to salvation, there are no extraneous commands or doctrines in the word of GOD. The idea of labeling certain Bible doctrines as essential and other teachings in Scripture as non-essential is not countenanced in Scripture and is a human invention *or* a satanic suggestion incorporated by humanity.

Once this barrier of separation over doctrinal differences has effectively been removed and certain of the elements of the confessions of faith have been declared non-essentials, the pathway is cleared for an ever-widening series of progressively larger conglomerations of purported Christian cooperation. Therefore, in a strange way, Fundamentalism, which was birthed from a desire of separation from liberalism, led quite naturally to the evolution of Cooperative Evangelism, which created the inclusion of liberalism. If it is deemed permissible, even noble, to cross over doctrinal boundaries in the name of defending the common faith, then it is surely acceptable to do so in the name of winning souls, since *there is no greater good* than the salvation of the lost or so the reasoning would be.

This second incentive to minimize the emphasis on distinctives, Cooperative Evangelism, is most identified with William Franklin (Billy) Graham, a Southern Baptist. The primary purpose of cooperative evangelism is supposedly to evangelize the lost. The cooperation pursued reaches over and beyond all of the doctrines and practices of the groups combining in the effort. From the beginning of Graham's crusades, the campaign efforts were organized very broadly to include the widest doctrinal base.[7] Eventually, this evangelistic broadness included the uniting of conservative and liberal Christians of all denominational persuasions, Protestant and Catholic. The de-emphasis on doctrine eroded the doctrinal distinctions of the cooperating groups.[8]

Graham and other Cooperative Evangelists conducted numbers of extensive citywide campaigns with thousands of attendees and hundreds of respondents. That some individuals were saved is not in dispute; however, the souls that the Cooperative Evangelists desired to *win to Jesus* were distributed among the mingled cooperating religious institutions for instruction in salvation and for discipleship. Consequently, the majority of the *converts* never bore fruit or else they were professors of Christianity who never were possessors of salvation.

Fundamentalism and Cooperative Evangelism have instilled a weakness of character into the popular Christian faith that has proven to be detrimental and not beneficial to genuine Christianity. The pursuit of numbers to sell the faith has progressively removed elements of the faith from the message. This has been especially injurious to Baptists, as it has softened the identification distinctives of being a Baptist to the point of nearly disappearing.

Efforts such as the *Moral Majority* founded by Independent Baptist Jerry Falwell and the *Purpose Driven Movement*[9] founded by Southern Baptist Rick Warren have further contributed to the demise of Baptist doctrines and practices among their followers.[10]

Falwell early identified himself as a Fundamentalist[11] and his television programming, large regional and national meetings, megachurch pastorate, and growing university positioned him to influence impressionable Baptists. His personal drift into increasingly less emphasis on doctrine and practice brought him into an open alignment with Convention Baptists before his death. The sincerity or salvation of neither man is questioned. Their energy and zeal is legendary. However, their ecumenical efforts have further weakened Baptist distinctiveness and encouraged an increasingly stronger non-denominational and inner-denominational approach.[12]

Two areas that historically have separated Baptists from both Protestantism and Catholicism are baptism and Communion. Major doctrinal areas are sacrificed when these two practices are surrendered or compromised. Unless Baptists reaffirm the uniqueness that identifies and distinguishes Baptists from other Christians, Baptists really have no reason for existing as Baptists. The distinctiveness that cause Baptists to exist has been sacrificed in the pursuit of unity.[13]

As the Nineteenth Century closed, Dr. J. B. Gambrell wrote: "As Baptist principles are peculiar to Baptists, every Baptist church, with all its appointments, from preacher to Sunday-school teacher, ought to stand, in the community where it holds forth the word, for something different from any other congregation. When a Baptist church thinks of itself as just one of the churches in a community, with no mission above others, it has become a very weak affair."[14]

Gambrell was correct. Baptists have been weakened by the compromise of both doctrine and practices by the association with interdenominational and non-denominational unions with fundamentalism and cooperative evangelism. Baptist strength lies in faithfulness to the word of GOD. *Keep that Ordinances* is the call for the return to a faithful reassertion of Baptist distinctiveness.

[1] Based upon the denominational affiliations of the sixty-four contributors to the 1909 publication of *The Fundamentals*, a twelve-volume set financed by Milton and Lyman Stewart.

[2] Modernists identified themselves as liberals by the middle of the last century and called themselves progressives by the beginning of this century.

[3] The acceptance of Higher Criticism by Charles Augustus Briggs and the subsequent conflict with the Princeton theologians brought the controversy within the Presbyterian Church front and center in the denomination. The early 1890s witnessed three separate heresy trials against Briggs; he survived the first two, but was defrocked in the third in 1893. This resulted in Briggs becoming an Episcopal priest in 1899. Henry Preserved Smith was convicted of heresy in 1894 and Arthur Cushman McGiffert resigned in 1898 to avoid a trial. By 1909, there was a battle over the attempt to ordain three Presbyterian ministers that refused to affirm the virgin birth.

In 1910, the General Assembly of the Presbyterian Church in the USA produced the a document entitled the Doctrinal Deliverance of 1910, declaring that the following doctrines are *necessary and essential* to the Christian faith:

"1. It is an essential doctrine of the Word of God and our Standards, that the Holy Spirit did so inspire, guide and move the writers of the Holy Scriptures as to keep them from error. Our Confession says [Chapter I, Section 10]: "The Supreme Judge, by whom all controversies of religion are to be determined, and all decrees of councils, opinions of ancient writers, doctrines of men, and private spirits, are to be examined, and in whose sentence we are to rest, can be no other but the Holy Spirit speaking in the Scriptures.

"2. It is an essential doctrine of the Word of God and our Standards, that our Lord Jesus Christ was born of the Virgin Mary. The Shorter Catechism states, Question 22: "Christ, the Son of God, became man, by taking to Himself a true body and a reasonable soul, being conceived by the power of the Holy Ghost, in the womb of the Virgin Mary, and born of her, yet without sin."

"3. It is an essential doctrine of the Word of God and our Standards, that Christ offered up "himself a sacrifice to satisfy divine justice, and to reconcile us to God." The Scripture saith Christ "once suffered for sins, the just for the unjust, that he might bring us to God, being put to death in the flesh, but quickened in the Spirit." [Cf. the Westminster Shorter Catechism, Q. 25]

"4. It is an essential doctrine of the Word of God and our Standards, concerning our Lord Jesus, that "on the third day he arose from the dead, with the same body in which he suffered; with which also he ascended into heaven, and there sitteth at the right hand of his Father, making intercession." [Cf. the Westminster Confession of Faith, Chapter VIII, Section 4]

"5. It is an essential doctrine of the Word of God as the supreme Standard of our faith, that the Lord Jesus showed his power and love by working mighty miracles. This working was not contrary to nature, but superior to it. "Jesus went about all the cities and villages, teaching in their synagogues, and preaching the gospel of the kingdom, and healing every sickness and every disease among the people" [Matthew 9:35]. These great wonders were signs of the divine power of our Lord, making changes in the order of nature. They were equally examples, to his Church, of charity and good-will toward all mankind.

"These five articles of faith are essential and necessary."

http://www.pcahistory.org/documents/deliverance.html

These doctrinal essentials were repudiated by the Auburn Affirmation of 1924 and rejected by the General Assembly in 1927 with a declaration that the denomination cannot require particular doctrines to be accepted before ordination.

Those five articles of faith become the impetus for the five fundamentals of the faith which formed the nucleus of the Fundamentalists.

4 1 Kings 18:1 And it came to pass *after* many days, that the word of the LORD came to Elijah in the third year, saying, Go, shew thyself unto Ahab; and I will send rain upon the earth. 2 And Elijah went to shew himself unto Ahab. And *there was* a sore famine in Samaria. 3 And Ahab called Obadiah, which *was* the governor of *his* house. (Now Obadiah feared the LORD

greatly: 4 For it was *so*, when Jezebel cut off the prophets of the LORD, that Obadiah took an hundred prophets, and hid them by fifty in a cave, and fed them with bread and water.) 5 And Ahab said unto Obadiah, Go into the land, unto all fountains of water, and unto all brooks: peradventure we may find grass to save the horses and mules alive, that we lose not all the beasts. 6 So they divided the land between them to pass throughout it: Ahab went one way by himself, and Obadiah went another way by himself. 7 And as Obadiah was in the way, behold, Elijah met him: and he knew him, and fell on his face, and said, *Art* thou that my lord Elijah? 8 And he answered him, I *am*: go, tell thy lord, Behold, Elijah *is here.* 9 And he said, What have I sinned, that thou wouldest deliver thy servant into the hand of Ahab, to slay me? 10 *As* the LORD thy God liveth, there is no nation or kingdom, whither my lord hath not sent to seek thee: and when they said, *He is* not *there*; he took an oath of the kingdom and nation, that they found thee not. 11 And now thou sayest, Go, tell thy lord, Behold, Elijah *is here.* 12 And it shall come to pass, *as soon as* I am gone from thee, that the Spirit of the LORD shall carry thee whither I know not; and *so* when I come and tell Ahab, and he cannot find thee, he shall slay me: but I thy servant fear the LORD from my youth. 13 Was it not told my lord what I did when Jezebel slew the prophets of the LORD, how I hid an hundred men of the LORD'S prophets by fifty in a cave, and fed them with bread and water? 14 And now thou sayest, Go, tell thy lord, Behold, Elijah *is here*: and he shall slay me. 15 And Elijah said, *As* the LORD of hosts liveth, before whom I stand, I will surely shew myself unto him to day. 16 So Obadiah went to meet Ahab, and told him: and Ahab went to meet Elijah.

[5] Identifiable Baptists among the writers are E. Y. Mullins, J. J. Reeve, Charles B. Williams, Thomas Spurgeon, George W. Lasher, and A. C. Dixon.

[6] Chapter 28 GOD IN CHRIST THE ONLY REVELATION OF THE FATHERHOOD OF GOD - By Robert E. Speer, Secretary of The Board of Foreign Missions of the Presbyterian Church, U.S.A., New York City.

[7] "The most impressive way to extend an official

invitation to Dr. Billy Graham for a united evangelistic crusade is to make it as all-inclusive as possible. In addition to the Ministerial Association, other Protestant religious and denominational bodies should be asked to join in the invitation. Many cities ask the Governor of the State; the U. S. Senators and Representatives; University and College Presidents; the Mayor; the newspaper, radio and television executives; leaders of industry and civic organizations to also join in the invitation. Such an invitation gives religious and civic leaders an opportunity to be vitally concerned and become a part of the crusade right from the start. Also, the wide impact of such an invitation is quite evident."
Taken from the document titled, *SUGGESTED PLAN OF ORGANIZATION FOR A BILLY GRAHAM CRUSADE.*
http://www2.wheaton.edu/bgc/archives/docs/haytxt.html
This was the original document that was provided to all inquiries as to holding a Billy Graham Crusade. **The restriction to *Protestant religious and denominational bodies* was removed before the second decade of the Graham crusades**.

[8] "When the Catholic Church opened the door to dialogue with Protestants in 1964, the leader welcoming them on other side of the doorway was evangelist and Southern Baptist minister Billy Graham. ... the nation's first Catholic president, John F. Kennedy, had Graham by his side in 1961 as they bowed their heads at a prayer breakfast. ... When one of Graham's most prominent Catholic supporters, Cardinal Richard Cushing of Boston, returned from a session of the Second Vatican Council in Rome, he met with Graham in a televised meeting, commended the evangelist's ministry and encouraged Catholics to listen to him. ... The new spirit of openness gradually defused tension in religious discourse in the United States. Graham forged relationships with Catholics up to and including Pope John Paul II, whom he met in Rome in 1981. His Billy Graham Evangelistic Association wouldn't hold a crusade unless a majority of local churches, eventually including Catholic churches, invited him."
http://www.usatoday.com/story/news/nation/2012/10/28/billy-graham-vatican-catholics/1627503/

[9] This is my term for the following that has risen around the books and campaigns by Warren.

[10] Warren is a signatory of "A Common Word" from the Yale Center for Faith and Culture. The document seeks to recognize the commonality of the Christian and Muslim belief systems. The document opens with the statement, "In the name of the Infinitely Good God whom we should love with all our Being." Is the next step in this walk of compromise to extend Christian fellowship to those outside the Christian faith?

[11] In 1982, Falwell began to publish *The Fundamentalist Journal*. The publication ceased publication in December 1989.

[12] Fundamentalists sacrificed distinctives for the defense of the integrity of Scripture. Cooperative Evangelists sacrificed the integrity of Scripture for souls. The Moral Majority sacrificed souls for morality. The current fad is sacrificing morality for acceptance.

[13] A search (April 22, 2014) of the website for Saddleback Church pastored by Rick Warren found the only use of the word *Baptist* was to identify one of the schools that Pastor Warren attended and to label the position of a guest speaker as within the Southern Baptist Convention. The tendency is to minimize the stigma of the word *Baptist.*

[14] Jeter, Jeremiah, *Baptist Principles Reset*; The Religious Herald Co, Richmond, VA, 1902. Part 2, Chapter 9, *Obligations of Baptists to Teach Their Principles*, J. B. Gambrell, D. D.

Ye shall do my judgments,
and keep mine ordinances,
to walk therein:
I am the LORD your God.
Leviticus 18:4

Now I praise you, brethren,
that ye remember me in all things,
and keep the ordinances,
as I delivered them to you.
1 Corinthians 11:2

He that answereth a matter
before he heareth it,
it is folly and shame unto him.
Proverbs 18:13

THE TWO ORDINANCES OF
THE LOCAL CHURCH

1

THE ORDINANCES OF THE CHURCH

The LORD Jesus, the Head of the church, decreed only two ordinances for His church. The apostle Paul uses this word *ordinance* specifically to identify Communion. His word is the plural *ordinances* because the apostle had discussed the other ordinance, *baptism*, in the first chapter of the first of the Epistles of Paul to the Corinthian church.[1]

> 1 Corinthians 11:2 Now I praise you, brethren, that ye remember me in all things, and keep the ordinances, as I delivered *them* to you. ... 23 For I have received of the Lord that which also I delivered unto you, That the Lord Jesus the *same* night in which he was betrayed took bread:

Unquestionably, the LORD Jesus established for His church the ordinances of baptism and the Table of the LORD with clear commands requiring obedience.

> Matthew 28:18 And Jesus came and spake unto them, saying, All power is giv-

en unto me in heaven and in earth. 19 Go ye therefore, and teach all nations, baptizing them in the name of the Father, and of the Son, and of the Holy Ghost: 20 Teaching them to observe all things whatsoever I have commanded you: and, lo, I am with you alway, *even* unto the end of the world. Amen.

Luke 22:19 And he took bread, and gave thanks, and brake *it*, and gave unto them, saying, This is my body which is given for you: this do in remembrance of me.

With the use of the word *ordinances*, baptism and Communion are identified as commands of the LORD. The word *command* has a legal association and the use of the word *legal* has a negative connotation among Baptists; nevertheless, the word *ordinance* is a legal term and moves baptism and Communion from *suggestions* to *binding commands*.[2] An ordinance has the force of law with penalties for non-compliance.

Surely, no blood-bought child of GOD would challenge the authority of the LORD Jesus to establish whatever ordinances for His church that He might chose. To deny Him the right to do so would be a strange proposal. Since both baptism and Communion are ordinances, the child of GOD will be either obedient or disobedient to both commands; no allowance for neutrality or evasion exists. The ordinances are of equal importance and neither may be avoided intentionally with impunity.

BAPTISM

Baptism is the public profession of faith, an act that is preformed in the likeness, the picture, of the believer's identification with the death, burial, and resurrection of Christ Jesus. Baptism is a onetime occurrence that is not a proper subject for repetition by the believer.

> Romans 6:3 Know ye not, that so many of us as were baptized into Jesus Christ were **baptized into his death**? 4 Therefore we are **buried with him by baptism** into death: that like as Christ was raised up from the dead by the glory of the Father, even so we also should walk in newness of life. 5 For if we have been **planted together in the likeness of his death**, we shall be also *in the likeness* of *his* resurrection: 6 Knowing this, that our old man is **crucified with *him***, that the body of sin might be destroyed, that henceforth we should not serve sin. 7 For he that is dead is freed from sin. 8 Now if we be **dead with Christ**, we believe that we shall also live with him: 9 Knowing that Christ being raised from the dead dieth no more; death hath no more dominion over him. 10 For in that he died, **he died unto sin once**: but in that he liveth, he liveth unto God.

COMMUNION

While the command concerning baptism is such that when baptism has been properly received baptism is not to be repeated, the instruction for the Table of the LORD is that the Remembrance is to be commemorated often.

> 1 Corinthians 11:25 After the same manner also *he took* the cup, when he had supped, saying, This cup is the new testament in my blood: this do ye, **as oft** as ye drink *it*, in remembrance of me. ... 26 For **as often** as ye eat this bread, and

drink this cup, ye do shew the Lord's death till he come.

Since Scripture does not stipulate the frequency of the remembrance, the times of observance are subject to the desires of each church to determine the times for the service. The instruction from the LORD Jesus is that the ordinance is to be repeated for He uses the terms "as oft as ye drink it" and "as often as ye eat." I do not understand this to suggest *often* in the sense of *frequently*, but *often* in the sense of *those times when it is observed*.

Those errorists that consider Communion as obtaining or helping to obtain salvation promote regular participation, if not daily attendance. The other extreme is the error of the Society of Friends (Quakers), the Salvation Army, and Christian Scientists, all of whom do not observe Communion.

Among Baptists, the observance is diverse. The Passover was a yearly remembrance and some Baptists hold Communion on an annual basis. Other Baptists have a service weekly, while others schedule the service on a monthly or quarterly basis. Random or sporadic would describe the rest.

The service is to be observed *often* enough that its importance is not neglected, but not *so often* that its significance becomes reduced by the repetition.

---

[1] This will be discussed later in detail. The apostle references the individuals that he had baptized into the church at Corinth ("baptized ... of you") and rejoiced in smallness of the number in that it reduced the likelihood of a personality cult being built around him. His statement that "Christ sent me not to baptize, but to preach" is not a denial of the properness of baptism, but a declaration of the fact that salvation was not located in or connected with the obedience of baptism, but is found in the response of faith in the Gospel message.

1 Corinthians 1:10 Now I beseech you, brethren, by the name of our Lord Jesus Christ, that ye all speak the same thing, and *that* there be no divisions among you; but *that* ye be perfectly joined together in the same mind and in the same judgment. 11 For it hath been declared unto me of you, my brethren, by them *which are of the house* of Chloe, that there are contentions among you. 12 Now this I say, that every one of you saith, I am of Paul; and I of Apollos; and I of Cephas; and I of Christ. 13 Is Christ divided? was Paul crucified for you? or were ye baptized in the name of Paul? 14 I thank God that I baptized none of you, but Crispus and Gaius; 15 Lest any should say that I had baptized in mine own name. 16 And I baptized also the household of Stephanas: besides, I know not whether I baptized any other. 17 For Christ sent me not to baptize, but to preach the gospel: not with wisdom of words, lest the cross of Christ should be made of none effect.

[2] *Merriam-Webster 11th Collegiate Dictionary* defines the word *ordinance* as follows: 1a: an authoritative decree or direction: ORDER; 1b: a law set forth by a governmental authority; specifically: a municipal regulation; 2: something ordained or decreed by fate or a deity; 3a: prescribed usage, practice, or ceremony; synonyms see LAW

THE ORDINANCE OF
BAPTISM

2

DEFINITION BEFORE DISCUSSION

Then they that gladly received his
word were baptized.
Acts 2:41

Before entering the serious tension always generated by the consideration of any controversy that is connected with doctrine, wisdom suggests that all of the participants in that discussion must agree on the definitions of the particular terms involved and they must consistently adhere to the use of only those definitions. No honest and meaningful deliberation can be achieved should any among those listening to or contributing to the discussion choose to use special meanings, secret definitions, or private interpretations for the Bible words or theological terms being discussed, whether that divergent use is accidental and unintentional or sly and surreptitious. Nothing constructive results from any doctrinal conversation that is conducted without those stipulations confining the discussion by all parties. The encounter will otherwise produce an unrecognized confusion among those involved, provide an outbreak of hostility between those involved, or project a purposefully planned deception by one or more of the participants.

Among the sinister subtleties of cultic teachers, making them an exceedingly dangerous attraction, while at the same time a deadly ambush, to immature or uninstructed, and, therefore, naive believers and other gullible victims, is the effective practice that all false prophets utilize. These spiritual deceivers delight in insidiously altering the historical definitions of basic Bible words and of disingenuously rephrasing traditional Bible doctrines so that the customary and scriptural meanings of these words are mutilated beyond repair and mutated beyond recognition and *doing so surreptitiously,* attempting to avoid detection. Then, with clever deceitful skill, these perverters of truth treacherously incorporate these new, radically different, unbiblical, *even anti-biblical,* malignant counterfeits into what appear to be commonly used spiritual or Scriptural phrases.

Consequently, the unsuspecting listener feels no urgency or necessity to seek any clarification connected with the words heard because he[1] is certain that the meaning intended is what is normally and commonly expected. This deliberate verbal duplicity weaves a skillfully camouflaged snare inviting the unwary into their web of deceit from which escape is very unlikely. What appears to the credulous listener as known and familiar terminology is in reality beguiling costuming that is skillfully and cleverly designed to disguise the heretical doctrine advocated by the alteration of truth in the camouflage of acceptable truth.[2]

These wondrous religious enchanters are vicious wolves in sheep's clothing, who survive by wresting Bible truths by *sleight of tongue* distortion and through using *tongue-is-faster-than-the-brain* manipulation. Words that the listener, the dictionaries of the language, and historical Christianity all receive as having a settled definition are corrupted and used with a bewitchment[3] that is fully intended by these spiritual wizards for a purpose and meaning that is entirely different from what the hearer could rightfully, even if naively, have expected or understood to have been meant.

Sadly, these human and satanic perversions of truths are not explained to the credulous initiate until that gullible individual is firmly ensnared and deeply entombed in the error or the cult. Very often, the *strange fire* of these bizarre, distorted meanings is veiled in the masquerade of being a *new mystery revelation* that is available only to those individuals that are *fortunate* enough to receive the secret.

Individuals and publications representing various groups use the same words. These include Baptists, Jehovah's Witnesses, Latter Day Saints, Roman Catholics, Charismatics, Methodists, Lutherans, Presbyterians, the World Wide Church of God, the Christian Science, the Unity School of Christianity, the Disciples of Christ, etc. These all identify themselves as Christians; and they each use words that are spelled identically and that are even pronounced indistinguishably. However, a sincere careful study of the doctrinal teachings of the individuals and groups and with the exercise of spiritual discernment gained by comparing those beliefs with the Scriptures,[4] those words are found to be not at all identical in meaning. The particular designed use by the different groups will be found to be highly distinguishable from each other.

Bluntly stated, the use of the same Bible words or theological terms is no indication, never acceptable proof, and *certainly no guarantee*, that the same meaning is intended by these varied groups; this is true of even the most basic and ordinary of words.[5] As strange as it might seem to some, these dangerous alterations include the most common words of Scripture such as *saved, justified, born again, heaven, hell, sin, prayer, grace*; even such words as *life, death, angels, God, Christ,* the *Holy Spirit* and many other terms receive the same insidious tampering. The word *baptism* must be included near the top on the list of these systematically and deliberately mutilated words.

Before entering this examination of the doctrine of baptism, it is imperative to define three particular terms that are relevant to the discussion: Christian, Christianity, and Christendom.[6] The following definitions are the most basic and generally accepted meanings of those three terms as they are used by the print and broadcast media and as they are used in daily conversation by the English-speaking world.

1. Christian: One who professes some level of acceptance of the *teachings* of Jesus Christ.

14

2. Christianity: The religion derived from Jesus Christ, based on the Bible as sacred Scriptures, and professed by the Eastern, Roman Catholic, and the various Protestant bodies.

3. Christendom: The part of the world in which the influence of Christianity has prevailed to affect morals, custom, and laws.

Though from a biblical position these definitions have serious flaws, I have chosen to use these three terms *according to these definitions* to avoid any confusion of meaning. Even so, please notice carefully the following objections concerning how these words are customarily used in media and conversation.

1. The word *Christendom* is used to encompass all citizens of any nation whose population is not predominantly Moslem, Jewish, Buddhist, or another non-Christian religion; this word has no suggestion of acceptance, application, or even personal acknowledgment of Christianity by any particular citizen of such a nation. The word speaks more of a moral and philosophical influence than it does of a relationship with Christ.

2. The word *Christianity* is used very broadly to include any individual or group that makes any claim whatsoever to appreciate the teachings of Jesus Christ in any extent, degree, manner, or form. In this manner, Christianity is connected with the *teachings* and not the *person* of Christ.

3. The word *Christian* is used in common speech with a multitude of meanings ranging from *commendably decent or generous*[7] to a person that has received the LORD Jesus Christ as personal Saviour. The word is not restricted to those that believe in the LORD Jesus for salvation or that try to live in accordance to His teachings. Unfortunately, even those that openly deny and repudiate the deity of Jesus of Nazareth are labeled as Christians.

Though I will use these words in compliance with these obviously *faulty* definitions, I will do so solely because that is the way these terms are commonly understood. The indisputable fact is to be emphasized, and strongly so, that the New Testament exclusively applies the word *Christian* to identify those individuals who are true (*genuine, saved, born again, regenerated*) disciples of the LORD Jesus Christ. A *Christian* as defined by the Biblical definition is very different from the *Christian* of colloquial speech.

Of these three terms, only the word *Christian* is used in the New Testament. In its first appearance in the New Testament, the *Christian* specifically identifies those individuals who were faithful baptized members of the church at Antioch.

> Acts 11:26 And when he had found him, he brought him unto Antioch. And it came to pass, that a whole year they assembled themselves with the church, and taught much people. And the disciples were called Christians first in Antioch.

In the other two instances where the word

16

Christian is applied in the New Testament, it is used with the unmistakable meaning of *one who identifies personally and publicly with the cause of Christ and with His followers.*

> Acts 26:28 Then Agrippa said unto Paul, Almost thou persuadest me to be a Christian.

> 1 Peter 4:16 Yet if any man suffer as a Christian, let him not be ashamed; but let him glorify God on this behalf.

The word *Christian* does not appear in any text in the New Testament other than the three that are cited and no other reasonable argument for the use or application of the term in any other manner can be made than the very restrictive and narrow meaning of a regenerated follower of the LORD Jesus Christ that has openly identified with fellow believers.

Though within Scripture, the word Christian has this unique and very precise limitation of use, sadly, that restriction does not hold true in either the secular or religious world today. The departure from the Scriptural pattern is sometimes a deliberate manipulation; but very often, it is simply a careless mistake. Whether intentionally or in error, the misuse of the word produces confusion over what is intended to be the meaning of the term *Christian* when the word is used in conversations or when found in publications.

With the existence of the definite possibility that the term *Christian* will not be understood in the strict Scriptural sense by all those who will read this work, another New Testament term that is used to identify the true followers of the LORD Jesus Christ will be used instead, the word **believer**.

This word **believer** is used synonymously with *Christian* in the New Testament and will identify in this discussion the individual who has received by personal faith and in the exercise of his own personal will the LORD Jesus Christ as Saviour and that has publically identified by the act of baptism with Christ. Believers are individuals who are not trusting in some work or act that might be undertaken that would grant or obtain salvation, but who are trusting *entirely and only* in the atonement of the shed blood of the Saviour applied by and through the grace of GOD.

> Acts 5:14 And believers were the more added to the Lord, multitudes both of men and women.

> 1 Timothy 4:12 Let no man despise thy youth; but be thou an example of the believers, in word, in conversation, in charity, in spirit, in faith, in purity.

Though I have emphasized the public profession by the Christian, my statements are not intended to deny the possibility of a person being a *secret* believer. The Scripture records that both Nicodemus and Joseph of Arimathaea were undeclared believers prior to the trial and the crucifixion of Christ. The fear of the Jewish leadership of that day kept Joseph and others silent regarding acceptance of the Gospel and may even have prevented some from receiving Christ.[8]

However, following Christ in secrecy is not the proper stance for a believer. In view of the caution of the LORD Jesus, the prayer of David that he might not be ashamed of his hope is

18

an appropriate prayer for the believer.[9]

> Mark 8:38 Whosoever therefore shall be ashamed of me and of my words in this adulterous and sinful generation; of him also shall the Son of man be ashamed, when he cometh in the glory of his Father with the holy angels. [10]

Very importantly, both Joseph of Arimathaea and Nicodemus found the courage to identify publically with Christ and they did so at the very time that His friends,[11] the apostles, had scattered from His presence and were only gathered behind closed doors for fear of persecution.[12] The secret disciples Joseph and Nicodemus became public disciples while the public disciples became secret disciples.

The message of the Gospel was from the beginning the message of the cross.[13] The preaching of the LORD Jesus included the potential of opposition, even from family members.[14]

Pressures existed during the ministry of Jesus of Nazareth and that opposition intensified soon after the crucifixion. The early chapters of the Book of Acts records the sufferings and death of many of the members of the church in Jerusalem.[15] Persecutions were not unusual and were not to be unexpected in the early churches and ought not to be considered startlingly when they come upon present churches and believers.

Paul endured severely heavy persecutions for the entirety of his life as a Christian.[16] It is proper to notice that those who are identified as Christians in 1 Peter were believers in the face of severe persecution.[17]

The LORD Jesus taught His disciples that persecutions were to be expected. Not only were harassment, discrimination, and mal- treatment to be anticipated, but the death of the cross was to be accepted willingly.

> Matthew 10:38 And he that taketh not his cross, and followeth after me, is not wor- thy of me.[18]

In the days of the New Testament, there were no nominal Christians. Being a Christian required commitment and dedication, follow- ing Christ was a way of living that encom- passed the entirety of one's existence. Being identified publically as a Christian could and often did cause the physical death of the believer.

Therefore, the act of obeying the LORD in entering the waters of baptism was not a frivolous decision. In the First Century, the person being baptized was willing to die for the obedience demonstrated in and by that act. Baptism was never foisted upon an unconscious person or administered to an uncomprehending baby. Baptism was always and only received by an individual capable of understanding the purpose and the reason for the act. The baptism was the willful, deliber- ate, and intentional response of commitment to the fulfillment of duty. No one was baptized in ignorance of the responsibilities that flowed from that baptism.

[1] The use of the third person singular pronoun **he** rather than the tedious **he or she**, the pretentious **s/he**, **(s)he**, the unintelligible **sie** and **hir**, or the strained artificial **they**, is (1) following the centuries long pattern of acceptable writing in the English language ["used in a generic sense or when the sex of the person is unspecified"—*Merriam-Webster 11th Collegiate Dictionary*], (2) honoring the pattern of the Authorized Version of the Scriptures, (3) a rejection of the condescending notion that female readers are intellectually incapable of comprehending the figure of speech (called *synecdoche*), where a part is used for the whole, *pars pro toto*, and (4) the absolute rejection of the agenda of the political-correctness-movement that has neutered intelligent conversation, polarized segments of the population into adversaries, and created a climate of intimidated speakers and writers.

I use the term *pretentious* in the dictionary-defined sense of "intended to seem to have a special quality or significance, but often seeming forced or overly clever in the pattern of e. e. cummings."

The same reasoning prompts me to use the word *man* as representing the entire human race when the word is not used in reference to a specific male.

Genesis 1:27 So God created man in his own image, in the image of God created he him; male and female created he them.

[2] 2 Corinthians 11:13 For such *are* false apostles, deceitful workers, transforming themselves into the apostles of Christ. 14 And no marvel; for Satan himself is transformed into an angel of light. 15 Therefore *it is* no great thing if his ministers also be transformed as the ministers of righteousness; whose end shall be according to their works.

[3] Galatians 3:1 O foolish Galatians, who hath bewitched you, that ye should not obey the truth, before whose eyes Jesus Christ hath been evidently set forth, crucified among you?

[4] Hebrews 5:14 But strong meat belongeth to them that are of full age, *even* those who by reason of use have their senses exercised to discern both good and evil.

5 A sitting President of the United States famously testified under oath that "It depends on what the meaning of the word 'is' is." *Representatives on President William Jefferson Clinton; Referral to the United States House of Representatives pursuant to Title 28, United States Code, § 595(c)*; Submitted by The Office of the Independent Counsel September 9, 1998; found under the section titled Summary of President's Grand Jury Testimony and referenced in footnotes 108 and 1091.

6 *Merriam-Webster 11th Collegiate Dictionary*, Merriam-Webster, Inc, 2003

7 *Merriam-Webster 11th Collegiate Dictionary*

8 John 19:38 And after this Joseph of Arimathaea, being a disciple of Jesus, but secretly for fear of the Jews, besought Pilate that he might take away the body of Jesus: and Pilate gave *him* leave. He came therefore, and took the body of Jesus.
Luke 23:50 And, behold, *there was* a man named Joseph, a counseller; *and he was* a good man, and a just: 51 (The same had not consented to the counsel and deed of them;) *he was* of Arimathaea, a city of the Jews: who also himself waited for the kingdom of God. 52 This *man* went unto Pilate, and begged the body of Jesus.
John 9:22 These *words* spake his parents, because they feared the Jews: for the Jews had agreed already, that if any man did confess that he was Christ, he should be put out of the synagogue.

9 Psalms 119:116 Uphold me according unto thy word, that I may live: and let me not be ashamed of my hope.

10 Luke 9:26 For whosoever shall be ashamed of me and of my words, of him shall the Son of man be ashamed, when he shall come in his own glory, and *in his* Father's, and of the holy angels.

11 John 15:15 Henceforth I call you not servants; for the servant knoweth not what his lord doeth: but I have called you friends; for all things that I have heard of my Father I have made known unto you.

12 Matthew 26:31 Then saith Jesus unto them, All ye shall be offended because of me this night: for it is written, I will smite the shepherd, and the sheep of the flock shall be scattered abroad. ... 56 But all this was

22

done, that the scriptures of the prophets might be fulfilled. Then all the disciples forsook him, and fled.

John 16:32 Behold, the hour cometh, yea, is now come, that ye shall be scattered, every man to his own, and shall leave me alone: and yet I am not alone, because the Father is with me.

John 20:19 Then the same day at evening, being the first *day* of the week, when the doors were shut where the disciples were assembled for fear of the Jews, came Jesus and stood in the midst, and saith unto them, Peace *be* unto you.

[13] Matthew 16:24 Then said Jesus unto his disciples, If any *man* will come after me, let him deny himself, and take up his cross, and follow me.

Mark 8:34 And when he had called the people *unto him* with his disciples also, he said unto them, Whosoever will come after me, let him deny himself, and take up his cross, and follow me.

Luke 9:23 And he said to *them* all, If any *man* will come after me, let him deny himself, and take up his cross daily, and follow me.

[14] Matthew 10:32 Whosoever therefore shall confess me before men, him will I confess also before my Father which is in heaven. 33 But whosoever shall deny me before men, him will I also deny before my Father which is in heaven. 10:34 Think not that I am come to send peace on earth: I came not to send peace, but a sword. 35 For I am come to set a man at variance against his father, and the daughter against her mother, and the daughter in law against her mother in law. 36 And a man's foes *shall be* they of his own household. 37 He that loveth father or mother more than me is not worthy of me: and he that loveth son or daughter more than me is not worthy of me. 38 And he that taketh not his cross, and followeth after me, is not worthy of me. 39 He that findeth his life shall lose it: and he that loseth his life for my sake shall find it. ... 16:24 Then said Jesus unto his disciples, If any *man* will come after me, let him deny himself, and take up his cross, and follow me. 25 For whosoever will save his life shall lose it: and whosoever will lose his life for my sake shall find it.

Mark 8:34 And when he had called the people *unto him* with his disciples also, he said unto them, Whosoever will come after me, let him deny himself, and take up his cross, and follow me. 35 For whosoever will save his life shall lose it; but whosoever shall lose his life for my sake and the gospel's, the same shall save it. 36 For what shall it profit a man, if he shall gain the whole world, and lose his own soul?

Luke 9:23 And he said to *them* all, If any *man* will come after me, let him deny himself, and take up his cross daily, and follow me. 24 For whosoever will save his life shall lose it: but whosoever will lose his life for my sake, the same shall save it. ... 12:8 Also I say unto you, Whosoever shall confess me before men, him shall the Son of man also confess before the angels of God: 9 But he that denieth me before men shall be denied before the angels of God.

15 Acts 4:1 And as they [Peter and John] spake unto the people, the priests, and the captain of the temple, and the Sadducees, came upon them, 2 Being grieved that they taught the people, and preached through Jesus the resurrection from the dead. 3 And they laid hands on them, and put *them* in hold unto the next day: for it was now eventide. ... 5 And it came to pass on the morrow, that their rulers, and elders, and scribes, 6 And Annas the high priest, and Caiaphas, and John, and Alexander, and as many as were of the kindred of the high priest, were gathered together at Jerusalem. 7 And when they had set them in the midst, ... 18 And they called them, and commanded them not to speak at all nor teach in the name of Jesus. ... So when they had further threatened them, they let them go, ... 5:17 Then the high priest rose up, and all they that were with him, (which is the sect of the Sadducees,) and were filled with indignation, 18 And laid their hands on the apostles, and put them in the common prison. ... 40 And to him they agreed: and when they had called the apostles, and beaten *them*, they commanded that they should not speak in the name of Jesus, and let them go. ... 6:12 And they stirred up the people, and the elders, and the scribes, and came upon *him*, [Stephen] and caught him, and brought *him* to the council, ... 7:54 When they heard these things, they were cut to the heart, and they gnashed on him with *their* teeth. ... 57 Then they cried out with a loud voice, and stopped their ears, and ran upon him with one

accord, 58 And cast *him* out of the city, and stoned *him*: ... 8:1 And Saul was consenting unto his death. And at that time there was a great persecution against the church which was at Jerusalem; and they were all scattered abroad throughout the regions of Judaea and Samaria, except the apostles. ... 3 As for Saul, he made havock of the church, entering into every house, and haling men and women committed *them* to prison. 4 Therefore they that were scattered abroad went every where preaching the word. ... 9:1 And Saul, yet breathing out threatenings and slaughter against the disciples of the Lord, went unto the high priest, 2 And desired of him letters to Damascus to the synagogues, that if he found any of this way, whether they were men or women, he might bring them bound unto Jerusalem.

[16] Acts 9:19 And when he had received meat, he was strengthened. Then was Saul certain days with the disciples which were at Damascus. 20 And straightway he preached Christ in the synagogues, that he is the Son of God. 21 But all that heard *him* were amazed, and said; Is not this he that destroyed them which called on this name in Jerusalem, and came hither for that intent, that he might bring them bound unto the chief priests? 22 But Saul increased the more in strength, and confounded the Jews which dwelt at Damascus, proving that this is very Christ. 23 And after that many days were fulfilled, the Jews took counsel to kill him: 24 But their laying await was known of Saul. And they watched the gates day and night to kill him. 25 Then the disciples took him by night, and let *him* down by the wall in a basket. 26 And when Saul was come to Jerusalem, he assayed to join himself to the disciples: but they were all afraid of him, and believed not that he was a disciple.

2 Corinthians 11:23 Are they ministers of Christ? (I speak as a fool) I *am* more; in labours more abundant, in stripes above measure, in prisons more frequent, in deaths oft. 24 Of the Jews five times received I forty *stripes* save one. 25 Thrice was I beaten with rods, once was I stoned, thrice I suffered shipwreck, a night and a day I have been in the deep; 26 *In* journeyings often, *in* perils of waters, *in* perils of robbers, *in* perils by *mine own* countrymen, *in* perils by the heathen, *in* perils in the city, *in* perils in the wilderness, *in* perils in the sea,

in perils among false brethren; 27 In weariness and painfulness, in watchings often, in hunger and thirst, in fastings often, in cold and nakedness. 28 Beside those things that are without, that which cometh upon me daily, the care of all the churches. 29 Who is weak, and I am not weak? who is offended, and I burn not? 30 If I must needs glory, I will glory of the things which concern mine infirmities. 31 The God and Father of our Lord Jesus Christ, which is blessed for evermore, knoweth that I lie not. 32 In Damascus the governor under Aretas the king kept the city of the Damascenes with a garrison, desirous to apprehend me: 33 And through a window in a basket was I let down by the wall, and escaped his hands.

¹⁷ 1 Peter 1:3 Blessed *be* the God and Father of our Lord Jesus Christ, which according to his abundant mercy hath begotten us again unto a lively hope by the resurrection of Jesus Christ from the dead, 4 To an inheritance incorruptible, and undefiled, and that fadeth not away, reserved in heaven for you, 5 Who are kept by the power of God through faith unto salvation ready to be revealed in the last time. 6 Wherein ye greatly rejoice, **though now for a season, if need be, ye are in heaviness through manifold temptations**: 7 That **the trial of your faith, being much more precious than of gold that perisheth, though it be tried with fire**, might be found unto praise and honour and glory at the appearing of Jesus Christ: ... 2:11 Dearly beloved, I beseech *you* as strangers and pilgrims, abstain from fleshly lusts, which war against the soul; 12 Having your conversation honest among the Gentiles: that, whereas they speak against you as evildoers, they may by *your* good works, which they shall behold, glorify God in the day of visitation. ... 3:14 **But and if ye suffer for righteousness' sake, happy *are ye*: and be not afraid of their terror, neither be troubled;** 15 But sanctify the Lord God in your hearts: and *be* ready always to *give* an answer to every man that asketh you a reason of the hope that is in you with meekness and fear: 16 Having a good conscience; that, whereas **they speak evil of you,** as of evildoers, they may be ashamed that falsely accuse your good conversation in Christ. 17 For *it is* better, if the will of God be so, that ye **suffer** for well doing, than for evil

doing. 18 For Christ also hath once suffered for sins, the just for the unjust, that he might bring us to God, being put to death in the flesh, but quickened by the Spirit: ... 4:12 Beloved, think it not strange concerning **the fiery trial** which is to try you, as though some strange thing happened unto you: 13 But rejoice, inasmuch as ye are partakers of Christ's sufferings; that, when his glory shall be revealed, ye may be glad also with exceeding joy. 14 If ye be **reproached for the name of Christ**, happy *are ye*; for the spirit of glory and of God resteth upon you: on their part he is evil spoken of, but on your part he is glorified. 15 But let none of you suffer as a murderer, or *as* a thief, or *as* an evildoer, or as a busybody in other men's matters. 16 **Yet if *any man suffer* as a Christian, let him not be ashamed; but let him glorify God on this behalf.** 17 For the time *is come* that judgment must begin at the house of God: and if *it* first *begin* at us, what shall the end *be* of them that obey not the gospel of God? 18 And if the righteous scarcely be saved, where shall the ungodly and the sinner appear? 19 Wherefore let them that **suffer** according to the will of God commit the keeping of their souls *to him* in well doing, as unto a faithful Creator.

[18] Somewhere along the path of preaching, taking up the cross has come to mean bearing a burden. However, the cross was never designed to be laid on someone to be a burden; it was placed there as the instrument of the death of that person.

3
WHAT IS BAPTISM?

Among those professing to be Christians, baptism is defined in ways that are confusing, conflicting, and contradictory. Baptism is variously described because the theology of what is the purpose of baptism divides the various groups. Baptism is made to fit the different modes and the purposes that the particular theological understandings require.

The basic division in the practice of baptism among Christians is a firm unbreachable separation between the majority of Christians that *baptize an individual to make that person a Christian* and the minority of Christians that will only *baptize a person after that person has made a credible confession of faith.*[1] This last position is known as believer's baptism, because it performs baptisms only after a profession of salvation.

All Christian entities, whether churches, denominations, sects, cults, etc., that practice any type of baptism will fall into one or the other of those two broad groups. Though it has always been the position of all true Baptists, the baptism of only those who are believers is practiced by the minority of Christians. Believer's baptism requires a person who is of the age, who has the understanding of what is being done, and who possesses the ability to give a credible confession of faith.

Additional differences exist within the larger group of Christians that associates baptism in some way with creating a Christian. Baptism is considered by some as the means of the removal of sin, *the actual and effective means of washing away sin.* Among these baptismal regenerationists, one will find considerable latitude of belief. Some teach that baptism only removes *original sin* and not committed sins; while others insist that all sins are washed away.

It is impossible to list all of the permutations that have risen. Some have taught that baptism was the means of salvation only for those believing Jews who were alive and who were baptized during the specific era between the ministry of John the Baptist until the day of that Paul turned to the Gentiles. Others hold that while baptism did save the Jewish believer before Pentecost, after Pentecost both the Jew and Gentile are saved by grace; giving baptism a different significance for this era of time than it held before Pentecost.

Baptism is practiced by some within the majority group as an action of pouring a small amount of water upon the head of a person, while others sprinkle drops of water on the head,[2] most often that of an infant. Some of this group will indeed baptize babies. The practice of baptizing babies is known as Paedobaptism.

Some will also baptize comatose individuals, because baptism is essential for entrance into heaven in their view.

Some will even practice proxy baptism, which is baptizing a substitute for someone who has died.

There are other differences within Christianity in the practice of baptism. Some permit *anyone* to perform the act of baptism on *any other* individual seeking baptism.[3] Under the canons of Roman Catholicism in the event of necessity due to imminent death, any person may baptize as long as the Trinitarian formula is used.[4]

Baptism of intent is acceptable by some groups for those who would have been baptized if they had had the opportunity, but that were unable to be baptized before they died. This is not a literal baptism, but the granting of credit for the *intention* of what might have been done if an opportunity or the knowledge had been available to the person.

Baptism in blood is considered valid by certain churches for those who died as martyrs for the faith, but who are presumed to have had a *valid* reason for never having been baptized. This baptism is also not a literal baptism, but it is the acceptance of the death of the person as a substitute in place of an actual baptism.

Among Christians, baptism is practiced through the sprinkling of water, the pouring of water, and the immersion into water; and some Christians recognize the validity of both affusion (sprinkling or pouring) and immersion, while others practice or accept any of the three modes. Among immersionists, some require flowing water. Others use a baptistery or any body of water. Some will only baptize outdoors, even if that should require breaking ice to enable baptism in the winter months; others will baptize indoors or outdoors without distinction. Some baptize face forward, while others lay the person backwards. Still others require a threefold immersion.

There are even those among the dispensationalists that contend *in this dispensation*[5] baptism is not a physical action but solely a spiritual undertaking performed by the Holy Spirit. They insist that *water* baptism lacks any real purpose of meaning for individuals who are alive today and that *water* baptism was never more than a practice restricted to those Jews who lived during the time span that began with the public ministry of John the Baptist and ended when the Apostle Paul publicly turned to the Gentiles.

Other Christians make a distinction between *spirit baptism* and *water baptism* and recognize both. Certain groups eliminate the so-called *water baptism* and acknowledge only the so-called *spirit baptism*.

As discussed earlier, baptism is often termed a uniting. The fundamental and serious issue that term produces is the question of what a person is joined by his baptism. Does baptism unite the believer to Christ or to a church?

Is a person baptized to obtain forgiveness of sins or is a person baptized in order to be added to the membership of a church? If baptism plays any part in a person's salvation, then, obviously, it unites that person to Christ. If however, baptism plays no part in salvation, then just as obviously, baptism unites a person to a church by his public profession.

Clearly, the evidence of the divisions among Christians over the act of baptism is easily documented, because of the many and varied views regarding baptism. It is equally apparent that the creeds of Christendom cannot be used as a safe guide to understand the meaning of baptism, since they contain, at best, the sincere reasonings of religious humanity and differ widely in form and meaning.

The truth concerning baptism can be found in one place and one place alone. That is within the word of GOD, the Bible. For the sincere child of GOD there can be only this one source of ultimate, total, complete, absolute, final authority for all matters of faith and practice. Human reasoning, however sincere or religious, is never a safe guide. Therefore, each religious utterance of man must be carefully examined and judged in the light of the teachings of Scripture.

That discernment must be constant and continual. The price of faithfulness to Christ and of fidelity to the word of GOD is persistent diligence in the exercise of discernment. To do otherwise, is to place the will and the words of a man or men above the will and the word of GOD.

That same irrational inversion was the exact situation existing during the days of the

33

earthly sojourn of the LORD Jesus Christ. The word of GOD was interpreted in such a way that it contradicted itself.

> Matthew 15:1 Then came to Jesus scribes and Pharisees, which were of Jerusalem, saying, 2 Why do thy disciples transgress the tradition of the elders? for they wash not their hands when they eat bread. 3 But he answered and said unto them, Why do ye also transgress the commandment of God by your tradition? 4 For God commanded, saying, Honour thy father and mother: and, He that curseth father or mother, let him die the death. 5 **But ye say**, Whosoever shall say to *his* father or *his* mother, *It is* a gift, by whatsoever thou mightest be profited by me; 6 And honour not his father or his mother, *he shall be free*. Thus have ye made the commandment of God of none effect by your tradition. 7 *Ye* hypocrites, well did Esaias prophesy of you, saying, 8 This people draweth nigh unto me with their mouth, and honoureth me with *their* lips; but their heart is far from me. 9 But in vain they do worship me, teaching *for* doctrines the commandments of men.

Any legitimate examination of the doctrine of baptism must be grounded firmly in the word of GOD and all conclusions reached must be based only and entirely upon the words of Scripture. All commandments of men, though they might be based upon the most logical of reasonings and the highest of intellectual judgments, must be weighed in the balance of Scripture.

When the traditions of men fall short of Scripture, they are to be rejected without debate or further consideration. For a believer to follow any other procedure is to engage in the entertainment of error and that is nothing short of spiritual folly.

Among the doctrines that have defined Baptists since the apostolic days is the foundation principle that Scripture is the *sole and final authority for all matters of faith and practice.* Though the Reformers adopted the slogan of *Sola Scriptura,* they did not practice *Sola Scriptura.* Unfortunately, the Protestants retained many traditions and customs of the system they sought to reform. In particular, the Reformers retained the concept of baptism as taught by the Roman Catholic Church [RCC].[6]

Scripture is not ambiguous regarding what constitutes baptism. Baptism is defined in the Bible by teaching and demonstrated by example. The teachings are clear and the examples are plain.

BAPTISM IS AN ACT OF IDENTIFICATION.

First, baptism is the identification of the believer with the LORD Jesus Christ.

Second, baptism is the identification of the believer with the local church.

FIRST, BAPTISM IS IDENTIFICATION WITH CHRIST.

In contrast to man-conceived doctrines and traditions, the word of GOD declares baptism to be an act of identification. Baptism is a twofold accomplishment.

Baptism is a step of obedience.

Baptism is the public profession of faith.

Baptism does not have any part in salvation—not in preparing for salvation, not in obtaining salvation, not in sealing for salvation, and not in retaining salvation. Most Christians have the understanding that baptism removes sin, at a minimum original sin.[7]

Galatians 3:27 is a particular passage that is often used to *prove* that baptism is *into Christ* meaning that baptism is the means of salvation.

> For as many of you as have been baptized into Christ have put on Christ.

However, when the context of that verse is considered, it becomes obvious that to *put on Christ* is to speak of the newness of life in Christ. Moreover, baptism cannot have any part in providing or obtaining salvation, because works do not justify.

> Romans 4:1 What shall we say then that Abraham our father, as pertaining to the flesh, hath found? 2 For if Abraham were justified by works, he hath *whereof* to glory; but not before God. 3 For what saith the scripture? Abraham believed God, and it was counted unto him for righteousness. 4 Now to him that worketh is the reward not reckoned of grace, but of debt. 5 But to him that worketh not, but believeth on him that justifieth the ungodly, his faith is counted for righteousness. 6 Even as David also describeth the blessedness of the man, unto whom God imputeth righteousness without works, 7 *Saying*, Blessed *are* they whose iniquities are forgiven, and whose sins are covered. 8 Blessed *is* the man to whom the Lord will not impute sin. 9 *Cometh* this blessedness then upon the circumcision *only*,

or upon the uncircumcision also? for we say that faith was reckoned to Abraham for righteousness. 10 How was it then reckoned? when he was in circumcision, or in uncircumcision? Not in circumcision, but in uncircumcision. 11 And he received the sign of circumcision, a seal of the righteousness of the faith which *he had yet* being uncircumcised: that he might be the father of all them that believe, though they be not circumcised; that righteousness might be imputed unto them also: 12 And the father of circumcision to them who are not of the circumcision only, but who also walk in the steps of that faith of our father Abraham, which *he had* being *yet* uncircumcised.

One does not obtain a right standing with the holy GOD of Heaven through the accomplishment of a particular work or a series of works. The words of verses four and five above cannot be drafted in any plainer language.

Now to him that worketh is the reward not reckoned of grace, but of debt. But to him that worketh not, but believeth on him that justifieth the ungodly, his faith is counted for righteousness.

Justification is not achieved; it is accepted. The path to justification is by grace through faith. This was true through the Old Testament and remains true today. No person ever was or ever will be saved by his own efforts. Salvation is now and always has been by grace.

This is the explanation of salvation provided in the Epistle to the Romans.

Romans 3:24 Being justified freely by his grace through the redemption that is in Christ Jesus:

Romans 4:16 Therefore *it is* of faith, that *it might be* by grace; to the end the promise might be sure to all the seed; not to that only which is of the law, but to that also which is of the faith of Abraham; who is the father of us all,

Romans 5:1 Therefore being justified by faith, we have peace with God through our Lord Jesus Christ:

Romans 11:6 And if by grace, then *is it* no more of works: otherwise grace is no more grace. But if *it be* of works, then is it no more grace: otherwise work is no more work.

This truth is expressed in the simplest of statements in Ephesians 2:8.

For by grace are ye saved through faith; and that not of yourselves: *it is* the gift of God:

The context for the misused verse in Galatians 3:27 clearly proclaims the vital connection of salvation and justification with faith. The context of a verse is that which is found in the verses that surround that verse. In the previous chapter of Galatians, the apostle is firm in emphasizing the same truth as in the Epistles of Romans and Ephesians.

Galatians 2:16 Knowing that a man is not justified by the works of the law, but by the faith of Jesus Christ, even we have believed in Jesus Christ, that we might be justified by the faith of Christ, and not by the works of the law: for by the works of the law shall no flesh be justified. ... 20 I am crucified with Christ: nevertheless I live; yet not I, but Christ liveth in me: and the life which I now live in the flesh I live by the faith of the Son of God, who loved me, and gave himself for me. 21 I do not

frustrate the grace of God: for if righteousness *come* by the law, then Christ is
dead in vain.

Verse twenty-one provides the strongest
possible affirmation of salvation by grace in
the English language as it declares that *if a
law could produce righteousness, Christ died
in vain.* The apostle would obviously have had
the Law of Moses in mind as these words are
written at the direction of the Holy Spirit;
however, in verse twenty-seven of chapter
three, he included all possible laws that might
have been given. The declaration is that if
were possible under any potential scenario for
obedience to any law to provide salvation,
then that law ought to have been given so that
righteousness could have been by that law.
The conclusion is that nothing that individual
man or collective humanity might accomplish
could provide righteousness under any
circumstance.

Therefore, every effort of an individual or
of the whole of unified mankind is doomed to
failure. Paul writes that the Galatians were
foolish to have allowed themselves to be
persuaded that they could obtain salvation
through some work or a lifetime of perfect
obedience to laws.

Galatians 3:1 O foolish Galatians, who
hath bewitched you, that ye should not
obey the truth, before whose eyes Jesus
Christ hath been evidently set forth, crucified among you? 2 This only would I learn
of you, Received ye the Spirit by the works
of the law, or by the hearing of faith? 3
Are ye so foolish? having begun in the
Spirit, are ye now made perfect by the
flesh? 4 Have ye suffered so many things

in vain? if *it be* yet in vain. 5 He therefore that ministereth to you the Spirit, and worketh miracles among you, *doeth he it* by the works of the law, or by the hearing of faith? 6 Even as Abraham believed God, and it was accounted to him for right-eousness. 7 Know ye therefore that they which are of faith, the same are the children of Abraham. 8 And the scripture, foreseeing that God would justify the heathen through faith, preached before the gospel unto Abraham, *saying*, In thee shall all nations be blessed. 9 So then they which be of faith are blessed with faithful Abraham. 10 For as many as are of the works of the law are under the curse: for it is written, Cursed *is* every one that continueth not in all things which are written in the book of the law to do them. 11 But that **no man is justified by the law in the sight of God**, *it is* evident: for, The just shall live by faith. 12 And the law is not of faith: but, The man that doeth them shall live in them. 13 Christ hath redeemed us from the curse of the law, being made a curse for us: for it is written, Cursed *is* every one that hangeth on a tree: 14 **That the blessing of Abraham might come on the Gentiles through Jesus Christ; that we might receive the promise of the Spirit through faith.** 15 Brethren, I speak after the manner of men; Though *it be* but a man's covenant, yet *if it be* confirmed, no man disannul-eth, or addeth thereto. 16 Now to Abraham and his seed were the promises made. He saith not, And to seeds, as of many; but as of one, And to thy seed, which is Christ. 17 And this I say, *that* the covenant, that was confirmed before of God in Christ, the law, which was four hundred and thirty years after, cannot disannul, that it should make the promise of none effect. 18 For if the inheritance *be* of the law, *it is* no more of promise: but God gave *it* to Abraham by promise. 19 Wherefore then *serveth* the law? It was added because of transgressions, till the seed should come to whom the promise was made; *and it was* ordained by angels in the hand of a mediator. 20 Now a mediator is not *a mediator* of one, but God is one. 21 *Is* the law then against the promises of God? **God forbid: for if there had been a law given which could have given life, verily righteousness should have been by the law.** 22 But the scripture hath concluded all under sin, **that the promise by faith of Jesus Christ might be given to them that believe.** 23 But before faith came, we were kept under the law, shut up unto the faith which should afterwards be revealed. 24 Wherefore the law was our schoolmaster *to bring us* unto Christ, that we might be justified by faith. 25 But after that faith is come, we are no longer under a schoolmaster. 26 For ye are all the children of God by faith in Christ Jesus. 27 For as many of you as have been baptized into Christ have put on Christ. 28 There is neither Jew nor Greek, there is neither bond nor free, there is neither male nor female: for ye are all one in Christ Jesus. 29 And if ye *be* Christ's, then are ye Abraham's seed, and heirs according to the promise.

The Holy Spirit moves Paul to focus his argument on two precepts. If obedience and fulfillment of any law *could have* provided eternal life, then

(1) that Law should have been given; and,

if that be true, then,

(2) Christ died in vain.

If GOD could have devised a law whereby even one individual could have achieved righteousness, then the death of Christ was meaningless. Calvary would have accomplished no more than might have accomplished by obeying that law; therefore, Jesus of Nazareth did not need to die. This means that the very concept of law-keeping salvation is not only meritless in that it does not attain the positive possession of righteousness; but it is blasphemous—it is a serious liability, in that the concept attributes to Christ a foolish and needless death that has no value.

According to the Holy Spirit, writing through the apostle, for the Galatian believers to have accepted such an untenable, unscriptural concept is evidence that they have been *bewitched. Merriam-Webster 11th Collegiate Dictionary* gives the definition of *bewitch* as "*to influence or affect especially injuriously by witchcraft; to cast a spell over; to attract as if by the power of witchcraft.*" The word *bewitched* is found three times in the Authorized Version and is connected with sorceries in two of the passages.[8] Sorcery is defined by *Merriam-Webster* as "*the use of power gained from the assistance or control of evil spirits especially for divining.*"

To believe false doctrine is keeping company with witchcraft and sorcery. To accept the premise that salvation might be accomplished without the atoning sacrifice of the blood of the LORD Jesus is to traffic with satanic elements. Idolatry, which is the ultimate example of false doctrine, is clearly an act of worship of Satan.

> Psalm 106:36 And they served their idols: which were a snare unto them. 37 Yea, they sacrificed their sons and their daughters unto devils, 38 And shed innocent blood, *even* the blood of their sons and of their daughters, whom they sacrificed unto the idols of Canaan: and the land was polluted with blood. 39 Thus were they defiled with their own works, and went a whoring with their own inventions.

> 1 Corinthians 10:20 But *I say*, that the things which the Gentiles sacrifice, they sacrifice to devils, and not to God: and I would not that ye should have fellowship with devils.

To attribute to baptism any participation to or even a relationship with the reception of salvation is to change the Gospel from a message of grace to a edict of works. To teach such a gospel of works is to teach a false gospel. To believe such a false gospel is to believe a lie.

> Romans 11:6 And if by grace, then *is it* no more of works: otherwise grace is no more grace. But if *it be* of works, then is it no more grace: otherwise work is no more work.

The testimony throughout the Scriptures is that salvation has never been achieved through human works either before or after the Law was given.

> Romans 4:2 For if Abraham were justified by works, he hath *whereof* to glory; but not before God. 3 For what saith the scripture? Abraham believed God, and it was counted unto him for righteousness. 4 Now to him that worketh is the reward not reckoned of grace, but of debt. 5 But to

43

him that worketh not, but believeth on him that justifieth the ungodly, his faith is counted for righteousness. 6 Even as David also describeth the blessedness of the man, unto whom God imputeth righteousness without works, 7 *Saying*, Blessed *are* they whose iniquities are forgiven, and whose sins are covered. 8 Blessed *is* the man to whom the Lord will not impute sin.

Baptism is not connected with the obtaining or the possessing of salvation; it is the testimony that salvation has been received. Baptism is a type, a picture. The antitype for baptism is not difficult to understand. Baptism is the type, the picture, or the likeness, of the threefold antitype death, burial, and resurrection of the Christ.[9]

Romans 6:4 Therefore we are buried **with** him by baptism into death: that **like as** Christ was raised up from the dead by the glory of the Father, **even so** we also should walk in newness of life. 5 For if we have been planted together **in the likeness** of his death, we shall be also *in the likeness* of *his* resurrection: 6 Knowing this, that our old man is crucified with *him*, that the body of sin might be destroyed, that henceforth we should not serve sin.

This walking in the *newness of life*, the putting *on of Christ*, that is to follow baptism being referred to in Romans chapter six is the same as the changes in the life of the *new man* described in Ephesians and Colossians.

Ephesians 4:17 This I say therefore, and testify in the Lord, that ye henceforth walk not as other Gentiles walk, in the vanity of their mind, 18 Having the understanding

44

darkened, being alienated from the life of God through the ignorance that is in them, because of the blindness of their heart: 19 Who being past feeling have given themselves over unto lasciviousness, to work all uncleanness with greediness. 20 But ye have not so learned Christ; 21 If so be that ye have heard him, and have been taught by him, as the truth is in Jesus: 22 That ye **put off concerning the former conversation the old man,** which is corrupt according to the deceitful lusts; 23 And be renewed in the spirit of your mind; 24 And that ye **put on the new man**, which after God is created in righteousness and true holiness. 25 Wherefore **putting away** lying, speak every man truth with his neighbour: for we are members one of another. 26 Be ye angry, and sin not: let not the sun go down upon your wrath: 27 Neither give place to the devil. 28 Let him that stole steal no more: but rather let him labour, working with *his* hands the thing which is good, that he may have to give to him that needeth. 29 Let no corrupt communication proceed out of your mouth, but that which is good to the use of edifying, that it may minister grace unto the hearers. 30 And grieve not the holy Spirit of God, whereby ye are sealed unto the day of redemption. 31 Let all bitterness, and wrath, and anger, and clamour, and evil speaking, be **put away** from you, with all malice: 32 And be ye kind one to another, tenderhearted, forgiving one another, even as God for Christ's sake hath forgiven you.

Colossians 3:1 If ye then be risen with Christ, seek those things which are above, where Christ sitteth on the right hand of God. 2 Set your affection on things above, not on things on the earth. 3 **For ye are dead, and your life is hid with Christ in God.** 4 When Christ, *who is* our life, shall appear, then shall ye also appear with him in glory. 5 Mortify therefore your members which are upon the earth; fornication, uncleanness, inordinate affection, evil concupiscence, and covetousness, which is idolatry: 6 For which things' sake the wrath of God cometh on the children of disobedience: 7 In the which ye also walked some time, when ye lived in them. 8 But now ye also **put off** all these; anger, wrath, malice, blasphemy, filthy communication out of your mouth. 9 Lie not one to another, seeing that ye have **put off the old man** with his deeds; 10 And have **put on the new** *man*, which is renewed in knowledge after the image of him that created him: 11 Where there is neither Greek nor Jew, circumcision nor uncircumcision, Barbarian, Scythian, bond *nor* free: but Christ *is* all, and in all. 12 **Put on** therefore, as the elect of God, holy and beloved, bowels of mercies, kindness, humbleness of mind, meekness, longsuffering; 13 Forbearing one another, and forgiving one another, if any man have a quarrel against any: even as Christ forgave you, so also *do* ye. 14 And above all these things *put on* charity, which is the bond of perfectness. 15 And let the peace of God rule in your hearts, to the which also ye are called in one body; and be ye thankful. 16 Let the word of Christ dwell in you richly in all wisdom; teaching and admonishing one another in psalms and hymns and spiritual songs, singing with grace in your hearts to the Lord. 17 And whatsoever ye do in word or deed, *do* all in the name of the Lord Jesus, giving thanks to God and the Father by him. ... 23 And whatsoever ye do, do *it* heartily, as to the Lord, and not unto men; 24 Knowing that of the Lord ye shall receive the reward of the inheritance: for ye serve the Lord Christ. 25 But he that doeth wrong shall receive for the wrong which he hath done: and there is no respect of persons.

Baptism does not remove *original* sin.

Baptism is not necessary for salvation.

Baptism is not the culmination of the process of salvation.

Baptism does not free from sin.[10]

Baptism does not obtain salvation.

Baptism is not the rebirth of a child of GOD.

Baptism does not remit sin.

Baptism has no part or portion in salvation

Baptism is identification with Christ.

SECOND, BAPTISM IS IDENTIFICATION WITH THE CHURCH.

The apostle Paul declares that baptism is into one body.

> 1 Corinthians 12:13 For by one Spirit are we all baptized into one body, whether we be Jews or Gentiles, whether we be bond or free; and have been all made to drink into one Spirit.

The context of this passage quite plainly identifies *the one body* in this text as the *local church of Corinth* to whom the Epistle was written. While I believe this is a self-evident conclusion gleaned from simply reading that text in its context, that understanding becomes inescapable when the Epistle is viewed as a whole. This might seem to be an obvious conclusion; however, that conclusion has escaped many commentators.

Several years ago, I worked through the Epistle marking every use of the second person personal pronouns. Without exception, those pronouns refer to the members of the church of GOD at Corinth as a body. Since I believe that exercise helped cement my understanding of the importance of the local church, I have included a *Single Issue Commentary* as Chapter 12 so that it might do the same for you.

When the trail of the second person personal pronouns is followed to its completion, the importance of the local church in Corinth and its relationship to Christ is established beyond question.[11] The pronoun *ye* refers in 1 Corinthians 12:27 to the members of the church in Corinth exactly as it does in every other use in the Epistle.

That church is to be respected by her members as the body of Christ.

> Now ye are the body of Christ, and members in particular.

This was not to suggest that the church at Corinth was the unique and only body of Christ, but that the church at Corinth was the body of Christ under discussion in chapter twelve of the Epistle.

Verse thirteen of this same chapter connects baptism and membership in the church at Corinth as united in a relationship that correlates with the pattern of the Book of Acts. The record of Acts 2 is that those who were baptized were added to the church at Jerusalem, which was the only church then in existence, by that act of baptism. Baptism was, according to this verse, the actual step of adding the person to the church in Jerusalem. Quite properly, that observation has led Baptists to describe baptism as the *introductory rite into the church.*

> Acts 2:41 Then they that gladly received his word were baptized: and the same day there were added *unto them* about three thousand souls. 42 And they continued stedfastly in the apostles' doctrine and fellowship, and in breaking of bread, and in prayers. 43 And fear came upon every soul: and many wonders and signs were done by the apostles. 44 And all that believed were together, and had all things common; 45 And sold their possessions and goods, and parted them to all *men,* as every man had need. 46 And they, continuing daily with one accord in the temple, and breaking bread from house to house, did eat their meat with gladness and singleness of heart, 47 Praising God, and having favour with all the people. And the Lord added to the church daily such as should be saved.

The Bible is emphatic that baptism never had and never will have anything to do with obtaining salvation. Baptism never saved anyone and never contributed anything towards the salvation of anyone in any era of time.

Within the New Testament, not a single example can be cited of an individual being baptized under the authority of a New Testament church *other than* a professing believer.

I believe there is a particular example that demonstrates the truth that baptism does not save. Acts chapter eight provides the instance of the baptism of Simon, who was baptized *upon* his profession of faith, but who was *never* a genuine believer.

> 13 Then Simon himself believed also: and when he was baptized, he continued with Philip, and wondered, beholding the miracles and signs which were done. ... 18 And when Simon saw that through laying on of the apostles' hands the Holy Ghost was given, he offered them money, 19 Saying, Give me also this power, that on whomsoever I lay hands, he may receive the Holy Ghost. 20 But Peter said unto him, Thy money **perish with thee**, because thou hast thought that the gift of God may be purchased with money. 21 **Thou hast neither part nor lot in this matter: for thy heart is not right in the sight of God**. 22 Repent therefore of this thy wickedness, and pray God, if perhaps the thought of thine heart may be forgiven thee. 23 For I perceive that **thou art in the gall of bitterness, and *in* the bond of iniquity**.

Simon had *neither part not lot in this matter* and was in *the bond of iniquity.* I understand this description of Simon to reveal that he has not been saved. Simon was like so many who believe *with the mind,* but not *with the heart.* He *believed,* but he *wondered.* He had an intellectual understanding but he lacked the *spiritual acceptance.* Simeon thought that the *gift of God* could be *purchased with money.* Like too many others, Simon was a baptized unbeliever, a man that had made a false profession of faith.

The disciples in Ephesus that Paul encounters as recorded in Acts chapter nineteen are an example of those who were baptized as improper subjects and without the proper authority.

> Acts 19:1 And it came to pass, that, while Apollos was at Corinth, Paul having passed through the upper coasts came to Ephesus: and finding certain disciples, 2 He said unto them, Have ye received the **Holy Ghost** since ye believed? And they said unto him, **We have not so much as heard whether there be any Holy Ghost**. 3 And he said unto them, Unto what then were ye baptized? And they said, Unto John's baptism. 4 Then said Paul, John verily baptized with the baptism of repentance, saying unto the people, **that they should believe on him which should come after him, that is, on Christ Jesus.** 5 **When they heard *this*,** they were baptized in the name of the Lord Jesus. 6 And when Paul had laid *his* hands upon them, the **Holy Ghost** came on them; and they spake with tongues, and prophesied. 7 And all the men were about twelve.

It seems clear that these individuals never heard John preach. A careful reading of the passage shows that they do not claim to have been baptized by John the Baptist. Their assertion is only that they were baptized *unto John's baptism*. In the same fashion as Apollos, they give evidence of having heard *about* John the Baptist, but having an insufficient or non-existent knowledge of Jesus of Nazareth as the Christ, Who was the fulfillment of the message of John.

1. These men did not know of the existence of the Holy Spirit. It is doubtful

that anyone could hear the preaching of John the Baptist and not know of the Holy Spirit; that doctrine was part of his testimony and his preaching.[12]

2. These individuals did not know that they were to believe on Him Who came after John the Baptist. It is certain that no one could hear the preaching of John the Baptist and not be aware that Christ Jesus was to come.[13] That was the entirety of his reason for preaching and it was his continuous message.

For these individuals not to know that Jesus had come these decades after the crucifixion is indication of a deficiency in their knowledge and the obvious lack of actual personal contact with John the Baptist and no contact with Jesus of Nazareth. Who performed their baptisms is textually unknown, but the evidence does not support a baptism by John the Baptist.

These deficiencies would make the baptism that they received unauthorized and invalid. The fact that these individuals had a terribly inadequate, incomplete, insufficient understanding of Jesus Christ would also invalidate their baptism regardless of where or under what authority it was received, as it would the baptism of any other individual.

Paul did not conduct a baptismal service for these individuals because they had been inadequately baptized by John and needed rebaptism with *Christian baptism*. Every apostle was baptized by John the Baptist as were the seventy; not one of the twelve or of the seventy was re-baptized. The baptism of

John was *Christian* baptism.

The only reasons for a person entering into the baptismal waters for the second time are:

The person was not saved when he was baptized.

The baptism was received as a part of obtaining salvation.

The baptism was not in accordance with the Biblical requirements as to method and authority.

Baptism has a purpose, but that purpose is for identification and not for the regeneration of the soul or removal of sin from the person. The person must have the ability to make a valid confession of faith.

While not all baptismal regenerationists will baptize unconscious individuals and infants, most Protestants that incorporate baptism as a part of salvation, even if that part is anticipatory, do encourage the baptism of infants. Such baptisms are not only permissible, they are required in Roman Catholicism.

Since *no passage of Scripture that concerns baptism ever even mentions a baby,* those that do baptize infants and do so as soon as possible following the birth, resort to three basic arguments to support the deed.

Compare baptism to circumcision as a sign of a covenant.

Insist that the use of the word *household* must include infants.

Argue that since baptism removes original sin, it would be wrong to deny babies the rite of baptism.

Other arguments are advanced, but they are largely an expansion of one of these three. The irrefutable record is that no infants were baptized within the pages of Holy Writ, while multiple adults are identified as being baptized or having been baptized.

In exact opposition to the idea of baptizing a person that does not have the capacity to believe, the Bible teaches that baptism is an act of obedience by a knowledgeable, willing, consenting believer; baptism is never an act that is to be undertaken by a sinner seeking salvation or performed on a person unawares.

The mode of baptism through the New Testament is immersion in water; no one is sprinkled with water, and no one has water poured upon his head. Those facts are incontrovertible. No baptismal bowls or baptismal pitchers appear anywhere in the text of the New Testament; that detail also is undeniable.

That baptism is immersion is evidenced both by the many clear scriptural examples and by the precise symbolism declared to be involved in the act of baptism. No legitimate textual support exists for any statement purporting that baptism as practiced by John the Baptist and the apostles, including Paul, could be understood as anything other than the immersion of a professing believer in water.

> Matthew 3:16 And Jesus, when he was baptized, went up straightway out of the water: and, lo, the heavens were opened unto him, and he saw the Spirit of God descending like a dove, and lighting upon him:

Mark 1:9 And it came to pass in those days, that Jesus came from Nazareth of Galilee, and was baptized of John in Jordan. 10 And straightway coming up out of the water, he saw the heavens opened, and the Spirit like a dove descending upon him:

Acts 8:38 And he commanded the chariot to stand still: and they went down both into the water, both Philip and the eunuch; and he baptized him. 39 And when they were come up out of the water, the Spirit of the Lord caught away Philip, that the eunuch saw him no more: and he went on his way rejoicing.

Romans 6:4 Therefore we are buried with him by baptism into death: that like as Christ was raised up from the dead by the glory of the Father, even so we also should walk in newness of life.

Baptism does not, indeed cannot, impart life. Baptism does not regenerate. Baptism does not seal in the anticipation of eventual faith. Instead of being a *birth*, either in the fact or in the type, baptism is clearly defined as a *burial* in type and an *identification* in fact.

Many excuses are offered to promote the suggestion that either sprinkling or pouring is or could be the mode of baptism employed. None of those pretexts, in spite of how well reasoned or good sounding they may be, are based upon the undeniable meaning of the word itself, nor could they honestly be so based.[14] Neither sprinkling or pouring fit the type that baptism is portraying—the death, burial, and resurrection of Christ Jesus.

Lacking either textual citation or linguistic support, the proponents advance *tradition, convenience, symbolism, or new revelation* as the authority for ignoring the New Testament pattern and introducing an altered form. Some insist that baptism may be accomplished through immersion, sprinkling, or pouring depending upon whichever satisfies the preference of the individual. These concepts are nothing more than the reasonings of men who are in open conflict with Scripture, no matter how sincere they might have been or are.

How baptism is administered is not determined based on popular vote. The form and purpose of baptism is established in the Scriptures. No one has the authority to conflict with or to contradict the settled word of GOD.

The appeal to only the Bible affirms that baptism does not symbolically convey the sprinkling of the blood or the out-pouring of the Holy Spirit. Baptism does not signify the washing away of sins.

Baptism is indeed a type, a representation; but baptism as a type unquestionably represents in Scripture the antitype, the threefold picture in one act: that of the death, the burial, and the resurrection of the LORD Jesus Christ. Baptism must represent that same type to us.

> Romans 6:4 Therefore we are buried with him by baptism into death: that like as Christ was raised up from the dead by the glory of the Father, even so we also should walk in newness of life.

> Colossians 2:12 Buried with him in baptism, wherein also ye are risen with him through the faith of the operation of God,

56

who hath raised him from the dead.

Besides the many examples of baptisms described in Scripture and along with the symbolism portrayed in the act of baptism, the very Greek words[15] that are brought into English as transliterations instead of translations, being *baptize, baptizing, baptized, baptism, baptisms,* and *Baptist,* can be understood literally only in the sense of an immersion, a dipping, a submergence. Absolutely no suggestion of pouring or sprinkling can be traced to the Greek words.

Even secular English dictionaries in giving the etymology of the English word *baptize,* freely recognize that this word (and all the other related words cited above are English descendants from the transliterated[16] Greek βαπτιζω, meaning "to immerse, submerge; to make whelmed (i.e. fully wet)."

Scholars of the Biblical Greek readily and boldly declare this same truth. The Greek Orthodox Church, also identified as the Eastern Orthodox Church, interestingly enough baptizes only by *immersion,* including those babies that are baptized into Orthodoxy! The Greek Orthodox at least understand the Greek word βαπτιζω.

The word *baptize* in any of its forms can only mean immersion, nothing except immersion, and nothing less than immersion to any individual who desires to honor the universally accepted meaning of the word—whether in Greek or English—whether in the act or in the type and *to obey the Scriptures.*

In spite of tradition, custom, or sincerity, baptism does not portray the sprinkling of the blood upon the altar, the out-pouring of the

Holy Spirit on the day of Pentecost, or the washing away of sins. The New Testament, the only reliable authority and source for the practice, is emphatic and unequivocal that baptism pictures the death, the burial, and the resurrection of the LORD Jesus Christ.

Valid baptism was by immersion in the days of the New Testament, and continued to be immersion through the intervening ages, and baptism remains immersion today. Baptism is immersion—and nothing else, and nothing less!

Tradition is wonderful to follow, and should be followed, but *only when and only if* the tradition has a biblical basis.

> 2 Thessalonians 2:15 Therefore, brethren, stand fast, and hold the traditions which ye have been taught, whether by word, or our epistle.

> 2 Thessalonians 3:6 Now we command you, brethren, in the name of our Lord Jesus Christ, that ye withdraw yourselves from every brother that walketh disorderly, and not after the tradition which he received of us.

When any tradition does not rise from a biblical foundation, then that tradition is either a doctrine of devils (always bad) or a commandment of men (which may be either good or bad). A good tradition may be worthy of being followed, but it is never binding. Tradition is not the same as Scripture and tradition must never be treated as if the tradition were Scripture by giving it the weight of Scripture. The warnings are exceptionally clear.

> 1 Timothy 4:1 Now the Spirit speaketh

expressly, that in the latter times some shall depart from the faith, giving heed to seducing spirits, and doctrines of devils;

Matthew 15:2 Why do thy disciples transgress the tradition of the elders? for they wash not their hands when they eat bread. 3 But he answered and said unto them, Why do ye also transgress the commandment of God by your tradition? ... 6 Thus have ye made the commandment of God of none effect by your tradition.[17]

Some traditions are not evil of themselves or in conflict with Scripture. Those may be followed safely, if they are appropriate. Examples of such traditions would be Sunday Morning Services, Sunday Schools, the times services start, and a host of others.

However, many traditions are evil and are in conflict with Scripture. Those ought to be avoided, and, if need be, resisted strenuously. Examples of these would include special clerical garb, unmarried clergy, prayers to saints, indulgences, and a near unlimited list of commandments originating with men (and, let us not forget, from women).

When the tradition does not originate from Scripture, it cannot be *binding* and will be in conflict with Scripture; it is *damning*. Any tradition that *lays aside, changes,* or *rejects* the commands of GOD did not originate with GOD, but comes from either humanity or devils.

For a Christian to allow any tradition to alter the clear teachings of the word of GOD concerning baptism is to be *spoiled* and having a *vain (empty, meaningless)* conversation (*manner of life*). He was not led by the Spirit of GOD; and when he does so, he is not following GOD, regardless how sincere or satisfied he might claim to be personally. Such an individual is simply following a leadership other than that of the Holy Spirit, and there are three possibilities as to the source of any false doctrine concerning baptism:

(1) the teaching of seducing spirits,

(2) the introduction of doctrines of devils, or

(3) the tradition or heresy propagated by some human. The individual may be sincere, but that person has been deceived.

> Colossians 2:8 Beware lest any man spoil you through philosophy and vain deceit, after the tradition of men, after the rudiments of the world, and not after Christ.

> 1 Peter 1:18 Forasmuch as ye know that ye were not redeemed with corruptible things, as silver and gold, from your vain conversation received by tradition from your fathers;

Any *new revelation* that would contradict Scripture or presume to *supersede* Scripture is either Satanic or human in origin; it cannot be authoritative and must be rejected entirely. No believer should ever allow anyone to use *new revelation* as the basis for anything! Revelation ceased with the closing of the canon of Scripture; there is no basis in Scripture to expect any new revelation today. In opposition to such vain anticipation, Scripture warns against following any alleged revelation that alters or reverses Scripture.

> Deuteronomy 13:1 If there arise among

you a prophet, or a dreamer of dreams, and giveth thee a sign or a wonder, 2 And the sign or the wonder come to pass, whereof he spake unto thee, saying, Let us go after other gods, which thou hast not known, and let us serve them; 3 Thou shalt not hearken unto the words of that prophet, or that dreamer of dreams: for the LORD your God proveth you, to know whether ye love the LORD your God with all your heart and with all your soul. 4 Ye shall walk after the LORD your God, and fear him, and keep his commandments, and obey his voice, and ye shall serve him, and cleave unto him. 5 And that prophet, or that dreamer of dreams, shall be put to death; because he hath spoken to turn *you* away from the LORD your God, which brought you out of the land of Egypt, and redeemed you out of the house of bondage, to thrust thee out of the way which the LORD thy God commanded thee to walk in. So shalt thou put the evil away from the midst of thee.

Proverbs 19:27 Cease, my son, to hear the instruction that causeth to err from the words of knowledge.

Isaiah 8:20 To the law and to the testimony: if they speak not according to this word, it is because there is no light in them.

Matthew 7:15 Beware of false prophets, which come to you in sheep's clothing, but inwardly they are ravening wolves. 16 Ye shall know them by their fruits. Do men gather grapes of thorns, or figs of thistles? 17 Even so every good tree bringeth forth good fruit; but a corrupt tree bringeth forth evil fruit. 18 A good tree cannot bring forth evil fruit, neither *can* a corrupt tree bring forth good fruit. 19 Every tree that bringeth not forth good fruit is hewn down, and cast into the fire. 20 Wherefore by their fruits ye shall know them. 21 Not every one that saith unto me, Lord, Lord, shall enter into the kingdom of heaven; but he that doeth the will of my Father which is in heaven. 22 Many will say to me in that day, Lord, Lord, have we not prophesied in thy name? and in thy name have cast out devils? and in thy name done many wonderful works? 23 And then will I profess unto them, I never knew you: depart from me, ye that work iniquity. 24 Therefore whosoever heareth these sayings of mine, and doeth them, I will liken him unto a wise man, which built his house upon a rock: 25 And the rain descended, and the floods came, and the winds blew, and beat upon that house; and it fell not: for it was founded upon a rock. 26 And every one that heareth these sayings of mine, and doeth them not, shall be likened unto a foolish man, which built his house upon the sand: 27 And the rain descended, and the floods came, and the winds blew, and beat upon that house; and it fell: and great was the fall of it. 28 And it came to pass, when Jesus had ended these sayings, the people were astonished at his doctrine: 29 For he taught them as *one* having authority, and not as the scribes.

Matthew 15:9 But in vain they do worship me, teaching for doctrines the commandments of men.

Romans 16:17 Now I beseech you, brethren, mark them which cause divisions and offences contrary to the doctrine which ye have learned; and avoid them. 18 For they that are such serve not our Lord Jesus

Christ, but their own belly; and by good words and fair speeches deceive the hearts of the simple.

Galatians 1:6 I marvel that ye are so soon removed from him that called you into the grace of Christ unto another gospel: 7 Which is not another; but there be some that trouble you, and would pervert the gospel of Christ. 8 But though we, or an angel from heaven, preach any other gospel unto you than that which we have preached unto you, let him be accursed. 9 As we said before, so say I now again, If any *man* preach any other gospel unto you than that ye have received, let him be accursed.

1 John 4:1 Beloved, believe not every spirit, but try the spirits whether they are of God: because many false prophets are gone out into the world. 2 Hereby know ye the Spirit of God: Every spirit that confesseth that Jesus Christ is come in the flesh is of God: 3 And every spirit that confesseth not that Jesus Christ is come in the flesh is not of God: and this is that *spirit* of antichrist, whereof ye have heard that it should come; and even now already is it in the world..

2 Peter 2:1 But there were false prophets also among the people, even as there shall be false teachers among you, who privily shall bring in damnable heresies, even denying the Lord that bought them, and bring upon themselves swift destruction.

The motivation for reconfiguring baptism from immersion to a more convenient mode, is sometimes justified as a *convenience* (such as the need to baptize comatose or dying individuals, those who have a physical inability to enter a baptismal pool, those who are infants,

63

etc.). Some groups promote such deviation from Scripture because *without exception* the concept of salvation which they teach requires in some fashion or to some extent baptism as the means to remove or to wash away sin. Their doctrine of salvation requires a mode of baptism that might be suitable for everyone, even if it must be a change from the teaching of Scripture!

Obviously, that doctrine provides the motivation behind their tampering with Scripture. The inventors transformed the mode of baptism to fit the theology that they taught. The groups that they engendered have followed their inventions as if the Holy Spirit devised them. They have laid *aside the commandment of GOD,* and instead *hold the tradition of men,* making *the commandment of GOD of none effect by* their new *traditions.*

¹ Even those entities that eschew the name Baptist will describe this position as baptistic.

² Through the second grade of school, I attended a Methodist Church. The pastor performed baptisms by dipping the bud of a red rose in a bowl of water and shaking that bud over the heads of those whom he baptized.

³ I once encountered a man that had baptized himself and who was offended when I would not recognize his act as a valid baptism. I would assume that he is not the only self-deluded individual that has performed this act.

⁴ Canon 849 Baptism, the gateway to the sacraments and necessary for salvation by actual reception or at least by desire, is validly conferred only by a washing of true water with the proper form of words. Through baptism men and women are freed from sin, are reborn as children of God, and, configured to Christ by an indelible character, are incorporated into the Church.
http://www.vatican.va/archive/ENG1104/_P2W.HTM
§2. When an ordinary minister is absent or impeded, a catechist or another person designated for this function by the local ordinary, or in a case of necessity any person with the right intention, confers baptism licitly.
Cannon 868 §2. An infant of Catholic parents or even of non-Catholic parents is baptized licitly in danger of death even against the will of the parents.
http://www.vatican.va/archive/ENG1104/_P2U.HTM
V. WHO CAN BAPTIZE?
§1256 The ordinary ministers of Baptism are the bishop and priest and, in the Latin Church, also the deacon. In case of necessity, anyone, even a non-baptized person, with the required intention, can baptize , by using the Trinitarian baptismal formula. The intention required is to will to do what the Church does when she baptizes. The Church finds the reason for this possibility in the universal saving will of God and the necessity of Baptism for salvation.
Catechism of the Catholic Church, Second Edition

⁵ Dispensationalists divide all history into sections of time during which GOD relates to His creation in different ways. The number of dispensations varies

among the different schools of Dispensationalism. Probably the most common number is seven.

6 "The word Protestant describes the protestation of the Reformers against the excesses of the Roman Catholic Church. While retaining many of the doctrines and practices of the RCC, Luther and others voiced a call for the reform of the RCC. It was the sale of indulgences (some of which were for sins that *might be* committed in the future), and other such excesses that spurred the public actions. As the RCC resisted, became intransient, and finally demanded subservient compliance, these individuals resisted the pressures and the dangers, refused to surrender their consciences, and retained their opposition. The courage required and the bravery demonstrated for those actions is undeniable; however, the divorcement was forced upon the Reformers. Separation from the RCC was certainly not their initial design or desire.

"They did not reject, certainly they did not repudiate, some of the central fundamental doctrines of the RCC. They desired only to reform—keeping some of the form and much of the substance, but reshaping the structure and the application.

"It is important to recognize that the disagreement was at first more against the *practices* of the RCC than it was against the *doctrines* of the RCC. However, as the move to reform failed, the movement became a division. In the process of time, the areas of doctrinal differences became a part of the rupture between the Reformers and the RCC and between the various Reformers themselves.

"It should be stated that both the RCC and the Reformers wrote of individuals and groups, which were identified by various names, that were outside of the RCC but that were separate from and not identified with the Reformers. These individuals and groups received pressure that escalated to persecution from both the Reformers and the RCC.

"Chief among the causes for the unity of the RCC and the Reformers in their pressure, which often became persecution, against those churches and individuals that were in existence prior to the Reformation, continued with a viable existence through the Reformation, remained firmly outside of the RCC, and that would not align with the Reformers, was the issue of believer's baptism. The RCC and the Reformers agreed that baptism, particularly infant baptism, was required and both the RCC and the Reformers were enraged that the validity of their common baptism would be questioned.

"The Reformers consistently maintained that the baptism that they had received by the authority of the RCC was valid. No record exists of a single Reformer having repudiated his RCC baptism and receiving believer's baptism after leaving or being excommunicated by the RCC.

"The commonality between all of the reformers and the RCC beyond their baptism, was a deep, bitter hatred for anyone who believed that the baptism of the RCC and the Reformers was invalid and who accordingly called for those who followed Christ to receive believer's baptism.

"Both the Reformers and the RCC gave those believers that were outside the RCC the derogatory name of the re-baptizers or Anabaptists to various groups that each considered dissidents or heretics. Historians have also used the name indiscriminately. Within those who were broadly labeled Anabaptists would have been individuals and churches that would not have an affinity for those others receiving the same brand at that time or in any other era. However, among those churches and individuals who were so labeled did exist some that retained and maintained the doctrine and practices of the apostolic churches. Not all of those identified by the RCC and the Reformers with the Anabaptist label were sound in the faith; however, some were. A similar situation exists with the name Baptist in the present age. The use of the name whether to self-identify or as a label applied by others does not guarantee either uniformity or accuracy in that application. Those believers rejected that name insisting that they did not *re-baptize* anyone; they were convinced that the baptism of infants was not Biblical, and therefore it was not a genuine baptism. These individuals and churches that were independent from both the RCC and the Reformers faithfully practiced the immersion of believers after and upon their profession of faith."

Manley, Jerald L., *The WILTED Tulip, 2013; ISBN 1493577387;* page 27.

7 **Catholicism** teaches: Since the New Testament era, the Catholic Church has always understood baptism differently, teaching that it is a sacrament which accomplishes several things, the first of which is the remission of sin, both original sin and actual sin—only original sin in the case of infants and young children, since they are incapable of actual sin; and both original and actual sin in the case of older persons. Peter explained what happens at baptism when he said, "Repent, and be baptized every one of you in the name of Jesus Christ for the forgiveness of your sins; and you shall receive the gift of the Holy Spirit" (Acts 2:38). But he did not restrict this teaching to adults. He added, "For the promise is to you and to your children and to all that are far off, every one whom the Lord our God calls to him" (2:39). We also read: "Rise and be baptized, and wash away your sins, calling on his name" (Acts 22:16). These commands are universal, not restricted to adults. Further, these commands make clear the necessary connection between baptism and salvation, a connection explicitly stated in 1 Peter 3:21: "Baptism ... now saves you, not as a removal of dirt from the body but as an appeal to God for a clear conscience, through the resurrection of Jesus Christ."
http://www.catholic.com/tracts/infant-baptism

Methodism teaches: Within the Methodist tradition, baptism has long been a subject of much concern, even controversy. John Wesley retained the sacramental theology which he received from his Anglican heritage. He taught that in baptism a child was cleansed of the guilt of original sin, initiated into the covenant with God, admitted into the church, made an heir of the divine kingdom, and spiritually born anew. He said that while baptism was neither essential to nor sufficient for salvation, it was the "ordinary means" that God designated for applying the benefits of the work of Christ in human lives.
http://www.umc.org/what-we-believe/by-water-and-the-spir it-a-united-methodist-understanding-of-baptism

Lutherans believe: Furthermore, Jesus said, "He who believes and is baptized shall be saved; he who believes

not shall be damned" (Mark 16:16). According to Jesus, ANYONE [sic] who does not believe in Him will be damned. Jesus makes no exception for infants. Babies will not be saved without faith in Jesus. Parents who think they are placing their children under God's grace by "dedicating" them are deceiving themselves. The only dedication that the New Testament knows of is the "dedication" that take place via baptism. That is why infants should be baptized. Like everyone else, they desperately need forgiveness. If infants die before they believe in Jesus, they will be eternally condemned. They, like everyone else, need to be baptized so that they can be born again. Jesus said, "unless one is born of water and the Spirit, he cannot enter the kingdom of God" (John 3:5). We believe that baptism is God's special means of grace for children by which He causes them to be born again. To keep them from baptism is to keep them from forgiveness and to endanger them with damnation.
http://www.orlutheran.com/html/trinfbap .html

[8] Acts 8:9 But there was a certain man, called Simon, which beforetime in the same city used sorcery, and bewitched the people of Samaria, giving out that himself was some great one:
Acts 8:11 And to him they had regard, because that of long time he had bewitched them with sorceries.
Galatians 3:1 O foolish Galatians, who hath bewitched you, that ye should not obey the truth, before whose eyes Jesus Christ hath been evidently set forth, crucified among you?

[9] Types are the illustration of the antitype, which is the fulfillment of the type. The type is usually the foreshadowing of the reality. I use the word type for baptism because it fits the pattern so very well; however, baptism is not a foreshadowing of its antitype. The reality of the death, burial, and resurrection of the LORD Jesus was prefigured by the baptisms performed by John the Baptist and the disciples of Christ during His earthly ministry. After the resurrection, baptism looks backward to the death, burial, and resurrection of Christ.

[10] Canon 849 Baptism, the gateway to the sacraments and necessary for salvation by actual reception or at least by desire, is validly conferred only by a

washing of true water with the proper form of words. Through baptism men and women are freed from sin, are reborn as children of God, and, configured to Christ by an indelible character, are incorporated into the Church.

http://www.vatican.va/archive/ENG1104/

[11] A few years ago at his request, I shared this commentary with a Baptist pastor. He soon gave the material back. He said that he started reading, but that he had stopped and would not finish. Somewhat sheepishly, he explained that he became convinced that if he actually did read to chapter twelve, he would have to change what he had preached was the meaning of verse twenty-seven. He said that he did not wish to face the awkwardness that changing his preaching might bring. Somehow, the truth of the text was less important than the potential of embarrassment for teaching the truth.

[12] Matthew 3:1 In those days came John the Baptist, preaching in the wilderness of Judaea, 2 And saying, Repent ye: for the kingdom of heaven is at hand. 3 For this is he that was spoken of by the prophet Esaias, saying, The voice of one crying in the wilderness, Prepare ye the way of the Lord, make his paths straight. 4 And the same John had his raiment of camel's hair, and a leathern girdle about his loins; and his meat was locusts and wild honey. 5 Then went out to him Jerusalem, and all Judaea, and all the region round about Jordan, 6 And were baptized of him in Jordan, confessing their sins. 7 But when he saw many of the Pharisees and Sadducees come to his baptism, he said unto them, O generation of vipers, who hath warned you to flee from the wrath to come? 8 Bring forth therefore fruits meet for repentance: 9 And think not to say within yourselves, We have Abraham to *our* father: for I say unto you, that God is able of these stones to raise up children unto Abraham. 10 And now also the axe is laid unto the root of the trees: therefore every tree which bringeth not forth good fruit is hewn down, and cast into the fire. 11 I indeed baptize you with water unto repentance: **but he that cometh after me is mightier than I, whose shoes I am not worthy to bear: he shall baptize you with the Holy Ghost,** and *with* fire: 12 Whose fan *is* in his hand, and he will

throughly purge his floor, and gather his wheat into the garner; but he will burn up the chaff with unquenchable fire. 13 Then cometh Jesus from Galilee to Jordan unto John, to be baptized of him. 14 But John forbad him, saying, I have need to be baptized of thee, and comest thou to me? 15 And Jesus answering said unto him, Suffer *it to be so* now: for thus it becometh us to fulfil all righteousness. Then he suffered him. 16 And Jesus, when he was baptized, went up straightway out of the water: and, lo, the heavens were opened unto him, and he saw the Spirit of God descending like a dove, and lighting upon him: 17 And lo a voice from heaven, saying, This is my beloved Son, in whom I am well pleased.

Mark 1:1 The beginning of the gospel of Jesus Christ, the Son of God; 2 As it is written in the prophets, Behold, I send my messenger before thy face, which shall prepare thy way before thee. 3 The voice of one crying in the wilderness, Prepare ye the way of the Lord, make his paths straight. 4 John did baptize in the wilderness, and preach the baptism of repentance for the remission of sins. 5 And there went out unto him all the land of Judaea, and they of Jerusalem, and were all baptized of him in the river of Jordan, confessing their sins. 6 And John was clothed with camel's hair, and with a girdle of a skin about his loins; and he did eat locusts and wild honey; 7 And preached, saying, **There cometh one mightier than I after me, the latchet of whose shoes I am not worthy to stoop down and unloose. 8 I indeed have baptized you with water: but he shall baptize you with the Holy Ghost.** 9 And it came to pass in those days, that Jesus came from Nazareth of Galilee, and was baptized of John in Jordan. 10 And straightway coming up out of the water, he saw the heavens opened, and the Spirit like a dove descending upon him: 11 And there came a voice from heaven, *saying,* Thou art my beloved Son, in whom I am well pleased.

John 1:5 John bare witness of him, and cried, saying, **This was he of whom I spake, He that cometh after me is preferred before me: for he was before me.** 16 And of his fulness have all we received, and grace for grace. 17 For the law was given by Moses, *but* grace and truth came by Jesus Christ. 18 No man hath seen

God at any time; the only begotten Son, which is in the bosom of the Father, he hath declared *him*. 19 And this is the record of John, when the Jews sent priests and Levites from Jerusalem to ask him, Who art thou? 20 And he confessed, and denied not; but confessed, I am not the Christ. 21 And they asked him, What then? Art thou Elias? And he saith, I am not. Art thou that prophet? And he answered, No. 22 Then said they unto him, Who art thou? that we may give an answer to them that sent us. What sayest thou of thyself? 23 He said, I *am* the voice of one crying in the wilderness, Make straight the way of the Lord, as said the prophet Esaias. 24 And they which were sent were of the Pharisees. 25 And they asked him, and said unto him, Why baptizest thou then, if thou be not that Christ, nor Elias, neither that prophet? 26 John answered them, saying, I baptize with water: **but there standeth one among you, whom ye know not; 27 He it is, who coming after me is preferred before me, whose shoe's latchet I am not worthy to unloose.** 28 These things were done in Bethabara beyond Jordan, where John was baptizing. 29 **The next day John seeth Jesus coming unto him, and saith, Behold the Lamb of God, which taketh away the sin of the world.** 30 **This is he of whom I said, After me cometh a man which is preferred before me: for he was before me. 31 And I knew him not: but that he should be made manifest to Israel, therefore am I come baptizing with water. 32 And John bare record, saying, I saw the Spirit** descending from heaven like a dove, and it abode upon him. 33 And I knew him not: but he that sent me to baptize with water, the same said unto me, Upon whom **thou shalt see the Spirit** descending, and remaining on him, the same is he which baptizeth with the **Holy Ghost**. 34 **And I saw, and bare record that this is the Son of God.** 35 Again the next day after John stood, and two of his disciples; 36 And looking upon Jesus as he walked, he saith, **Behold the Lamb of God!** 37 And the two disciples heard him speak, and they followed Jesus.

¹³ John 1: 14 And the Word was made flesh, and dwelt among us, (and we beheld his glory, the glory as of the only begotten of the Father,) full of grace and truth. 15 John bare witness of him, and cried, saying,

This was he of whom I spake, He that cometh after me is preferred before me: for he was before me. 16 And of his fulness have all we received, and grace for grace. 17 For the law was given by Moses, *but* grace and truth came by Jesus Christ. 18 No man hath seen God at any time; the only begotten Son, which is in the bosom of the Father, he hath declared *him.* 19 And this is the record of John, when the Jews sent priests and Levites from Jerusalem to ask him, Who art thou? 20 And he confessed, and denied not; but confessed, I am not the Christ. 21 And they asked him, What then? Art thou Elias? And he saith, I am not. Art thou that prophet? And he answered, No. 22 Then said they unto him, Who art thou? that we may give an answer to them that sent us. What sayest thou of thyself? 23 He said, I *am* the voice of one crying in the wilderness, Make straight the way of the Lord, as said the prophet Esaias. 24 And they which were sent were of the Pharisees. 25 And they asked him, and said unto him, Why baptizest thou then, if thou be not that Christ, nor Elias, neither that prophet? 26 John answered them, saying, I baptize with water: but there standeth one among you, whom ye know not; 27 He it is, who coming after me is preferred before me, whose shoe's latchet I am not worthy to unloose. 28 These things were done in Bethabara beyond Jordan, where John was baptizing. 29 The next day John seeth Jesus coming unto him, and saith, Behold the Lamb of God, which taketh away the sin of the world. 30 This is he of whom I said, After me cometh a man which is preferred before me: for he was before me. 31 And I knew him not: but that he should be made manifest to Israel, therefore am I come baptizing with water. 32 And John bare record, saying, I saw the Spirit descending from heaven like a dove, and it abode upon him. 33 And I knew him not: but he that sent me to baptize with water, the same said unto me, Upon whom thou shalt see the Spirit descending, and remaining on him, the same is he which baptizeth with the Holy Ghost. 34 And I saw, and bare record that this is the Son of God. 35 Again the next day after John stood, and two of his disciples; 36 And looking upon Jesus as he walked, he saith, Behold the Lamb of God!

John 3:23 And John also was baptizing in AEnon near to Salim, because there was much water there: and they came, and were baptized. 24 For John was not yet cast into prison. 25 Then there arose a question between *some* of John's disciples and the Jews about purifying. 26 And they came unto John, and said unto him, Rabbi, he that was with thee beyond Jordan, to whom thou barest witness, behold, the same baptizeth, and all *men* come to him. 27 John answered and said, A man can receive nothing, except it be given him from heaven. 28 Ye yourselves bear me witness, that I said, I am not the Christ, but that I am sent before him. 29 He that hath the bride is the bridegroom: but the friend of the bridegroom, which standeth and heareth him, rejoiceth greatly because of the bridegroom's voice: this my joy therefore is fulfilled. 30 He must increase, but I *must* decrease. 31 He that cometh from above is above all: he that is of the earth is earthly, and speaketh of the earth: he that cometh from heaven is above all. 32 And what he hath seen and heard, that he testifieth; and no man receiveth his testimony. 33 He that hath received his testimony hath set to his seal that God is true. 34 For he whom God hath sent speaketh the words of God: for God giveth not the Spirit by measure *unto him.* 35 The Father loveth the Son, and hath given all things into his hand. 36 He that believeth on the Son hath everlasting life: and he that believeth not the Son shall not see life; but the wrath of God abideth on him.

14 For instance Methodists do not restrict baptism to immersion, but do so without citing any Biblical text to support the use of sprinkling or pouring.

"There are two forms or modes of baptism: immersion and sprinkling or pouring. **[Apparently, sprinkling and pouring are being considered as one mode.]** Each of these forms seems to have good spiritual backing and is deeply meaningful to millions. Sprinkling is the form of baptism, which has been practiced by the vast majority of Christians down through the centuries. For United Methodists, sprinkling or pouring, symbolizes our cleansing from sin. It roots in certain biblical expressions, such as Ezekiel 36:25, 27, "I will sprinkle clean water upon you, and you shall be clean...And I will put my spirit within you, and cause you to walk in my statutes." (See also Isaiah 44:3-5; Joel 2:28-29; and especially Acts 2:1-4, 14-18, and 37-39.) Just as Jesus, at his baptism was anointed by the Holy Spirit, so are we at ours. This is what the poured or sprinkled water symbolizes.

United Methodists also recognize the validity of another form of baptism, namely immersion. The symbolism of immersion, based largely on Romans, chapter 6, is that of dying with Christ to sin and rising with him to a renewed life. Immersion is a biblical form of baptism, and we accept into our membership, without requiring our form of baptism, anyone who has been immersed and who continues to adhere to his/her baptismal faith."

http://www.smyrnafirstumc.org/meaning-and-mode-of-baptism

[15] 907 βαπτιζω baptize from a derivative of 911; to immerse, submerge; to make whelmed (i.e. fully wet); used only (in the New Testament) of ceremonial ablution, especially (technically) of the ordinance of Christian baptism:—Baptist, baptize, wash.

908. βαπτισμα baptisma from 907; baptism (technically or figuratively):—baptism.

909. βαπτισμος baptismos from 907; ablution (ceremonial or Christian):—baptism, washing.

910 βαπτιστης Baptistes from 907; a baptizer, as an epithet of Christ's forerunner:—Baptist.

SwordSearcher, Strong's Greek Dictionary

[16] *Merriam-Webster 11th Collegiate Dictionary* defines *transliterate* as "to represent or spell in the characters of another alphabet."

[17] Mark 7:1 Then came together unto him the Pharisees, and certain of the scribes, which came from Jerusalem. 2 And when they saw some of his disciples eat bread with defiled, that is to say, with unwashen, hands, they found fault. 3 For the Pharisees, and all the Jews, except they wash *their* hands oft, eat not, holding the tradition of the elders. 4 And *when they come* from the market, except they wash, they eat not. And many other things there be, which they have received to hold, *as* the washing of cups, and pots, brasen vessels, and of tables. 5 Then the Pharisees and scribes asked him, Why walk not thy disciples according to the tradition of the elders, but eat bread with

unwashen hands? 6 He answered and said unto them, Well hath Esaias prophesied of you hypocrites, as it is written, This people honoureth me with *their* lips, but their heart is far from me. 7 Howbeit in vain do they worship me, teaching *for* doctrines the commandments of men. 8 For laying aside the commandment of God, ye hold the tradition of men, *as* the washing of pots and cups: and many other such like things ye do. 9 And he said unto them, Full well ye reject the commandment of God, that ye may keep your own tradition. 10 For Moses said, Honour thy father and thy mother; and, Whoso curseth father or mother, let him die the death: 11 But ye say, If a man shall say to his father or mother, *It is* Corban, that is to say, a gift, by whatsoever thou mightest be profited by me; *he shall be free.* 12 And ye suffer him no more to do ought for his father or his mother; 13 Making the word of God of none effect through your tradition, which ye have delivered: and many such like things do ye.

4

WHY IS A PERSON BAPTIZED?

Though many teach that a person is baptized to *wash away sin* or to *be born again,* the Bible not only does not teach such doctrine, the Bible teaches the exact opposite. The water of baptism cannot remove the stains of sin; let alone remove its presence. Sin is a spiritual issue between a person and the Holy GOD of Heaven; therefore, it is not possible that physical water has the ability to remove for sin—not even when combined with a religious ceremony.

Primarily, a believer is to be baptized because to do so is to obey the clear command of the LORD Jesus Christ. For a believer to choose not to be baptized is to choose to disobey that command.

> Matthew 28:18-20 And Jesus came and spake unto them, saying, All power is given unto me in heaven and in earth. Go ye therefore, and teach all nations, baptizing them in the name of the Father, and of the Son, and of the Holy Ghost: Teaching

them to observe all things whatsoever I have commanded you: and, lo, I am with you alway, even unto the end of the world. Amen.

If the LORD Jesus explicitly commanded the disciples to baptize believers, (and He did), He was at the same time, without question, also implicitly commanding the believers to submit to being baptized. Obviously, for a professing believer not to obey this direct command of the LORD Jesus Christ is for that believer to be disobedient, even rebellious.

Though there are those who declare that *water baptism*, which term never appears in Scripture, is not a valid practice for believers today, it must be admitted by all that no command to cease baptizing believers in water can be found anywhere in the New Testament.

Generally, these individuals refer to themselves as *Pauline*, claiming by that name to follow the apostle Paul. As the authority for this change to the threefold commission of the LORD Jesus Christ, a phrase is lifted from 1 Corinthians, chapter 1, verse 17,

For Christ sent me not to baptize, but to preach the gospel.

The most casual reader that is not predisposed to a contrary position of the context of this verse will quickly discover that the Apostle had a very specific issue in mind when he said that he was not sent to baptize, because Paul identifies specific individuals that he *did* baptize. The church at Corinth had divided into groups that had loyalaty to the preacher who baptized them. Paul was strongly rebuking this factionalism which served to denominationalize within the church at Corinth.

> 1 Corinthians 1:1 Paul, called *to be* an apostle of Jesus Christ through the will of God, and Sosthenes *our* brother, 2 Unto the church of God which is at Corinth, to them that are sanctified in Christ Jesus, called *to be* saints, with all that in every place call upon the name of Jesus Christ our Lord, both theirs and ours: 3 Grace *be* unto you, and peace, from God our Father, and *from* the Lord Jesus Christ. ... 10 Now I beseech you, brethren, by the name of our Lord Jesus Christ, that ye all speak the same thing, and *that* there be no divisions among you; but *that* ye be perfectly joined together in the same mind and in the same judgment. 11 For it hath been declared unto me of you, my brethren, by them *which are of the house* of Chloe, that there are contentions among you. 12 Now this I say, that every one of you saith, I am of Paul; and I of Apollos; and I of Cephas; and I of Christ. 13 Is Christ divided? was Paul crucified for you? or were ye baptized in the name of Paul? 14 I thank God that I baptized none of you, but Crispus and Gaius; 15 Lest any should say that I had baptized in mine own name. 16 And I baptized also the household of Stephanas: besides, I know not whether I baptized any other. 17 For Christ sent me not to baptize, but to preach the gospel: not with wisdom of words, lest the cross of Christ should be made of none effect. 18 For the preaching of the cross is to them that perish foolishness; but unto us which are saved it is the power of God.

The Apostle was dealing with the issue of sectarianism—*not the doctrine of baptism.* He was declaring that the loyalty of believers is supposed to be to the Lord and Saviour—not to one of the messengers. The clarion call to de-emphasize the messenger needs proclamation in this day even as it did in the day of Paul, perhaps more so.[1] The larger problem today is that some of the self-promoted messengers were not sent by the Head of the Church[2] and are quite content to amass followers.

Greater evidence of a major change in the commandment of Christ must be required by any earnest and sincere believer than the mere assumption based upon one verse—and that verse having been lifted out of its context and considered as an isolated text from the rest of the New Testament. The teaching that baptism is *not valid for believers in this dispensation* does not rest upon a declaration of Scripture, but instead is based entirely upon an arrogant supposition made by those who approach Scripture with preconceived presumptions.

This doctrine of *no-baptism-in-this-age* is certainly not based upon a clear declaration of Scripture; moreover, that teaching repudiates the emphatic record of the ministry of Paul. *If* the Apostle taught that baptism was not to be practiced upon those who became believers through his ministry and *if* he ceased baptizing believers, some evidence of this must exist in the inspired historical account of that ministry, the Book of Acts.

No such indication is found in the Book of Acts or in the Epistles of Paul. Contrariwise, when one studies the ministry of the Apostle, it becomes clear that Paul and his traveling companions continued to baptize converts. This is true even after Paul speaks of turning to the Gentiles.

> Acts 13:46 Then Paul and Barnabas waxed bold, and said, It was necessary that the word of God should first have been spoken to you: but seeing ye put it from you, and judge yourselves unworthy of everlasting life, lo, we turn to the Gentiles.

This statement is considered evidence by some ultra dispensationalists that the words of the apostle established a new dispensation. However, the inspired testimony is that baptisms by the apostle continued.

> Acts 16:1 Then came he to Derbe and Lystra: and, behold, a certain disciple was there, named Timotheus, the son of a certain woman, which was a Jewess, and believed; but his father *was* a Greek: 2 Which was well reported of by the brethren that were at Lystra and Iconium. 3 Him would Paul have to go forth with him; and took and circumcised him because of the Jews which were in those quarters: for they knew all that his father was a Greek. 4 And as they went through the cities, they delivered them the decrees for to keep, that were ordained of the apostles and elders which were at Jerusalem. 5 And so were the churches established in the faith, **and increased in number** daily.

This *increase in number* is only understandable when cross-referenced to previous passages in the Book of Acts.

> Acts 2:41 Then they that gladly received his word were **baptized**: and the same day there were **added** unto them about three thousand souls.

Acts 2:47 Praising God, and having favour with all the people. And the Lord **added** to the church daily such as should be saved.

It seems obvious that the additions to the church were through baptism; therefore, for the churches to which Paul and Timothy ministered to have an *increase in number* would require the baptism of those converts. However, for those who might consider that phrase as indirect evidence, unmistakable direct refutation is found only verses away as the record of the journey of Paul and his company continues.

Acts 16:12 And from thence to Philippi, which is the chief city of that part of Macedonia, *and* a colony: and we were in that city abiding certain days. 13 And on the sabbath we went out of the city by a river side, where prayer was wont to be made; and we sat down, and spake unto the women which resorted *thither*. 14 And a certain woman named Lydia, a seller of purple, of the city of Thyatira, which worshipped God, heard *us*: whose heart the Lord opened, that she attended unto the things which were spoken of Paul. 15 **And when she was baptized, and her household**, she besought *us*, saying, If ye have judged me to be faithful to the Lord, come into my house, and abide *there*. And she constrained us. 16 And it came to pass, as we went to prayer, a certain damsel possessed with a spirit of divination met us, which brought her masters much gain by soothsaying: 17 The same followed Paul and us, and cried, saying, These men are the servants of the most high God, which shew unto us the way of salvation. 18 And this did she many days. But Paul, being grieved, turned and said to the spirit, I command thee in the name of Jesus Christ to come out of her. And he came out the same hour. 19 And when her masters saw that the hope of their gains was gone, they caught Paul and Silas, and drew *them* into the marketplace unto the rulers, 20 And brought them to the magistrates, saying, These men, being Jews, do exceedingly trouble our city, 21 And teach customs, which are not lawful for us to receive, neither to observe, being Romans. 22 And the multitude rose up together against them: and the magistrates rent off their clothes, and commanded to beat *them*. 23 And when they had laid many stripes upon them, they cast *them* into prison, charging the jailor to keep them safely: 24 Who, having received such a charge, thrust them into the inner prison, and made their feet fast in the stocks. 25 And at midnight Paul and Silas prayed, and sang praises unto God: and the prisoners heard them. 26 And suddenly there was a great earthquake, so that the foundations of the prison were shaken: and immediately all the doors were opened, and every one's bands were loosed. 27 And the keeper of the prison awaking out of his sleep, and seeing the prison doors open, he drew out his sword, and would have killed himself, supposing that the prisoners had been fled. 28 But Paul cried with a loud voice, saying, Do thyself no harm: for we are all here. 29 Then he called for a light, and sprang in, and came trembling, and fell down before Paul and Silas, 30 And brought them out, and said, Sirs, what must I do to be saved? 31 And they said, Believe on the Lord Jesus Christ, and thou shalt be saved, and thy house. 32 And they spake unto him the word of the Lord, and to all that were in his house. 33 And he took them the same hour of the night, and washed *their* stripes; **and was baptized**, he and all his, straightway.

Continuing in the Book of Acts to chapter 18, we find the Apostle in the city of Corinth where he is actively connected with the baptizing of *several individuals*. It is worthy of repetition, these baptisms occur *after* Paul declares that he will turn to the Gentiles.

It is that *turning* to the Gentiles by Paul that marks the contrived line of demarcation of a new dispensation to the ultra-dispensationalists. However, the Biblical record is that the church at Corinth was founded *after Paul turned to the Gentiles*—and there is not one iota of evidence that he changed his message or his practices whatsoever.

Acts 18:1 After these things Paul departed from Athens, and came to Corinth; 2 And found a certain Jew named Aquila, born in Pontus, lately come from Italy, with his wife Priscilla; (because that Claudius had commanded all Jews to depart from Rome:) and came unto them. 3 And because he was of the same craft, he abode with them, and wrought: for by their occupation they were tentmakers. 4 And he reasoned in the synagogue every sabbath, and persuaded the Jews and the Greeks. 5 And when Silas and Timotheus were come from Macedonia, Paul was pressed in the spirit, and testified to the Jews *that* Jesus *was* Christ. 6 And when they opposed themselves, and blasphemed, he shook *his* raiment, and said unto them, Your blood *be* upon your own heads; I *am* clean: **from henceforth I will go unto**

the Gentiles. 7 And he departed thence, and entered into a certain *man's* house, named Justus, *one* that worshipped God, whose house joined hard to the synagogue. 8 And Crispus, the chief ruler of the synagogue, believed on the Lord with all his house; and **many of the Corinthians hearing believed, and were baptized.**

Not only did the Apostle and his companions continue to baptize believers and to do so after he *turned to the Gentiles*, but the very night that he baptized those believers in Corinth, the LORD appeared to Paul, speaking encouragement to continue his ministry in the city and without administering any rebuke to him for baptizing those believers.

Acts 18:9 Then spake the Lord to Paul in the night by a vision, Be not afraid, but speak, and hold not thy peace: 10 For I am with thee, and no man shall set on thee to hurt thee: for I have much people in this city. 11 And he continued *there* a year and six months, teaching the word of God among them.

The ministry of the Apostle shows no indication of alteration to his message or methodology anywhere in the following chapters of Acts or in his Epistles.

Acts 19:1 And it came to pass, that, while Apollos was at Corinth, Paul having passed through the upper coasts came to Ephesus: and finding certain disciples, 2 He said unto them, Have ye received the Holy Ghost since ye believed? And they said unto him, We have not so much as heard whether there be any Holy Ghost. 3 And he said unto them, Unto what then were ye baptized? And they said, Unto

John's baptism. 4 Then said Paul, John verily baptized with the baptism of repentance, saying unto the people, that they should believe on him which should come after him, that is, on Christ Jesus. 5 When they heard *this*, they were baptized in the name of the Lord Jesus.

The obvious conclusion and the only honest verdict that may be drawn from these verses is that baptism remains the valid commandment of the LORD Jesus Christ. The commission of Matthew 28 remains in effect; it has not been revised or rescinded.

Matthew 28:18 And Jesus came and spake unto them, saying, All power is given unto me in heaven and in earth. 19 Go ye therefore, and teach all nations, baptizing them in the name of the Father, and of the Son, and of the Holy Ghost: 20 Teaching them to observe all things whatsoever I have commanded you: and, lo, I am with you alway, *even* unto the end of the world. Amen.

As previously shown, baptism is the public identification of the believer both with the LORD Jesus Christ and with the New Testament church authorizing the baptism.

Therefore, a person is to be baptized individually and personally as a public testimony of his own faith. No possibility of baptism of an infant in the hope that one day he would believe is suggested. No hint of *baptism in blood* or of *baptism of intent* is found in the New Testament. The concept of baptizing someone as a proxy for a dead person in the attempt to impute obedience to the deceased so that they might enter heaven comes from somewhere other than an honest understanding of the Bible.

Through his baptism, the person declares "I have been saved and I now intend to live for my LORD and Saviour." The person being baptized is making a public statement of his personal faith; that profession is a statement that there is an intention *to walk in newness of life.* By submitting to baptism, the believer is also declaring his intent not to forsake the assembling together with that church.

The Biblical declaration is that for a person to refuse to follow the command of the LORD Jesus to be baptized is a serious act of disobedience. Baptism is not a matter of individual personal preference of the believer as to the mode. The only safe definition of baptism is found within the Scriptures, where it is defined with clarity by both command and example. The choice of whether to be baptized by immersion, by pouring, by sprinkling, or not to be baptized at all is not left to the individual; but rather the choices open to the believer are only two—either to be obedient or to be disobedient.

Baptism is not optional; it is the command of the Son of GOD. The believer who is baptized in obedience to the command of His LORD is obedient. The believer who chooses not to be baptized is disobedient to the commands of His LORD.

That baptism is a command of the LORD Jesus is indisputable.

> Matthew 28:18 And Jesus came and spake unto them, saying, All power is given unto me in heaven and in earth. 19 Go ye therefore, and teach all nations, baptizing them in the name of the Father, and of

the Son, and of the Holy Ghost: 20 Teaching them to observe all things whatsoever I
have commanded you: and, lo, I am with
you alway, *even* unto the end of the world.
Amen.

That the LORD Jesus intended for His
commands to be obeyed is undeniable.

Matthew 5:19 Whosoever therefore shall
break one of these least commandments,
and shall teach men so, he shall be called
the least in the kingdom of heaven: but
whosoever shall do and teach *them*, the
same shall be called great in the kingdom
of heaven.

John 14:15 If ye love me, keep my commandments. ... 21 He that hath my commandments, and keepeth them, he it is
that loveth me: and he that loveth me
shall be loved of my Father, and I will love
him, and will manifest myself to him. ...
23 Jesus answered and said unto him, If a
man love me, he will keep my words: and
my Father will love him, and we will come
unto him, and make our abode with him.

1 John 5:2 By this we know that we love
the children of God, when we love God,
and keep his commandments. ... 3 For
this is the love of God, that we keep his
commandments: and his commandments
are not grievous.

For a believer to disobey any command of
Christ is for that believer to be so presumptu-
ous, so arrogant, so idolatrous as to set
himself above those commands. It is to teach
unwholesome words. The consequences of
disobedience is *envy, strife, railings, and evil
surmising.*

1 Timothy 6:3 If any man teach otherwise,
and consent not to wholesome words,

even the words of our Lord Jesus Christ, and to the doctrine which is according to godliness; 4 He is proud, knowing nothing, but doting about questions and strifes of words, whereof cometh envy, strife, railings, evil surmisings,

The sincere believer will avoid unwholesome words and evil surmising. He will not entangle himself in doting about questions and striving over words.

The believer who honestly wishes to obey his LORD will be immersed under the authority of a New Testament church as soon as possible after his confession of faith. He has no other option; indeed, the honest believer would desire none.

---

1 It is intriguing to wonder what the apostle might think of the abundance of ministries named for the "preacher." Saul of Tarsus Ministries hardly seems in keeping with the passage.

One could understand a Diotrephes or a Simeon of Samaria building a ministry of self glorification; however, John the Baptist ha the mission statement "He must increase, but I *must* decrease" (John 3:30).

3 John 1:9 I wrote unto the church: but Diotrephes, who loveth to have the preeminence among them, receiveth us not.

Acts 8:9 But there was a certain man, called Simon, which beforetime in the same city used sorcery, and bewitched the people of Samaria, giving out that himself was some great one: 10 To whom they all gave heed, from the least to the greatest, saying, This man is the great power of God. 11 And to him they had regard, because that of long time he had bewitched them with sorceries. 12 But when they believed Philip preaching the things concerning the kingdom of God, and the name of Jesus Christ, they were baptized, both men and women. 13 Then Simon himself believed also: and when he was baptized, he continued with Philip, and wondered, beholding the miracles and signs which were done. ... 18 And when Simon saw that through laying on of the apostles' hands the Holy Ghost was given, he offered them money, 19 Saying, Give me also this power, that on whomsoever I lay hands, he may receive the Holy Ghost.

3 John 1:9 I wrote unto the church: but Diotrephes, who loveth to have the preeminence among them, receiveth us not.

2 Ephesians 1:22 And hath put all *things* under his feet, and gave him *to be* the head over all *things* to the church,

Ephesians 5:23 For the husband is the head of the wife, even as Christ is the head of the church: and he is the saviour of the body.

Colossians 1:18 And he is the head of the body, the church: who is the beginning, the firstborn from the dead; that in all *things* he might have the preeminence.

5

WHO IS BAPTIZED?

Baptism is *only* for a believer and *only* upon a credible, competent, personal profession of faith and *only* upon the authority of a local New Testament church. Therefore, *only* those who have given a credible confession of faith are to be considered as being acceptable candidates for baptism.

A scenario vital for an understanding of baptism is found in the ministry of Philip, an evangelist from the church at Jerusalem.[1]

> Acts 8:26 And the angel of the Lord spake unto Philip, saying, Arise, and go toward the south unto the way that goeth down from Jerusalem unto Gaza, which is desert. 27 And he arose and went: and, behold, a man of Ethiopia, an eunuch of great authority under Candace queen of the Ethiopians, who had the charge of all her treasure, and had come to Jerusalem for to worship, 28 Was returning, and sitting in his chariot read Esaias the proph-

et. 29 Then the Spirit said unto Philip, Go near, and join thyself to this chariot. 30 And Philip ran thither to *him*, and heard him read the prophet Esaias, and said, Understandest thou what thou readest? 31 And he said, How can I, except some man should guide me? And he desired Philip that he would come up and sit with him. 32 The place of the scripture which he read was this, He was led as a sheep to the slaughter; and like a lamb dumb before his shearer, so opened he not his mouth: 33 In his humiliation his judgment was taken away: and who shall declare his generation? for his life is taken from the earth. 34 And the eunuch answered Philip, and said, I pray thee, of whom speaketh the prophet this? of himself, or of some other man? 35 Then Philip opened his mouth, and began at the same scripture, and preached unto him Jesus.

Notice that the specific question of exactly what might hinder or prevent a person from being baptized is both asked and answered in this passage.

Acts 8:36 And as they went on *their* way, they came unto a certain water: and the eunuch said, See, *here is* water; **what doth hinder me to be baptized?** 37 And Philip said, **If thou believest with all thine heart, thou mayest.** And he answered and said, I believe that Jesus Christ is the Son of God. 38 And he commanded the chariot to stand still: and they went down both into the water, both Philip and the eunuch; and he baptized him.

The only hindrance to the baptism of this Ethiopian official would have been his personal expression of unbelief; that is, Philip would not baptize him if he rejected the gospel message of salvation in Christ Jesus. Whether a person has received the LORD Jesus Christ as Saviour must be settled *before* that individual enters the waters of baptism. Upon hearing this man confess his faith in Christ, Philip, who was commissioned as an evangelist by the church at Jerusalem, entered the waters with the Ethiopian and baptized him.

This same pattern is found consistently through the New Testament: baptism always follows faith *and* the declaration of that faith. Baptism is the public profession of the personal confession faith.

John 4:1 When therefore the Lord knew how the Pharisees had heard that Jesus made and baptized more disciples than John

This passage testifies that the subjects of baptism were *made* disciples *before* they were baptized. The wording is unmistakable: "Jesus ... baptized disciples." The LORD Jesus made disciples and those disciples were baptized. Neither He nor His apostles baptized non-believers. The old Baptist slogan, *Into the Blood before into the water,* states the case clearly and properly.

The only procedure provided in the commission of Matthew 28 for a believing person to give a public confession or acknowledgment of his belief in the LORD Jesus Christ is by following His command and entering the waters of baptism. Scripture does not speak about *walking an aisle* or *taking a soul-winner's hand* as a declaration of faith; but it does command each believer to be baptized in obedience to His command.

John 14:23 Jesus answered and said unto him, If a man love me, he will keep my words: and my Father will love him, and we will come unto him, and make our abode with him.

John 15:14 Ye are my friends, if ye do whatsoever I command you.

Matthew 10:32 Whosoever therefore shall confess me before men, him will I confess also before my Father which is in heaven.

---

¹ Acts 6:5 And the saying pleased the whole multitude: and they chose Stephen, a man full of faith and of the Holy Ghost, and Philip, and Prochorus, and Nicanor, and Timon, and Parmenas, and Nicolas a proselyte of Antioch: 6 Whom they set before the apostles: and when they had prayed, they laid *their* hands on them.

Acts 21:8 And the next *day* we that were of Paul's company departed, and came unto Caesarea: and we entered into the house of Philip the evangelist, which was *one* of the seven; and abode with him.

6
WHEN IS A BELIEVER BAPTIZED?

The examples of the New Testament clearly indicate that a believer is to be baptized as soon as is possible after the individual receives the LORD Jesus Christ as his personal Saviour. No biblical precedent exists that could be offered that would permit a willful, rebellious, deliberate delay by any believer. The only biblical reason for waiting is a delay to be certain that the individual fully understands what salvation involves and why he is being baptized.

Historically, Baptists have referred to baptism as *the first step of obedience for the believer.* This was based upon *the order* of the commission in the Gospels of Matthew and Mark and the examples from Acts.

1. The Gospel is preached.

2. Those that believe the Gospel are to be baptized.

3. Those that are baptized are to be taught.

Matthew 28:18 And Jesus came and spake unto them, saying, All power is given unto me in heaven and in earth. 19 Go ye therefore, and teach all nations, baptizing them in the name of the Father, and of the Son, and of the Holy Ghost: 20 Teaching them to observe all things whatsoever I have commanded you: and, lo, I am with you alway, *even* unto the end of the world. Amen.

Mark 16:15 And he said unto them, Go ye into all the world, and preach the gospel to every creature. 16 He that believeth and is baptized shall be saved; but he that believeth not shall be damned.

Acts 2:41 Then they that gladly received his word were baptized: and the same day there were added unto them about three thousand souls.

Acts 2:47 Praising God, and having favour with all the people. And the Lord added to the church daily such as should be saved.

Acts 8:12 But when they believed Philip preaching the things concerning the kingdom of God, and the name of Jesus Christ, they were baptized, both men and women. ... 35 Then Philip opened his mouth, and began at the same scripture, and preached unto him Jesus. 36 And as they went on *their* way, they came unto a certain water: and the eunuch said, See, *here is* water; what doth hinder me to be baptized? 37 And Philip said, If thou believest with all thine heart, thou mayest. And he answered and said, I believe that Jesus Christ is the Son of God. 38 And he commanded the chariot to stand still: and they went down both into the water, both Philip and the eunuch; and he baptized him. 39 And when they were come up out of the water, the Spirit of the Lord caught away Philip, that the eunuch saw him no more: and he went on his way rejoicing.

Acts 10:47 Can any man forbid water, that these should not be baptized, which have received the Holy Ghost as well as we? 48 And he commanded them to be baptized in the name of the Lord. Then prayed they him to tarry certain days.

Acts 16:30 And brought them out, and said, Sirs, what must I do to be saved? 31 And they said, Believe on the Lord Jesus Christ, and thou shalt be saved, and thy house. 32 And they spake unto him the word of the Lord, and to all that were in his house. 33 And he took them the same hour of the night, and washed *their* stripes; and was baptized, he and all his, straightway.

When the individual is able to give a credible confession of faith, that person is a proper candidate for baptism, but not before. No other barrier ought to be erected. The only biblical reason for delaying baptism is to be certain that the individual fully understands salvation and baptism, the relationship of the two, and the purpose of baptism.

Baptism is not an act that is to be performed on a baby, young child, or a person that is unconscious. The only proposed justification for doing so is the erroneous belief that baptism has a role in salvation.

It is equally wrong to baptize any person that was unaware, misinformed, or confused regarding the reason or purpose for baptism or that is incapable of understanding why he is being baptized. Baptism requires a conscious decision.

Additionally, baptizing an individual who believed that the act of baptism would wash away his sins would be to participate in propagating *another gospel*. That involvement in advancing heresy would not be an insignificant matter.

> Galatians 1:6 I marvel that ye are so soon removed from him that called you into the grace of Christ unto another gospel: 7 Which is not another; but there be some that trouble you, and would pervert the gospel of Christ. 8 But though we, or an angel from heaven, preach any other gospel unto you than that which we have preached unto you, let him be accursed. 9 As we said before, so say I now again, If any *man* preach any other gospel unto you than that ye have received, let him be accursed.

Baptism is the identification of the believer with his LORD and Saviour *and* the identification with the church of the LORD Jesus. It is the willful, conscious, intentional decision to obey the command of the LORD Jesus to follow Him. No person is a proper candidate for baptism that is mentally incompetent or intellectually incapable to comprehend what is being done to him or that is incognizant of the purpose of his baptism. To do otherwise would be an unscriptural act.

Biblical precedent shows that baptism should follow salvation as soon as is reasonably possible. The only *rational* delay is to prepare the candidate for baptism.

Baptism is never anticipatory of some future act of faith in Scripture; baptism always follows salvation. The commission of Matthew 28 makes this unalterable order abundantly clear.

> Matthew 28:18 And Jesus came and spake unto them, saying, All power is given unto me in heaven and in earth. 19 Go ye therefore, and teach all nations, baptizing them in the name of the Father, and of the Son, and of the Holy Ghost: 20 Teaching them to observe all things whatsoever I have commanded you: and, lo, I am with you alway, *even* unto the end of the world. Amen.

Remember that the disciples were commanded to go everywhere doing three things, and fulfilling those three things in a specified order:

1. teaching the Gospel (Mark 16:15 "preach the gospel to every creature") to all who would listen,

2. baptizing all those who received the Gospel, and,

3. teaching all of those who had been baptized to observe the other commands of Christ.

Any additional teaching beyond the simple Gospel of the converts followed *after* the person had submitted to the ordinance of baptism. For a believer to refuse to take this *first step of obedience* in following the command of his LORD and Saviour to be baptized is for that believer to take willful, deliberate steps of disobedience.

Every displeasing believer refusing to follow the known revealed will of his Heavenly Father demonstrates not only an unwillingness to be instructed, but also a lack of love for the Saviour.

John 14:15 If ye love me, keep my commandments.

John 14:21 He that hath my commandments, and keepeth them, he it is that loveth me: and he that loveth me shall be loved of my Father, and I will love him, and will manifest myself to him.

By his act of rebellion, the person is grieving the Holy Spirit; and, therefore, he will not be taught or led by the Holy Spirit until that willful course of sinful action is repented and changed.

The *authorized* pattern given to the disciples for them to follow in their ministries is not in doubt.

First: The Gospel is to be proclaimed.

Second: Those who accept the Gospel message are to be baptized.

Third: Those who have been baptized are to be taught the commands of Christ.

Except for the baptism of Jesus of Nazareth by John the Baptist, this pattern was followed for every baptism recorded in the New Testament. This included:

1. those baptisms by John before the ministry of Christ began,

2. those baptisms administered by both John the Baptist and the apostles during the ministry of Christ, and

3. those baptisms recorded in the Book of Acts and mentioned in the Epistles.

This pattern is the only acceptable standard for every legitimate New Testament church since the ministry of the Apostles ended. It is the only legitimate standard by which to judge any baptism.

Baptism *follows* salvation; baptism never

precedes salvation.

Baptism *should* follow salvation; baptism ought not be avoided or circumvented.

Baptism is not an option, it is commanded. While the passage has been frequently cited, its repetition is warranted because of its clarity.

> Matthew 28:18 And Jesus came and spake unto them, saying, All power is given unto me in heaven and in earth. 19 **Go ye** therefore, and **teach** all nations, **baptizing** them in the name of the Father, and of the Son, and of the Holy Ghost: 20 **Teaching** them to observe all things whatsoever I have **commanded** you: and, lo, I am with you alway, *even* unto the end of the world. Amen.

> Acts 10:47 Can any man forbid water, that these should not be baptized, which have received the Holy Ghost as well as we? 48 **And he commanded them to be baptized in the name of the Lord**. Then prayed they him to tarry certain days.

Once a regenerated person understands what baptism is and why he should be baptized, it is puzzling as to why any blood-bought, heaven-bound, child of GOD would desire not to identify with the One Who loved him and Who gave Himself for him. Since it is not a lack of knowledge, it has to have a distasteful reason.

Is it willful rebellion?

Is it a lack of love and appreciation?

Is it uncomfortableness with being identified with Jesus of Nazareth or with His church?

Whatever the reason or the rationalization,

those believers that choose not to obey the command of the LORD will suffer an embarrassingly heavy penalty.

Mark 8:38 Whosoever therefore shall be ashamed of me and of my words in this adulterous and sinful generation; of him also shall the Son of man be ashamed, when he cometh in the glory of his Father with the holy angels.

Luke 9:26 For whosoever shall be ashamed of me and of my words, of him shall the Son of man be ashamed, when he shall come in his own glory, and in his Father's, and of the holy angels.

7

WHERE IS A BELIEVER BAPTIZED?

The only scriptural stipulations concerning the *where* of baptism is "into the water" and "with water." The phrase "into the water" implies a sufficient quantity of water that allows at least two men to enter the water so that one man may bury the other beneath the waters. This is borne out by the testimony of Scripture. When the LORD Jesus was baptized, He is said to come up out of the waters of the Jordan River.[1] It is stated that both Philip and the eunuch *went down into the water.*

> Acts 8:36-38 And as they went on their way, they came unto a certain water: and the eunuch said, See, here is water; what doth hinder me to be baptized? And Philip said, If thou believest with all thine heart, thou mayest. And he answered and said, I believe that Jesus Christ is the Son of God. And he commanded the chariot to stand still: and they went down both **into the water**, both Philip and the eunuch;

and he baptized him.

John 1:26-28 John answered them, saying, I baptize **with water**: but there standeth one among you, whom ye know not; He it is, who coming after me is preferred before me, whose shoe's latchet I am not worthy to unloose. These things were done in Bethabara beyond Jordan, where John was baptizing.

The one scriptural requirement concerning a physical location for baptism is *much water*. That quantity of water requires a depth sufficient to submerge briefly an adult by lowering that person backwards into the water.[2] That lowering into the water establishes that the water must not only have a sufficient depth, but also have a sufficient length.

John 3:22 After these things came Jesus and his disciples into the land of Judaea; and there he tarried with them, and baptized. 23 And John also was baptizing in AEnon near to Salim, because there was **much water** there: and they came, and were baptized.

Acts 8:35 Then Philip opened his mouth, and began at the same scripture, and preached unto him Jesus. 36 And as they went on *their* way, they came unto a certain water: and the eunuch said, See, *here is* water; what doth hinder me to be baptized? 37 And Philip said, If thou believest with all thine heart, thou mayest. And he answered and said, I believe that Jesus Christ is the Son of God. 38 And he commanded the chariot to stand still: and **they went down both into the water,** both Philip and the eunuch; and he baptized him. 39 And when they were come

up out of the water, the Spirit of the Lord caught away Philip, that the eunuch saw him no more: and he went on his way rejoicing.

There is no requirement in Scripture for *flowing water* or outdoor baptisms. There is no prohibition in Scripture regarding indoor baptisms. The only applicable standard is *much water*, which is to say sufficient water to immerse or to cover completely the believer, in a manner that pictures a burial.

---

¹ Matthew 3:16 And Jesus, when he was baptized, went up straightway out of the water: and, lo, the heavens were opened unto him, and he saw the Spirit of God descending like a dove, and lighting upon him:
Mark 1:9 And it came to pass in those days, that Jesus came from Nazareth of Galilee, and was baptized of John in Jordan. 10 And straightway coming up out of the water, he saw the heavens opened, and the Spirit like a dove descending upon him:

² I realize that some do baptize by lowering the person forward, but that does not seem to me to represent burial.

8

WHO BAPTIZES THE BELIEVER?

The commission of Matthew 28 was not given exclusively to the Apostles, else it would have ceased with their death, as did the authority to heal the sick, cast out devils, and to raise the dead.[1] Since no doctrine conveying *apostolic succession* or the establishment of a priestly line can be found within Scripture; such a concept must be rejected. This idea is a tradition of men, but it is not a biblical teaching.

This commission could not have been given to every Christian to exercise as his responsibility and at his volition, otherwise any eight or nine year old believer (some would baptize even younger children) could baptize a playmate. Such a premise must be disputed as being an absurdity.

The commission to baptize was given to the New Testament church; therefore, baptism is under the control and direction of a local New Testament church. Consequently, baptism is valid only when administered with the granted authority of a New Testament church.

> Matthew 28:18-20 And Jesus came and spake unto them, saying, All power is given unto me in heaven and in earth. Go ye therefore, and teach all nations, baptizing them in the name of the Father, and of the Son, and of the Holy Ghost: Teaching them to observe all things whatsoever I have commanded you: and, lo, I am with you alway, even unto the end of the world. Amen.

The key question regarding valid scriptural baptism is "Is it possible today to identify a New Testament church?" Scripture provides a clear description that any sincere Bible student will discover by reading the word of GOD.

A New Testament church as defined by the New Testament is a body of believers (1 Corinthians 12:27[2]) immersed upon a credible confession of faith in the LORD Jesus Christ (Romans 6:3-4; Acts 8:36-38[3]), having but two offices—that of pastor and, as needed, deacons (1 Timothy 3:1-13; Acts 6:1-7[4]), autonomous in polity—that is having the absolute of self-government, totally free from any and all interference by a hierarchy of either individuals or organizations (Matthew 18:17[5]), void of all organic ties with any other church, save a bond of fellowship (2 Corinthians 8:18-24[6]), banded together by a covenant of faith for the observance of the commands of her sole Head and LORD, Jesus Christ, in work, worship, witness, and the observance of the two ordinances (Matthew 28:19-20, 1 Corinthians 1:2,18, 23-33[7]), with one and only one authority for all matters of faith and practice—the word of GOD (Matthew 4:4, 2 Timothy 3:15-17[8]).

My personal experience would indicate and my study of history would confirm that the nearly unanimous majority of existing and historical churches meeting these qualifications would be self-identified as a Bible-believing Baptist church.

Unless a person has been baptized upon the authority of a New Testament church, his baptism is not valid and should not be recognized by any New Testament church. The *baptism* would have been administered without conforming to the Scriptural ordinance of baptism; and, lacking the authority of Scripture, the baptism is not baptism at all.

The situation of an invalid baptism is similar as when a *marriage* is performed without legal authority or right; it is not recognized by the government as a marriage. To perform weddings, a person must have the authority to do so. It is not legal and actually illegal for any individual to decide that he will begin to marry couples without benefit of authority. This is true even should the persons so married declare with all sincerity that they are satisfied and happy.

I once dealt with a sincere young couple who *did the job* themselves. (That was their word choice description of their wedding.) They had decided one day to exchange vows between the two of them without benefit of license or legally acceptable authority. They were a lovely couple and most sincere; but they were not married. They came to understand the impropriety of their actions and secured the recognition of a marriage license and were legally married. Any marriage performed without proper authority is not recognized as valid.

In theology, this kind of invalid baptism is called *alien baptism* The issue is never a matter of whether the individual involved is satisfied? The only legitimate question concerning baptism is whether the requirements of Scripture are satisfied?

The Bible is the only source and the only authority for all matters of faith and practice for Bible believers. While some individuals tend to alter the word of GOD by addition or subtraction of words at the exercise of their will to satisfy their own personal feelings and theological ideas and others redefine the words to fit preconceived theological positions, all such practices are sinful, arrogant, rebellious, prideful, and never demonstrates a spiritual attitude. It will ultimately bring the judgment of the GOD of the word.

Therefore, setting aside the traditions of religion and the reasonings of men, leaving the practices of various Christian denominations, forgetting about the influence of personal feelings and family background or ties, and basing our decision entirely within the context of Scripture, the only honest conclusion concerning baptism is that baptism is the one time rite or act of immersion in water exclusively intended for the believer, the child or GOD, whereby that believer personally and publicly identifies himself or herself with both his LORD and Saviour and with a local New Testament church by whose authority the baptism is administered.

Nothing else and everything else will not be a baptism that is in obedience to the command of the LORD Jesus.

¹ Matthew 10:1 And when he had called unto *him* his twelve disciples, he gave them power *against* unclean spirits, to cast them out, and to heal all manner of sickness and all manner of disease. ... 5 These twelve Jesus sent forth, and commanded them, saying, Go not into the way of the Gentiles, and into *any* city of the Samaritans enter ye not: 6 But go rather to the lost sheep of the house of Israel. 7 And as ye go, preach, saying, The kingdom of heaven is at hand. 8 Heal the sick, cleanse the lepers, raise the dead, cast out devils: freely ye have received, freely give.

² 1 Corinthians 12:27 Now ye are the body of Christ, and members in particular.

³ Romans 6:3 Know ye not, that so many of us as were baptized into Jesus Christ were baptized into his death? 4 Therefore we are buried with him by baptism into death: that like as Christ was raised up from the dead by the glory of the Father, even so we also should walk in newness of life.

Acts 8:36 And as they went on *their* way, they came unto a certain water: and the eunuch said, See, *here is* water; what doth hinder me to be baptized? 37 And Philip said, If thou believest with all thine heart, thou mayest. And he answered and said, I believe that Jesus Christ is the Son of God. 38 And he commanded the chariot to stand still: and they went down both into the water, both Philip and the eunuch; and he baptized him.

⁴ 1 Timothy 3:1 This *is* a true saying, If a man desire the office of a bishop, he desireth a good work. 2 A bishop then must be blameless, the husband of one wife, vigilant, sober, of good behaviour, given to hospitality, apt to teach; 3 Not given to wine, no striker, not greedy of filthy lucre; but patient, not a brawler, not covetous; 4 One that ruleth well his own house, having his children in subjection with all gravity; 5 (For if a man know not how to rule his own house, how shall he take care of the church of God?) 6 Not a novice, lest being lifted up with pride he fall into the condemnation of the devil. 7 Moreover he must have a good report of them which are without; lest he fall into reproach and the snare of the devil. 8 Likewise *must* the deacons *be* grave, not doubletongued, not given to much wine, not

greedy of filthy lucre; 9 Holding the mystery of the faith in a pure conscience. 10 And let these also first be proved; then let them use the office of a deacon, being *found* blameless. 11 Even so *must their* wives *be* grave, not slanderers, sober, faithful in all things. 12 Let the deacons be the husbands of one wife, ruling their children and their own houses well. 13 For they that have used the office of a deacon well purchase to themselves a good degree, and great boldness in the faith which is in Christ Jesus.

Acts 6:1 And in those days, when the number of the disciples was multiplied, there arose a murmuring of the Grecians against the Hebrews, because their widows were neglected in the daily ministration. 2 Then the twelve called the multitude of the disciples *unto them*, and said, It is not reason that we should leave the word of God, and serve tables. 3 Wherefore, brethren, look ye out among you seven men of honest report, full of the Holy Ghost and wisdom, whom we may appoint over this business. 4 But we will give ourselves continually to prayer, and to the ministry of the word. 5 And the saying pleased the whole multitude: and they chose Stephen, a man full of faith and of the Holy Ghost, and Philip, and Prochorus, and Nicanor, and Timon, and Parmenas, and Nicolas a proselyte of Antioch: 6 Whom they set before the apostles: and when they had prayed, they laid *their* hands on them. 7 And the word of God increased; and the number of the disciples multiplied in Jerusalem greatly; and a great company of the priests were obedient to the faith.

[5] Matthew 18:17 And if he shall neglect to hear them, tell *it* unto the church: but if he neglect to hear the church, let him be unto thee as an heathen man and a publican.

[6] 2 Corinthians 8:18 And we have sent with him the brother, whose praise *is* in the gospel throughout all the churches; 19 And not *that* only, but who was also chosen of the churches to travel with us with this grace, which is administered by us to the glory of the same Lord, and *declaration of* your ready mind: 20 Avoiding this, that no man should blame us in this abundance which is administered by us: 21 Providing for honest things, not only in the sight of the Lord, but

also in the sight of men. 22 And we have sent with them our brother, whom we have oftentimes proved diligent in many things, but now much more diligent, upon the great confidence which *I have* in you. 23 Whether *any do inquire* of Titus, *he is* my partner and fellowhelper concerning you: or our brethren *be inquired of, they are* the messengers of the churches, *and* the glory of Christ. 24 Wherefore shew ye to them, and before the churches, the proof of your love, and of our boasting on your behalf.

7 Matthew 28:19 Go ye therefore, and teach all nations, baptizing them in the name of the Father, and of the Son, and of the Holy Ghost: 20 Teaching them to observe all things whatsoever I have commanded you: and, lo, I am with you alway, *even* unto the end of the world. Amen.

1 Corinthians 1:2 Unto the church of God which is at Corinth, to them that are sanctified in Christ Jesus, called *to be* saints, with all that in every place call upon the name of Jesus Christ our Lord, both theirs and ours:

1 Corinthians 1:18 For the preaching of the cross is to them that perish foolishness; but unto us which are saved it is the power of God.

1 Corinthians 1:23 But we preach Christ crucified, unto the Jews a stumblingblock, and unto the Greeks foolishness; 24 But unto them which are called, both Jews and Greeks, Christ the power of God, and the wisdom of God. 25 Because the foolishness of God is wiser than men; and the weakness of God is stronger than men. 26 For ye see your calling, brethren, how that not many wise men after the flesh, not many mighty, not many noble, *are called*: 27 But God hath chosen the foolish things of the world to confound the wise; and God hath chosen the weak things of the world to confound the things which are mighty; 28 And base things of the world, and things which are despised, hath God chosen, *yea*, and things which are not, to bring to nought things that are: 29 That no flesh should glory in his presence. 30 But of him are ye in Christ Jesus, who of God is made unto us wisdom, and righteousness, and sanctification, and redemption: 31 That, according as it is written, He that glorieth, let him glory in the Lord.

[8] Matthew 4:4 But he answered and said, It is written, Man shall not live by bread alone, but by every word that proceedeth out of the mouth of God.

2 Timothy 3:15 And that from a child thou hast known the holy scriptures, which are able to make thee wise unto salvation through faith which is in Christ Jesus.

2 Timothy 4:22 The Lord Jesus Christ *be* with thy spirit. Grace *be* with you. Amen.

9

A QUESTION FACING ALL BELIEVERS.

Have you been baptized since you were saved?

Yes_____ No_____

If your answer is no, you should consider exactly why you have not chosen to be obedient to the command of the LORD Jesus. You need to examine your decision not to submit yourselves to your LORD and Saviour. I submit that you should read the next chapter slowly and carefully.

10

A QUESTION FOR THE BELIEVER WHO HAS NOT BEEN BAPTIZED

Why is it that you have not followed the LORD Jesus in believer's baptism in obedience to His command?

Maybe you did not know you were supposed to be baptized.

Maybe you have not had an opportunity to be baptized.

Maybe you have never before been shown or understood the truth about baptism.

Maybe you realize that you listened to some person rather than the LORD.

Maybe you were misguided or even taught wrongly about baptism.

Maybe there are family pressures that have prompted you to avoid baptism.

Maybe you been embarrassed or ashamed to take a public stand for the One Who died for your sins.

Maybe you have been fearful about being

121

pushed under the waters of baptism.

Maybe you considered baptism too lightly.

Whatever the reason, *if you are physically able to do so and refuse to be baptized,* what possible answer will you give to your Saviour for this deliberate act of disobedience and rebellion?

Think this situation through. If you are saved, having by faith trusted the LORD to forgive you of your sins and to keep you out of hell, why are you unwilling to follow the command of the LORD to be baptized?

Let me ask you this pointed question: How could you trust the Son of GOD for eternal salvation, and not trust Him, with the same kind of faith as that which saved you, to know what is best for you in this matter of baptism. Do you not believe that He will help you to be able to be obedient to His will and His word?

Even if you are afraid of entering the water for fear of drowning, would you not accept that He is able to protect you? Would you not believe that He will honor you if you obey? Will He not give you the grace to obey?

If you have been saved, but you have not submitted to Biblical baptism, you have only one question to face. *Are you willing to obey the command of your LORD and submit to believer's baptism?*

Is this your testimony? "I am saved. I know that I am trusting only in the shed blood of the LORD Jesus Christ to atone for my sins. I know that the LORD Jesus Christ rose literally and bodily from the grave for my justification. I know that I have personally received Him as my own personal Saviour. I am willing to follow the command of my LORD and Saviour and submit myself to the ordinance of scriptural baptism."

Yes_____ No_____

If your answer is *"No, I am not willing to be baptized,"* then I must honestly confront you with the truth.

Your action raises a serious doubt as to whether or not you are actually saved. You are certainly willfully and deliberating deciding to disobey the LORD Jesus Christ, and you are doing so willfully and knowingly. You are in open defiant rebellion against the word of GOD; and, therefore, you are contrary to the GOD of the word.

If you *are* saved, I warn you that you should expect to be chastened for this sinful disobedience. Every true believer receives chastisement for sin.

> Hebrews 12:5 And ye have forgotten the exhortation which speaketh unto you as unto children, My son, despise not thou the chastening of the Lord, nor faint when thou art rebuked of him: 6 For whom the Lord loveth he chasteneth, and scourgeth every son whom he receiveth. 7 If ye endure chastening, God dealeth with you as with sons; for what son is he whom the father chasteneth not? 8 **But if ye be without chastisement, whereof all are partakers, then are ye bastards, and not sons.** 9 Furthermore we have had fathers of our flesh which corrected *us*, and we gave *them* reverence: shall we not much rather be in subjection unto the Father of spirits, and live? 10 For they verily for a few days chastened *us* after their own pleasure; but he for *our* profit, that *we*

might be partakers of his holiness. ... 25 See that ye refuse not him that speaketh. For if they escaped not who refused him that spake on earth, much more *shall not* we *escape*, if we turn away from him that *speaketh* from heaven: 26 Whose voice then shook the earth: but now he hath promised, saying, Yet once more I shake not the earth only, but also heaven. 27 And this *word*, Yet once more, signifieth the removing of those things that are shaken, as of things that are made, that those things which cannot be shaken may remain. 28 Wherefore we receiving a kingdom which cannot be moved, **let us have grace, whereby we may serve God acceptably with reverence and godly fear:** 29 For our God *is* a consuming fire.

I beg you to repent and to do so before you are chastened. Do not continue to live after a planned course of rebellion.

11

A QUESTION FOR THE BELIEVER WHO HAS BEEN BAPTIZED

If you have been baptized, then the single question you must ask and answer is "Were you scripturally baptized?"

It is not at all important whether you were then or are now satisfied or whether someone else was then or is now satisfied. The single issue facing you today is whether your baptism was satisfying to the LORD. Your motive is not the question; your obedience is the only issue.

Were you baptized in obedience to the command of some individual?

Did you accept a baptism derived through some religious philosophy?

Were you baptized in obedience to the command of the LORD Jesus?

The following questions may enable you to determine whether your baptism was scripturally valid or not.

I was baptized upon my profession of faith, after I was born again?

Yes_____ No_____

If you were trusting in your baptism to have any role in saving you, such as removing original sin or being the act of obedience required to be saved when you were baptized or if you are now trusting that your baptism somehow contributed to your gaining eternal life, then you are still as lost today as you were before you were *baptized*. There is no salvation, none whatsoever, available in or through baptism.

If you are trusting in your baptism to wash away your sins, you are actually trusting in your works and not in the grace of GOD. You need to have "repentance from dead works and faith toward God."[1]

I was baptized by immersion in water?

Yes_____ No_____

I was baptized under the authority of a New Testament church?

Yes_____ No_____

I was *buried in baptism and was raised to walk in newness of life* as my identification with the LORD Jesus Christ and with His church?

Yes_____ No_____

Unless you can answer honestly and factually with an unqualified yes to each of the above questions, you have not been scripturally baptized. This is true regardless who might feel satisfied with that baptism. Whatever you received, it was not Bible baptism. If you are saved, you are an unbaptized believer.

You have a genuine need to be baptized. For you now to refuse to obey the command of your LORD and Saviour makes you a rebellious child who is both out of the will of your GOD and out of fellowship with your Heavenly Father.

Debate and delay concerning this matter are sin. You need to be obedient to your LORD. The simple issue for you to face is obedience, your personal conformity to the word of GOD, and not personal feelings of satisfaction.

> John 14:23 Jesus answered and said unto him, If a man love me, he will keep my words: and my Father will love him, and we will come unto him, and make our abode with him.

> John 15:14 Ye are my friends, if ye do whatsoever I command you.

If your answers reveal that you have not yet been baptized in obedience to and in compliance with Scripture, then you face one more question.

---

[1] Hebrews 6:1 Therefore leaving the principles of the doctrine of Christ, let us go on unto perfection; not laying again the foundation of repentance from dead works, and of faith toward God,

12

A QUESTION FOR THE BELIEVER WHOSE BAPTISM WAS NOT SCRIPTURAL

Now that you know what you should do about being baptized in obedience to the LORD'S command, what will you do with this knowledge? You cannot plead ignorance of your obligation or ignore what you now know to be your responsibility.

If you are physically able to be immersed, are you willing to submit yourself in obedience and to seek scriptural baptism?

Yes_____ No_____

If you are not presently physically able to be immersed, are you willing to submit yourself in obedience and to seek scriptural baptism as soon as you are physically able to be immersed?

Yes_____ No_____

If you answer that you are not willing to be baptized, then please read the following verse:

Luke 6:46 And why call ye me, Lord, Lord, and do not the things which I say?

Can you conceive of any answer other than physical inability that could possibly justify your refusal to obey the LORD that He will accept? I know of none.

Would it not be so much better for you to be obedient to the will of GOD than for you to have to face the disapproval and the chastisement of the Heavenly Father upon your life? Do you understand that when you stand before the Judgment Seat of Christ, your disobedience will cause you the loss of reward?

Baptism is not presented as a small insignificant issue in Scripture and baptism ought not to considered a nonessential in your life. Baptism is not some minor command; but, even if baptism were the least of the commands of Christ, you should still submit in obedience.

Matthew 5:18-19 For verily I say unto you, Till heaven and earth pass, one jot or one tittle shall in no wise pass from the law, till all be fulfilled. Whosoever therefore shall break one of these least commandments, and shall teach men so, he shall be called the least in the kingdom of heaven: but whosoever shall do and teach them, the same shall be called great in the kingdom of heaven.

For a believer to choose not to keep the command of Christ is for that believer to display a lack of love for Him.

John 14:21 He that hath my commandments, and keepeth them, he it is that loveth me: and he that loveth me shall be loved of my Father, and I will love him, and will manifest myself to him. ... 15 If ye love me, keep my commandments.

Your baptism is central to your relationship to your LORD. Certainly, an individual could be saved and never be baptized. That person could live a long life and when he died he would go to heaven. The question is why on earth would anyone want to refuse to obey the command of the LORD Jesus.

What profit could there be for you in deliberate disobedience?

What motive could there be in refusing to follow the example and the command of the Saviour that died for you?

Why would a believer desire to live out of fellowship with his Heavenly Father?

What joy will come from facing Christ and confessing that you have been rebellious?

What possible reason can justify your refusal to be baptized?

Those are serious questions worthy of consideration.

Has the Spirit of GOD touched your heart about baptism? If you have any desire to be baptized, that urging came from the Holy Spirit. He is leading you to be obedient to the word of GOD.

> Romans 8:5 For they that are after the flesh do mind the things of the flesh; but they that are after the Spirit the things of the Spirit. 6 For to be carnally minded *is* death; but to be spiritually minded *is* life and peace. 7 Because the carnal mind *is* enmity against God: for it is not subject to the law of God, neither indeed can be. 8 So then they that are in the flesh cannot please God. 9 But ye are not in the flesh,

but in the Spirit, if so be that the Spirit of God dwell in you. Now if any man have not the Spirit of Christ, he is none of his. 10 And if Christ *be* in you, the body *is* dead because of sin; but the Spirit *is* life because of righteousness. 11 But if the Spirit of him that raised up Jesus from the dead dwell in you, he that raised up Christ from the dead shall also quicken your mortal bodies by his Spirit that dwelleth in you. 12 Therefore, brethren, we are debtors, not to the flesh, to live after the flesh. 13 For if ye live after the flesh, ye shall die: but if ye through the Spirit do mortify the deeds of the body, ye shall live. 14 For as many as are led by the Spirit of God, they are the sons of God. 15 For ye have not received the spirit of bondage again to fear; but ye have received the Spirit of adoption, whereby we cry, Abba, Father. 16 The Spirit itself beareth witness with our spirit, that we are the children of God: 17 And if children, then heirs; heirs of God, and joint-heirs with Christ; if so be that we suffer with *him*, that we may be also glorified together. 18 For I reckon that the sufferings of this present time *are* not worthy *to be compared* with the glory which shall be revealed in us. ... 26 Likewise the Spirit also helpeth our infirmities: for we know not what we should pray for as we ought: but the Spirit itself maketh intercession for us with groanings which cannot be uttered. ... 28 And we know that all things work together for good to them that love God, to them who are the called according to *his* purpose. ... 31 What shall we then say to these things? If God *be* for us, who *can be* against us?

Would you like to be submissive to the will

of GOD? Are you willing to trust GOD for any strength that you might need? If so, then determine today that you will be obedient.

Philippians 2:13 For it is God which worketh in you both to will and to do of his good pleasure. 14 Do all things without murmurings and disputings:

I will follow the example of the LORD and I will obey His command. I will seek Biblical baptism at the earliest opportunity.

Yes_____ No_____

MY BAPTISM

Thou hast said, exalted Jesus,
Take thy cross and follow Me;
Shall the word with terror seize us?
Shall we from the burden flee?
Lord, I'll take it, and rejoicing follow Thee.
While this liquid tomb surveying,
Emblem of my Saviour's grave,
Shall I shun its brink, betraying
Feelings worthy of a slave?
No; I'll enter: Jesus entered Jordan's wave.
Blest the sign which thus reminds me,
Saviour, of Thy love for me;
But more blest the love that binds me
In its deathless bonds to Thee
Oh, what pleasure, buried with my Lord to be.
Should it rend some fond connection,
Should I suffer shame or loss,
Yet the fragrant, blest reflection,
I have been where Jesus was,
Will revive me when I faint beneath the cross.
Fellowship with Him possessing,
Let me die to earth and sin:
Let me rise to enjoy the blessing
Which the faithful soul shall win:
May I ever follow where my Lord has been.

—John Eustace Giles, 1837

THE ORDINANCE OF COMMUNION

13

DEFINING THE REMEMBRANCE

Following his baptism, the believer is to observe the single church observance commissioned by the LORD Jesus. The believer has been instructed "this do in remembrance of Me." However, the commission was not given to individuals for a private personal observance; the command for remembrance was given to the church for a cooperate assembled gathering.

The command "this do" was not given to singular individuals, but to the collective whole of the assembled church. The LORD Jesus did not command the disciples as individuals to (using *thee*), but He spoke to them as a body of believers (using *you* and *ye*).

1 Corinthians 11:24 And when he had given thanks, he brake *it*, and said, Take, eat: this is my body, which is broken for **you**: this do in remembrance of me. 25 After the same manner also *he took* the cup, when he had supped, saying, This

cup is the new testament in my blood: this
do **ye**, as oft as **ye** drink *it*, in remembrance of me.

Notice that the next verse is not a quota-
tion of what the LORD Jesus said to the
assembled disciples in the upper room, but is
an admonition addressed by Paul to the
church at Corinth.

26 For as often as ye eat this bread, and
drink this cup, ye do shew the Lord's
death till he come.

The only clear records of Communion services in Scripture are those held in the upper
room[1] the night before the death of Jesus of
Nazareth and the rebuke for improper conduct in 1 Corinthians 11:18-34.[2] Many
understand the phrase "breaking of bread" to
be an identification of a Communion service.
It may be such an recognition, but the phrase
certainly is not used exclusively for the
Communion service.[3]

As Paul writes to the Corinthian church
regarding the mishandling of the observance
of Communion, he addressed the church as a
unit that has *come together in the church.*[4] The
individual believer is to participate with his
church in a time of coming together.

Communion is not to be observed by individuals or by families. Communion is also not
a service for organizations to commemorate.
As is baptism, Communion is an ordinance
for the church to administer and to observe.

The chronological setting for the institution of the ordinance is found in three of the
Gospels. Following the eating of the Passover
meal, the LORD Jesus took the third cup,
called the *Cup of Redemption* in the Jewish

Seder, and gave it a new significance.[5]

> Luke 22:20 Likewise also the cup after supper, saying, **This cup is the new testament in my blood**, which is shed for you.

> 1 Corinthians 11:25 After the same manner also *he took* the cup, when he had supped, saying, **This cup is the new testament in my blood**: this do ye, as oft as ye drink *it*, in remembrance of me.

Jesus of Nazareth provided the redemption of His shed blood. In addition to the multiple times that He described what would be done to Him in Jerusalem, the LORD Jesus addresses His sacrificial death at the Passover meal. He speaks of His body as being broken and of His blood as being shed. He told the disciples that His body would be broken for them and His blood would be shed for them. In doing so, Jesus of Nazareth was explaining that His dying directly involved them, and was to be considered by them as being personal for them.[6]

Matthew 26
26 And as they were eating, Jesus took bread, and blessed *it*, and brake *it*, and gave *it* to the disciples, and said, Take, eat; this is my body. 27 And he took the cup, and gave thanks, and gave *it* to them, saying, Drink ye all of it; 28 For this is my blood of the new testament, which is shed for many for the remission of sins.

Mark 14
22 And as they did eat, Jesus took bread, and blessed, and brake *it*, and gave to them, and said, Take, eat: this is my body. 23 And he took the cup, and when he had given thanks, he gave *it* to them: and they all drank of it. 24 And he said unto them, This is my blood of the new testament, which is shed for many.

> Luke 22
>
> 19 And he took bread, and gave thanks, and brake *it*, and gave unto them, saying, This is my body which is given for you: this do in remembrance of me. 20 Likewise also the cup after supper, saying, This cup *is* the new testament in my blood, which is shed for you.

The LORD Jesus does not *name* the service of the bread and the cup and it is not until the apostle is moved to record the Epistle to the Corinthian church that the three Biblical names are recorded. The Saviour did use one very special word to identify this service: the word *Remembrance*. No other word summarizes and identifies the Table of the LORD as well as does the word *Remembrance*.

The Communion of the LORD'S Supper at the Table of the LORD is the ordinance of Remembrance.

> 1 Corinthians 1 Corinthians 10:16 The cup of blessing which we bless, is it not the **communion** of the blood of Christ? The bread which we break, is it not the communion of the body of Christ? ... 21 Ye cannot drink the cup of the Lord, and the cup of devils: ye cannot be partakers of **the Lord's table**, and of the table of devils. ... 11:1 Be ye followers of me, even as I also *am* of Christ. 2 Now I praise you, brethren, that ye remember me in all things, and keep the ordinances, as I delivered *them* to you. ... 17 Now in this that I declare *unto you* I praise *you* not, that ye come together not for the better, but for the worse. 18 For first of all, when ye come together in the church, I hear that there be divisions among you; and I partly believe it. 19 For there must be also here-

sies among you, that they which are approved may be made manifest among you. 20 When ye come together therefore into one place, *this* is not to eat **the Lord's supper**. 21 For in eating every one taketh before *other* his own supper: and one is hungry, and another is drunken. 22 What? have ye not houses to eat and to drink in? or despise ye the church of God, and shame them that have not? What shall I say to you? shall I praise you in this? I praise *you* not. 23 For I have received of the Lord that which also I delivered unto you, That the Lord Jesus the *same* night in which he was betrayed took bread: 24 And when he had given thanks, he brake *it,* and said, Take, eat: this is my body, which is broken for you: **this do in remembrance of me.** 25 After the same manner also *he took* the cup, when he had supped, saying, This cup is the new testament in my blood: **this do ye,** as oft as ye drink *it,* **in remembrance of me**. 26 For as often as ye eat this bread, and drink this cup, ye do shew the Lord's death till he come. 27 Wherefore whosoever shall eat this bread, and drink *this* cup of the Lord, unworthily, shall be guilty of the body and blood of the Lord. 28 But let a man examine himself, and so let him eat of *that* bread, and drink of *that* cup. 29 For he that eateth and drinketh unworthily, eateth and drinketh damnation to himself, not discerning the Lord's body. 30 For this cause many *are* weak and sickly among you, and many sleep. 31 For if we would judge ourselves, we should not be judged. 32 But when we are judged, we are chastened of the Lord, that we should not be condemned with the world. 33 Wherefore, my brethren, when ye come

together to eat, tarry one for another. 34
And if any man hunger, let him eat at
home; that ye come not together unto
condemnation. And the rest will I set in
order when I come.

The broken bread and the cup are titled
within the Scriptures as Communion, the
LORD'S Table, and the LORD'S Supper. Men
have called it by the non-Biblical terms of the
Eucharist [English transliteration of the Greek
for *gratitude*] and the *Mass* [the word has the
basic meaning of a dismissal] among other
titles.[7] In doing so, non-Biblical significances
and non-Biblical benefits have been alleged
for the observance.

When the apostle was moved to write to
the church at Corinth regarding the Table of
the LORD, he did so to address misconduct at
the service. It is worthy of noticing that within
this first generation of churches serious errors
of doctrine and practice rose within those
churches. It would be naïve to believe that no
such errors would rise in churches today.

The old truths must be taught continu-
ously[8] or else error will creep in and eventually dominate. The agricultural admonition is a
fitting reminder that we must not allow the
boundaries to be removed.

Proverbs 22:28 Remove not the ancient
landmark, which thy fathers have set.

[1] The only time that the LORD Jesus is recorded as having sung is after the institution of the Communion. That event is defined by the Holy Spirit as having occurred in the midst of the church.

Matthew 26:30 And when they had sung an hymn, they went out into the mount of Olives.

Mark 14:26 And when they had sung an hymn, they went out into the mount of Olives.

Hebrews 2:12 Saying, I will declare thy name unto my brethren, in the midst of the church will I sing praise unto thee.

[2] 1 Corinthians 11:18 For first of all, when ye come together in the church, I hear that there be divisions among you; and I partly believe it. 19 For there must be also heresies among you, that they which are approved may be made manifest among you. 20 When ye come together therefore into one place, *this* is not to eat the Lord's supper. 21 For in eating every one taketh before *other* his own supper: and one is hungry, and another is drunken. 22 What? have ye not houses to eat and to drink in? or despise ye the church of God, and shame them that have not? What shall I say to you? shall I praise you in this? I praise *you* not. 23 For I have received of the Lord that which also I delivered unto you, That the Lord Jesus the *same* night in which he was betrayed took bread: 24 And when he had given thanks, he brake *it*, and said, Take, eat: this is my body, which is broken for you: this do in remembrance of me. 25 After the same manner also *he took* the cup, when he had supped, saying, This cup is the new testament in my blood: this do ye, as oft as ye drink *it*, in remembrance of me. 26 For as often as ye eat this bread, and drink this cup, ye do shew the Lord's death till he come. 27 Wherefore whosoever shall eat this bread, and drink *this* cup of the Lord, unworthily, shall be guilty of the body and blood of the Lord. 28 But let a man examine himself, and so let him eat of *that* bread, and drink of *that* cup. 29 For he that eateth and drinketh unworthily, eateth and drinketh damnation to himself, not discerning the Lord's body. 30 For this cause many *are* weak and sickly among you, and many sleep. 31 For if we would judge ourselves, we should not be judged. 32 But when we are judged, we are

145

chastened of the Lord, that we should not be condemned with the world. 33 Wherefore, my brethren,
when ye come together to eat, tarry one for another. 34
And if any man hunger, let him eat at home; that ye
come not together unto condemnation. And the rest will
I set in order when I come.

3 The LORD Jesus did not observe Communion with
Cleopas and his wife on the evening of the Resurrection. Luke 24:35 And they told what things *were done*
in the way, and how he was known of them in breaking
of bread.
Furthermore, the three other passages that are cited as
evidence of Communion observances do not collectively
lend themselves to that interpretation. While Acts 2:42
might be so understood, Acts 2:46 and 20:11 speak of
eating and convey the image of a meal and not a
Communion. Acts 2:42 And they continued stedfastly
in the apostles' doctrine and fellowship, and in
breaking of bread, and in prayers. ... 46 And they,
continuing daily with one accord in the temple, and
breaking bread from house to house, did eat their meat
with gladness and singleness of heart, ... 20:11 When
he therefore was come up again, and had broken bread,
and eaten, and talked a long while, even till break of
day, so he departed.

4 1 Corinthians 11:18 ... when ye come together in
the church ... 20 When ye come together therefore into
one place ... 33 ... when ye come together to eat ... 34
... come not together unto condemnation.

5 The Seder has four cups that are a part of the
service. The cups in the order of the service are titled
the Cup of Sanctification, of Blessing, of Redemption,
and of Acceptance. The cups were named based upon
Exodus 6:6 Wherefore say unto the children of Israel, I
am the LORD, and [**CUP 1**] I will bring you out from
under the burdens of the Egyptians, and [**CUP 2**] I will
rid you out of their bondage, and [**CUP 3**] I will redeem
you with a stretched out arm, and with great judgments: 7 And [**CUP 4**] I will take you to me for a people,
and I will be to you a God: and ye shall know that I *am*
the LORD your God, which bringeth you out from
under the burdens of the Egyptians.
To these four cups, a fifth was added. This was the Cup
of Elijah. The tradition of the Seder includes an empty

146

chair at the table. This chair was anticipatory of the coming of Elijah to announce the Messiah.

⁶ **Matthew** 16:21 From that time forth began Jesus to shew unto his disciples, how that he must go unto Jerusalem, and suffer many things of the elders and chief priests and scribes, and be killed, and be raised again the third day. ... 17:12 But I say unto you, That Elias is come already, and they knew him not, but have done unto him whatsoever they listed. Likewise shall also the Son of man suffer of them. ... 17:22 And while they abode in Galilee, Jesus said unto them, The Son of man shall be betrayed into the hands of men: 23 And they shall kill him, and the third day he shall be raised again. And they were exceeding sorry. ... 20:17 And Jesus going up to Jerusalem took the twelve disciples apart in the way, and said unto them, 18 Behold, we go up to Jerusalem; and the Son of man shall be betrayed unto the chief priests and unto the scribes, and they shall condemn him to death, 19 And shall deliver him to the Gentiles to mock, and to scourge, and to crucify *him*: and the third day he shall rise again. ... 20:28 Even as the Son of man came not to be ministered unto, but to minister, and to give his life a ransom for many. ... 26:1 And it came to pass, when Jesus had finished all these sayings, he said unto his disciples, 2 Ye know that after two days is *the feast of* the passover, and the Son of man is betrayed to be crucified. ... 26:19 And the disciples did as Jesus had appointed them; and they made ready the passover. 20 Now when the even was come, he sat down with the twelve. 21 And as they did eat, he said, Verily I say unto you, that one of you shall betray me. 22 And they were exceeding sorrowful, and began every one of them to say unto him, Lord, is it I? 23 And he answered and said, He that dippeth *his* hand with me in the dish, the same shall betray me. 24 The Son of man goeth as it is written of him: but woe unto that man by whom the Son of man is betrayed! it had been good for that man if he had not been born. 25 Then Judas, which betrayed him, answered and said, Master, is it I? He said unto him, Thou hast said. 26 And as they were eating, Jesus took bread, and blessed *it*, and brake *it*, and gave *it* to the disciples, and said, Take, eat; this is my body. 27 And he took the cup, and gave thanks,

and gave *it* to them, saying, Drink ye all of it; 28 For this is my blood of the new testament, which is shed for many for the remission of sins. 29 But I say unto you, I will not drink henceforth of this fruit of the vine, until that day when I drink it new with you in my Father's kingdom. 30 And when they had sung an hymn, they went out into the mount of Olives. 31 Then saith Jesus unto them, All ye shall be offended because of me this night: for it is written, I will smite the shepherd, and the sheep of the flock shall be scattered abroad. 32 But after I am risen again, I will go before you into Galilee. ... 26:52 Then said Jesus unto him, Put up again thy sword into his place: for all they that take the sword shall perish with the sword. 53 Thinkest thou that I cannot now pray to my Father, and he shall presently give me more than twelve legions of angels? 54 But how then shall the scriptures be fulfilled, that thus it must be?

Mark 8:31 And he began to teach them, that the Son of man must suffer many things, and be rejected of the elders, and *of* the chief priests, and scribes, and be killed, and after three days rise again. ... 9:31 For he taught his disciples, and said unto them, The Son of man is delivered into the hands of men, and they shall kill him; and after that he is killed, he shall rise the third day. 32 But they understood not that saying, and were afraid to ask him. ... 10:32 And they were in the way going up to Jerusalem; and Jesus went before them: and they were amazed; and as they followed, they were afraid. And he took again the twelve, and began to tell them what things should happen unto him, 33 *Saying*, Behold, we go up to Jerusalem; and the Son of man shall be delivered unto the chief priests, and unto the scribes; and they shall condemn him to death, and shall deliver him to the Gentiles: 34 And they shall mock him, and shall scourge him, and shall spit upon him, and shall kill him: and the third day he shall rise again.

Luke 9:21 And he straitly charged them, and commanded *them* to tell no man that thing; 22 Saying, The Son of man must suffer many things, and be rejected of the elders and chief priests and scribes, and be slain, and be raised the third day. ... 9:28 And it came to pass about an eight days after these sayings, he took

Peter and John and James, and went up into a mountain to pray. 29 And as he prayed, the fashion of his countenance was altered, and his raiment *was* white *and* glistering. 30 And, behold, there talked with him two men, which were Moses and Elias: 31 Who appeared in glory, and spake of his decease which he should accomplish at Jerusalem. ... 9:21 And he straitly charged them, and commanded *them* to tell no man that thing; 22 Saying, The Son of man must suffer many things, and be rejected of the elders and chief priests and scribes, and be slain, and be raised the third day. 23 And he said to *them* all, If any *man* will come after me, let him deny himself, and take up his cross daily, and follow me. 24 For whosoever will save his life shall lose it: but whosoever will lose his life for my sake, the same shall save it. 25 For what is a man advantaged, if he gain the whole world, and lose himself, or be cast away? ... 9:43 And they were all amazed at the mighty power of God. But while they wondered every one at all things which Jesus did, he said unto his disciples, 44 Let these sayings sink down into your ears: for the Son of man shall be delivered into the hands of men. 45 But they understood not this saying, and it was hid from them, that they perceived it not: and they feared to ask him of that saying. ... 12:50 But I have a baptism to be baptized with; and how am I straitened till it be accomplished! ... 18:31 Then he took *unto him* the twelve, and said unto them, Behold, we go up to Jerusalem, and all things that are written by the prophets concerning the Son of man shall be accomplished. 32 For he shall be delivered unto the Gentiles, and shall be mocked, and spitefully entreated, and spitted on: 33 And they shall scourge *him*, and put him to death: and the third day he shall rise again. 34 And they understood none of these things: and this saying was hid from them, neither knew they the things which were spoken.

John 2:18 Then answered the Jews and said unto him, What sign shewest thou unto us, seeing that thou doest these things? 19 Jesus answered and said unto them, Destroy this temple, and in three days I will raise it up. 20 Then said the Jews, Forty and six years was this temple in building, and wilt thou rear it up in three days? 21 But he spake of the temple of his body. 22

When therefore he was risen from the dead, his disciples remembered that he had said this unto them; and they believed the scripture, and the word which Jesus had said. ... 3:14 And as Moses lifted up the serpent in the wilderness, even so must the Son of man be lifted up: ... 4:34 Jesus saith unto them, My meat is to do the will of him that sent me, and to finish his work. ... 7:6 Then Jesus said unto them, My time is not yet come: but your time is alway ready. 7 The world cannot hate you; but me it hateth, because I testify of it, that the works thereof are evil. 8 Go ye up unto this feast: I go not up yet unto this feast; for my time is not yet full come. ... 7:10 But when his brethren were gone up, then went he also up unto the feast, not openly, but as it were in secret. ... 10:15 As the Father knoweth me, even so know I the Father: and I lay down my life for the sheep. ... 10:17 Therefore doth my Father love me, because I lay down my life, that I might take it again. 18 No man taketh it from me, but I lay it down of myself. I have power to lay it down, and I have power to take it again. This commandment have I received of my Father. ... 12:23 And Jesus answered them, saying, The hour is come, that the Son of man should be glorified. 24 Verily, verily, I say unto you, Except a corn of wheat fall into the ground and die, it abideth alone: but if it die, it bringeth forth much fruit. 25 He that loveth his life shall lose it; and he that hateth his life in this world shall keep it unto life eternal. 26 If any man serve me, let him follow me; and where I am, there shall also my servant be: if any man serve me, him will *my* Father honour. 27 Now is my soul troubled; and what shall I say? Father, save me from this hour: but for this cause came I unto this hour. 28 Father, glorify thy name. Then came there a voice from heaven, *saying*, I have both glorified *it*, and will glorify *it* again. ... 12:31 Now is the judgment of this world: now shall the prince of this world be cast out. 32 And I, if I be lifted up from the earth, will draw all *men* unto me. ... 13:31 Therefore, when he was gone out, Jesus said, Now is the Son of man glorified, and God is glorified in him. 32 If God be glorified in him, God shall also glorify him in himself, and shall straightway glorify him. ... 16:28 I came forth from the Father, and am come into the world: again, I leave the

world, and go to the Father. ... 17:1 These words spake
Jesus, and lifted up his eyes to heaven, and said,
Father, the hour is come; glorify thy Son, that thy Son
also may glorify thee: ... 17:11 And now I am no more
in the world, but these are in the world, and I come to
thee. Holy Father, keep through thine own name those
whom thou hast given me, that they may be one, as we
are. ... 17:18 As thou hast sent me into the world, even
so have I also sent them into the world. ... 18:11 Then
said Jesus unto Peter, Put up thy sword into the
sheath: the cup which my Father hath given me, shall I
not drink it?

7 The following names of the Eucharist are listed in
section 5 of Compendium of the Catechism.
What are the names for this sacrament?
The unfathomable richness of this sacrament is
expressed in different names which evoke its various
aspects. The most common names are: the Eucharist,
Holy Mass, the Lord's Supper, the Breaking of the
Bread, the Eucharistic Celebration, the Memorial of the
passion, death and Resurrection of the Lord, the Holy
Sacrifice, the Holy and Divine Liturgy, the Sacred
Mysteries, the Most Holy Sacrament of the Altar, and
Holy Communion.
THE SACRAMENT OF THE EUCHARIST, Compendium
of the Catechism of the Catholic Church.
http://www.santorosario.net/english/mass/4.htm

8 2 Peter 1:12 Wherefore I will not be negligent to
put you always in remembrance of these things, though
ye know *them*, and be established in the present truth.
13 Yea, I think it meet, as long as I am in this tabernacle, to stir you up by putting *you* in remembrance;
14 Knowing that shortly I must put off *this* my
tabernacle, even as our Lord Jesus Christ hath shewed
me. 15 Moreover I will endeavour that ye may be able
after my decease to have these things always in
remembrance.

14

PREPARING FOR THE REMEMBRANCE SERVICE

W hen a church gathers together for the Remembrance Service, the Scriptures require that a firm, clear caution should be issued by the pastor to all who would present themselves before the Table of the LORD to participate in the observance of the church ordinance of the LORD'S Supper. All who are in attendance must be aware of the purpose for which the service is conducted and understand the Biblical requirements for participation.

Following that somber explanation and warning, before the church proceeds with the observance of Communion, a definite and defined opportunity for self-examination must be provided to all who have gathered. No one should be pressured to participate that has not given solemn and serious self-examination of his heart and of his life with an honest desire to discern any sinful acts, thoughts, or motives, whether these might be of commission or of omission. No one should be permitted to participate that has not been both warned and provided opportunity to do so.

In the allotment of time, an occasion for sincere repentance over the sin that might be brought to mind by the Holy Spirit must be included. It is as necessary that those in attendance are given the explanation of the purpose and the warning of participation as it is to provide appropriate time for repentance and confession.

The time for explanation of the service, the warning regarding personal preparation, and the provision for confession and repentance must not be perfunctorily or hastily accomplished. The LORD'S Supper must not be approached improperly or observed indifferently.

It is my conviction that it is the better practice for the church to have a special service for the Communion service and not to observe the Table of the LORD as merely an extension of a regular service. This procedure requires those that attend to have come with the mind already engaged in the purpose and to have prepared for the involvement in the service.

Those familiar with the service have a tendency to find it commonplace after the initial observances and Communion begins to lose the specialness that it must hold in the life of the believer. Those who are beginning to participate need to be fully aware of the importance of the observance. The explanation of the purpose accomplishes for both exactly what each needs.

The Saviour identified the observance of this ordinance as a *remembrance.*[1] It is a commemoration that is intended as a memorial to keep the sacrificial death of the Son of GOD in the mind of the believer.

Each believer must be challenged often never to forget that eternal salvation was not obtained lightly or cheaply. The LORD Jesus Christ gave Himself as our Passover Lamb, purchasing our atonement with His broken body and His shed blood.

The Table where His Supper is placed is His chosen Memorial of that sacrificial death. The physical elements of the unleavened bread and the fruit of the vine *do not become* the literal flesh or the actual blood of the LORD Jesus Christ; however, as His selected and appointed picture, they do represent, on this Table in this service, the broken body and the shed blood of our LORD and Saviour.

The church at Corinth misused the Table of the LORD. The purpose was forgotten and an apparently lavish banquet had developed. The LORD'S Supper is not a meal. The apostle rebukes the concept of a feasting time.

The Supper of the LORD has only two elements on the Table of the LORD: the broken bread and the cup. The broken bread is required to be unleavened and the cup with the fruit of the vine is also required to be unleavened. The first element symbolizes His broken body and the second element represents His shed blood.

The bread and the fruit of the vine that night in the Upper Room were on the table as part of the preparation for the Passover. The

Scriptures are emphatic that during the Passover every leavening agent was prohibited. So emphatic was this command that no leaven of any amount could remain in the home of the Israelite during the time of the Passover preparation or observance.[2]

> Exodus 12:19 Seven days **shall there be no leaven found in your houses**: for **whosoever eateth that which is leavened, even that soul shall be cut off** from the congregation of Israel, whether he be a stranger, or born in the land. ... 13:7 Unleavened bread shall be eaten seven days; and there shall no leavened bread be seen with thee, **neither shall there be leaven seen with thee in all thy quarters**.

The Biblical pattern for the bread of the Communion is unleavened; no leaven was permitted to be in the home where the Passover meal was prepared. The Jewish Matzo is a proper and easily obtainable bread to use for the Communion service. It is found commercially prepared in both square and round loaves, which have more the form of large crackers and are far more modern than the matzos used in the days of the Bible.

© Roman Sigaev - Fotolia.com. Used by permission

The form and features of the modern Matzos are capable of being incorporated into an illustration of what the bread represents. The absence of leaven might be seen as speaking of the sinlessness of the Son of man. The tiny holes may be used to picture the piercings that Son of GOD suffered. The stripes might remind of the stripes that were laid on Him.

Recipes for matzos are readily obtainable and it may be prepared rolled flat or in a loaf.

Finding grape juice without additives or preservatives is not a difficulty in these days of organic foods. The juice served for Communion is to be *without fermentation.*

To argue as some do for fermented grape juice, commonly identified as wine, as having been on the table in the Upper Room for the Passover observed by Jesus of Nazareth is to demonstrate a level of Biblical literacy *that is to be pitied.* No meal prepared for the Passover could have included *anything* leavened, and that included the fruit of the vine. The cup that night was filled with the fruit of the vine according to the three records.

> Matthew 26:29 But I say unto you, I will not drink henceforth of this fruit of the vine, until that day when I drink it new with you in my Father's kingdom.
>
> Mark 14:25 Verily I say unto you, I will drink no more of the fruit of the vine, until that day that I drink it new in the kingdom of God.
>
> Luke 22:18 For I say unto you, I will not drink of the fruit of the vine, until the kingdom of God shall come.

Simple, pure grape juice is the Biblical pattern for the *beverage* for the Communion service. The evidence is irrefutable that leaven could not be involved in any substance used in the Passover service from which the LORD Jesus instituted the service of Remembrance.

The juice in the cup represents the very blood of the LORD Jesus, the sinless Saviour. It is inconceivable that something containing leaven, which is the consistent type of sin in Scripture, would even be considered as a suitable representation for the blood of the Son of GOD. Walter Wilson wrote, In every place where leaven is mentioned, it is a type of evil teachings, evil doctrines, and evil practices. ... always to be put away and cast out as an unclean thing. ... Nothing good is ever compared to leaven. Nothing good is ever said about leaven. ... There is no place in the Bible where leaven is spoken of in an approving way, nor is it ever related to anything good.[3]

The two elements involved in the service of Remembrance of the death of the LORD Jesus are both unleavened. They cannot biblically be otherwise. The representations must have Scriptural integrity and must faithfully present the Son of GOD.

The service of Remembrance is to have special significance each time it is observed. While it is an ordinance and therefore binding to be observed, it is to be a service where attendance and participation is to be motivated by love and not from duty.

Believers, therefore, are to approach humbly the LORD'S Supper at the Table of the LORD in holy Communion with the One Who died for them and with the earnest desire to testify of His atoning death until He returns. Participation is not to be engaged casually or carelessly; however, believers are to partake faithfully and regularly and to do so willingly and joyfully.

Above all, this Table is not for the unbeliever who hopes to earn merit before GOD or to gain salvation by approaching this Table. Nor is it for the disobedient believer who has willfully failed to follow the LORD'S command to be baptized or is otherwise unfaithful to the LORD. The Supper is not for a insubordinate believer that hopes somehow to gain righteousness and to have his rebellion overlooked by coming to this Table.

There is no special grace gained in partaking at the Table of the LORD. There is no physical healing found, no spiritual forgiveness earned, and no righteousness granted through receiving the elements from this Table.

Anyone harboring such motives is strongly warned not to partake of the elements of the LORD'S Supper—to disregard that warning is for that rebellious soul to invite the judgment of the LORD.

Those who meet the requirements of Scripture are to be welcomed. Upon the authority of Scripture, all others are to be denied admission to the Table of the LORD.

[1] *Merriam-Webster 11th Collegiate Dictionary* defines *remembrance* as follows. #3 and #5 are the definitions that bear upon our understanding of this word as a description of Communion.
1: the state of bearing in mind
2 a: the ability to remember: MEMORY b: the period over which one's memory extends
3: an act of recalling to mind
4: a memory of a person, thing, or event
5 a: something that serves to keep in or bring to mind: REMINDER b: COMMEMORATION, MEMORIAL; c: a greeting or gift recalling or expressing friendship or affection
[2] Exodus 12:1 And the LORD spake unto Moses and Aaron in the land of Egypt, saying, 2 This month *shall be* unto you the beginning of months: it *shall be* the first month of the year to you. 3 Speak ye unto all the congregation of Israel, saying, In the tenth *day* of this month they shall take to them every man a lamb, according to the house of *their* fathers, a lamb for an house: 4 And if the household be too little for the lamb, let him and his neighbour next unto his house take *it* according to the number of the souls; every man according to his eating shall make your count for the lamb. 5 Your lamb shall be without blemish, a male of the first year: ye shall take *it* out from the sheep, or from the goats: 6 And ye shall keep it up until the fourteenth day of the same month: and the whole assembly of the congregation of Israel shall kill it in the evening. 7 And they shall take of the blood, and strike *it* on the two side posts and on the upper door post of the houses, wherein they shall eat it. 8 And they shall eat the flesh in that night, roast with fire, and unleavened bread; *and* with bitter *herbs* they shall eat it. 9 Eat not of it raw, nor sodden at all with water, but roast *with* fire; his head with his legs, and with the purtenance thereof. 10 And ye shall let nothing of it remain until the morning; and that which remaineth of it until the morning ye shall burn with fire. 11 And thus shall ye eat it; *with* your loins girded, your shoes on your feet, and your staff in your hand; and ye shall eat it in haste: it *is* the LORD'S passover. 12 For I will pass through the land of Egypt this night, and will

smite all the firstborn in the land of Egypt, both man and beast; and against all the gods of Egypt I will execute judgment: I *am* the LORD. 13 And the blood shall be to you for a token upon the houses where ye *are*: and when I see the blood, I will pass over you, and the plague shall not be upon you to destroy *you*, when I smite the land of Egypt. 14 And this day shall be unto you for a memorial; and ye shall keep it a feast to the LORD throughout your generations; ye shall keep it a feast by an ordinance for ever. 15 Seven days shall ye eat unleavened bread; even the first day ye shall put away leaven out of your houses: for whosoever eateth leavened bread from the first day until the seventh day, that soul shall be cut off from Israel. 16 And in the first day *there shall be* an holy convocation, and in the seventh day there shall be an holy convocation to you; no manner of work shall be done in them, save *that* which every man must eat, that only may be done of you. 17 And ye shall observe *the feast of* unleavened bread; for in this selfsame day have I brought your armies out of the land of Egypt: therefore shall ye observe this day in your generations by an ordinance for ever. 18 In the first *month*, on the fourteenth day of the month at even, ye shall eat unleavened bread, until the one and twentieth day of the month at even. 19 **Seven days shall there be no leaven found in your houses: for whosoever eateth that which is leavened, even that soul shall be cut off from the congregation of Israel, whether he be a stranger, or born in the land.** 20 Ye shall eat nothing leavened; in all your habitations shall ye eat unleavened bread. 21 Then Moses called for all the elders of Israel, and said unto them, Draw out and take you a lamb according to your families, and kill the passover. 22 And ye shall take a bunch of hyssop, and dip *it* in the blood that *is* in the bason, and strike the lintel and the two side posts with the blood that *is* in the bason; and none of you shall go out at the door of his house until the morning. 23 For the LORD will pass through to smite the Egyptians; and when he seeth the blood upon the lintel, and on the two side posts, the LORD will pass over the door, and will not suffer the destroyer to come in unto your houses to smite *you*. 24 And ye shall observe this thing for an ordinance to thee and to thy sons for ever. 25 And it shall come to pass, when ye be come to the land which the LORD will give you, according as he hath promised, that ye shall keep this service. 26 And it shall come to pass, when your children shall say unto you, What mean ye by this service? 27 That ye shall say, It *is* the sacrifice of the LORD'S passover, who passed over the houses of the children of Israel in Egypt, when he smote the Egyptians, and delivered our houses. And the people bowed the head and worshipped. 28 And the children of Israel went away, and did as the LORD had commanded Moses and Aaron, so did they.

Exodus 13:1 And the LORD spake unto Moses, saying, 2 Sanctify unto me all the firstborn, whatsoever openeth the womb among the children of Israel, *both* of man and of beast: it *is* mine. 3 And Moses said unto the people, Remember this day, in which ye came out from Egypt, out of the house of bondage; for by strength of hand the LORD brought you out from this *place*: there shall no leavened bread be eaten. 4 This day came ye out in the month Abib. 5 And it shall be when the LORD shall bring thee into the land of the Canaanites, and the Hittites, and the Amorites, and the Hivites, and the Jebusites, which he sware unto thy fathers to give thee, a land flowing with milk and honey, that thou shalt keep this service in this month. 6 Seven days thou shalt eat unleavened bread, and in the seventh day *shall be* a feast to the LORD. 7 **Unleavened bread shall be eaten seven days; and there shall no leavened bread be seen with thee, neither shall there be leaven seen with thee in all thy quarters.**

Exodus 23:15 Thou shalt keep the feast of unleavened bread: (thou shalt eat unleavened bread seven days, as I commanded thee, in the time appointed of the month Abib; for in it thou camest out from Egypt: and none shall appear before me empty:) ... 34:25 Thou shalt not offer the blood of my sacrifice with leaven; neither shall the sacrifice of the feast of the passover be left unto the morning.

3 "In every place where leaven is mentioned, it is a type of evil teachings, evil doctrines, and evil practices. It is always to be put away and cast out as an unclean thing. The gospel is never called leaven. Nothing good is

ever compared to leaven. Nothing good is ever said about leaven. In every place it is mentioned, leaven is defiling and is to be put away. (See also Ex 12:15; Le 2:11; 1Co 5:6.)

"Mt 13:33 The leaven in this case is a type of evil doctrines, taught by the apostate church. The woman is the apostate church, the meal is the Word of God, the leaven is wrong and evil teachings concerning the Word of God. Every false religion mixes false teachings in with the Scriptures and thereby poisons those who eat it. The leaven is never the gospel. There is no place in the Bible where leaven is spoken of in an approving way, nor is it ever related to anything good.

Unleavened

"1Co 5:7 Since the word is used to describe the bread in which there is no fermenting yeast, so now it is used to describe the church in which there are no ungodly sinners, none of the Devil's children, but only those who have been washed in the blood of the Lamb, made pure and beautiful in Christ. No evil doctrines would be permitted in such a church."

SwordSearcher, Wilson's Dictionary of Bible Types, Leaven.

A Proposed Service of Remembrance

15

REMEMBERING THE CRUCIFIXION OF OUR LORD AND SAVIOUR

In evil long I took delight,
Unawed by shame or fear,
Till a new object struck my sight,
And stopped my wild career.
I saw One hanging on a tree,
In agonies and blood;
He fixed His languid eyes on me,
As near His cross I stood.
Oh, never, till my latest breath,
Shall I forget that look!
It seemed to charge me with His death,
Though not a word He spoke
A second look He gave,
Which said, "I freely all forgive;
This blood is for thy ransom paid;
I die that thou mayst live."
Thus, while His death my sin displays
In all its blackest hue,
Such is the mystery of GRACE,
It seals my pardon too.

John Newton

IN REMEMBRANCE

Arranged For Responsive Reading[1]

To prepare our hearts, let us consider the sacrificial death of the Lamb of GOD.

PASTOR:

And he bearing his cross went forth into a place which is called Calvary, which is in the Hebrew, Golgotha, which is, being interpreted, The place of a skull. And when they were come to the place,

CONGREGATION:

there they crucified him,

PASTOR:

and the malefactors, two thieves, were crucified with him, one on the right hand, and another on the left and Jesus in the midst. And Pilate wrote a title, a superscription, and put it on the cross over his head. And the writing was,

CONGREGATION:

THIS IS JESUS OF NAZARETH THE KING OF THE JEWS.

PASTOR:

This title then read many of the Jews: for the place where Jesus was crucified was nigh to the city: and it was written in Hebrew, and Greek, and Latin.

Then said the chief priests of the Jews to Pilate, Write not, The King of the Jews; but that he said, I am King of the Jews.

CONGREGATION:

Pilate answered, What I have written I have written.

PASTOR:

Then the soldiers, when they had crucified Jesus, took his garments, and made four parts, to every soldier a part; and also his coat: now the coat was without seam, woven from the top throughout.

They said therefore among themselves, Let us not rend it, but cast lots for it, whose it shall be; that the scripture might be fulfilled, which saith, They parted my raiment among them, and for my vesture and upon my vesture they did cast lots.

CONGREGATION:

These things therefore the soldiers did.

PASTOR:

Then said Jesus, Father, forgive them; for they know not what they do.

CONGREGATION:

And sitting down they watched him there;

PASTOR:

Now there stood by the cross of Jesus his

mother, and his mother's sister, Mary the wife of Cleophas, and Mary Magdalene. When Jesus therefore saw his mother, and the disciple standing by, whom he loved, he saith unto his mother,

CONGREGATION:

Woman, behold thy son!

PASTOR:

Then saith he to the disciple,

CONGREGATION:

Behold thy mother!

PASTOR:

And from that hour that disciple took her unto his own home.

CONGREGATION:

And the people stood beholding.

PASTOR:

And the rulers also with them derided him, saying, He saved others; let him save himself, if he be Christ, the chosen of God. And they that passed by reviled him, wagging their heads, and saying, Thou that destroyest the temple, and buildest it in three days, save thyself.

CONGREGATION:

If thou be the Son of God, come down from the cross.

PASTOR:

Likewise also the chief priests mocking him, with the scribes and elders, said, He saved others; himself he cannot save. If he be the King of Israel, let him now come down from the cross, and we will believe him. He trusted in God; let him deliver him now, if he will have him:

CONGREGATION:

for he said, I am the Son of God.

PASTOR:

The thieves also, which were crucified with him, cast the same in his teeth. And the soldiers also mocked him, coming to him, and offering him vinegar, saying,

CONGREGATION:

If thou be the king of the Jews, save thyself.

PASTOR:

And one of the malefactors which were hanged railed on him, saying,

CONGREGATION:

If thou be Christ, save thyself and us.

PASTOR:

But the other answering rebuked him, saying, Dost not thou fear God, seeing thou art in the same condemnation? And we indeed justly; for we receive the due reward of our deeds: but this man hath done nothing amiss. And he said unto Jesus,

CONGREGATION:

Lord, remember me when thou comest into thy kingdom.

PASTOR:

And Jesus said unto him. Verily I say unto

thee. To day shalt thou be with me in paradise. And it was about the sixth hour,

CONGREGATION:

and there was a darkness over all the earth

PASTOR:

And about the ninth hour Jesus cried with a loud voice, saying, Eli, Eli. lama sabachthani? that is to say. My God, my God, why hast thou forsaken me? After this, Jesus knowing that all things were now accomplished, that the scripture might be fulfilled, saith,

CONGREGATION:

I thirst.

PASTOR:

Some of them that stood there, when they heard that, said,

CONGREGATION:

This man calleth for Elias.

PASTOR:

Now there was set a vessel full of vinegar And straightway one of them ran, and took a sponge, and filled it with vinegar, and put it upon hyssop, a reed, and put it to his mouth and gave him to drink. The rest said,

CONGREGATION:

Let be, let us see whether Elias will come to save him.

PASTOR:

When Jesus therefore had received the

vinegar, he said, with a loud voice

CONGREGATION:

It is finished:

PASTOR:

And the sun was darkened, until the ninth hour. And he bowed his head, and said,

CONGREGATION:

Father, into thy hands I commend my spirit:

PASTOR:

and having said thus, he gave up—yielded up—the ghost. And, behold, the veil of the temple was rent in twain from the top to the bottom in the midst; and the earth did quake, and the rocks rent, And the graves were opened; and many bodies of the saints which slept arose, And came out of the graves after his resurrection, and went into the holy city, and appeared unto many. Now when the centurion which stood over against him, saw that he so cried out, and gave up the ghost, he glorified God, saying,

CONGREGATION:

Certainly this was a righteous man. Truly this man was the Son of God.

PASTOR:

And when they that were with him, watching Jesus, saw the earthquake, and those things that were done, they feared greatly, saying,

CONGREGATION:

Truly this was the Son of God.

PASTOR:

With these words in our minds and in our hearts, let each consider that these things were done to the Son of GOD to obtain our redemption. Let us examine our lives and prepare our hearts for the time of Remembrance at the Communion of the LORD'S Supper Table of the LORD.

PASTOR:

The Apostle Paul was moved by the Holy Spirit to write "unto the church of God which is at Corinth" concerning the LORD'S Supper:

> For I have received of the Lord that which also I delivered unto you, That the Lord Jesus the same night in which He was betrayed took bread: And when He had given thanks, He brake it, and said, Take, eat: this is My body, which is broken for you: this do in remembrance of Me. After the same manner also He took the cup, when He had supped, saying, This cup is the New Testament in My blood: this do ye, as oft as ye drink it, in remembrance of Me. For as often as ye eat this bread, and drink this cup, ye do show the Lord's death till He come. Wherefore whosoever shall eat this bread, and drink this cup of the Lord, unworthily, shall be guilty of the body and blood of the Lord. But let a man examine himself, and so let him eat of that bread, and drink of that cup. For he that eateth and drinketh unworthily, eateth and drinketh damnation to himself, not discerning the Lord's body. For this cause many are weak and sickly among you, and many sleep. For if we would judge ourselves, we should not be judged. But when we are judged, we are chastened of the

Lord, that we should not be condemned with the world. Wherefore, my brethren, when ye come together to eat, tarry one for another. (1 Corinthians 11:23-33)

The word of the living GOD declares that it is necessary both to examine one's self and to tarry for others before any believer participates in the Communion Service.

It is written, "Let a man examine himself."

It is also written, "Wherefore, when ye come together to eat, tarry one for another."

Therefore, as we prepare ourselves so that we might properly approach the Table of the LORD to observe the Communion of the body and blood of the LORD Jesus Christ, it is essential that, as a church, we do faithfully pause so that the members of the church might honestly, privately, diligently, and throughly examine themselves individually.

This is not to be considered a light matter, but an issue most serious, perhaps requiring repentance, restitution, or reconciliation. Our relationship with GOD and with others is to be right.[2]

> For he that eateth and drinketh unworthily, eateth and drinketh damnation to himself, not discerning the Lord's body. For this cause many are weak and sickly among you, and many sleep. For if we would judge ourselves, we should not be judged. But when we are judged, we are chastened of the Lord, that we should not be condemned with the world.

However, it is also essential that we each respectfully pause, having either restored our own fellowship with our GOD or rekindled our own affection for our Saviour, to pray for our fellows members to do as we have done.

Therefore, for these purposes, this Congregation is called and assembled to an extended season of prayer.

Let us go before the Throne of grace to find mercy for our sins of omission and for our sins of commission. Let us be certain that we are prepared in heart and mind for this service of Remembrance of the broken body and the shed blood of our Saviour.

Having been before the Throne of grace to obtain mercy, we may approach the Table of the LORD in Remembrance of the sacrifice of the Son of GOD.

The Congregation shall now sing the hymn, *When I Survey The Wondrous Cross.*

> When I survey the wondrous cross
> On which the Prince of glory died,
> My riches gain, I count but loss,
> And pour contempt on all my pride.
> Forbid it Lord, that I should boast,
> Save in the death of Christ my God;
> All the vain things that charm me most,
> I sacrifice them to His blood.
> See, from His head, His hands, His feet,
> Sorrow and love flow mingled down—
> Did e'er such love and sorrow meet,
> Or thorns compose so rich a crown.
> Were the whole realm of nature mine,
> That were a present far too small;
> Love so amazing, so divine,
> Demands my soul, my life, my all.

PASTOR:

And when the hour was come, He sat down, and the twelve apostles with Him. And He said unto them, With desire I have desired to eat this passover with you before I suffer:

For I say unto you, I will not any more eat thereof, until it be fulfilled in the kingdom of GOD.[3]

Let us return to the Throne of grace in prayer as we remember that the LORD Jesus Christ was sent by the Father to be the Sacrifice for our sins.

PASTOR:

And as they were eating, He took bread, and gave thanks, and blessed it, and brake it, and gave it to the disciples, saying, Take, eat;

As the Deacons receive and distribute the unleavened bread, the Congregation will sing the hymn *Near the Cross*. The chorus shall be sung only after the last verse.

Jesus, keep me near the cross,
there a precious fountain
Free to all—a healing stream,
flows from Calvary's mountain.
Near the cross, a trembling soul,
Love and Mercy found me;
There the Bright and Morning Star
sheds its beams around me.
Near the cross! O Lamb of God,
bring its scenes before me;
Help me walk from day to day,
with its shadows o'er me.
Near the cross, I'll watch and wait,
hoping trusting, ever,
Till I reach the golden strand,
just beyond the river.

Chorus:

In the cross, in the cross,
Be my Glory ever;
Till my raptured soul shall find,
Rest beyond the river.

Let us return to the Throne of grace in prayer as we remember that the body of the

LORD Jesus Christ was broken for us.

PASTOR:

This is My body which is given for you, which is broken for you:

CONGREGATION:

This do in remembrance of Me.

The unleavened bread is now eaten.

PASTOR:

Likewise, after the same manner also He took the cup after supper and gave it to them, saying, Drink ye all of it;

As the Deacons receive and distribute the Fruit of the Vine, the Congregation will sing the hymn *There Is A Fountain*. The hymn shall be shortened by omitting the repetitive refrains.

There is a fountain filled with blood
drawn from Immanuel's veins,
And sinners plunged beneath that flood
lose all their guilty stains.
The dying thief rejoiced to see
that fountain in his day,
And there, may I, though vile as he,
wash all my sins away.
Dear dying Lamb, Thy precious blood
shall never lose its pow'r.
T'll all the ransomed church of God
be saved to sin no more;
E'er since by faith I saw the stream
Thy flowing wounds supply,
Redeeming love has been my theme
and shall be till I die;
When this poor lisping stamm'ring tongue
lies silent in the grave,
Then in a nobler, sweeter song,
I'll sing Thy pow'r to save.

Let us return to the Throne of grace in prayer as we remember that the blood of the LORD Jesus Christ was shed for us.

PASTOR:

For this cup is My blood of the New Testament, which is shed for many for the remission of sins.

CONGREGATION:

This do ye, as oft as ye drink it, in remembrance of Me.

PASTOR:

But I say unto you, I will not drink henceforth of this fruit of the vine, until that day when I drink it new with you in the kingdom of God, in My Father's kingdom.

CONGREGATION:

And they all drank of it.

The Fruit of the Vine is now drunk.

As the Deacons retrieve the empty cups, the Congregation will sing the hymn *Amazing Grace.*

> Amazing grace, how sweet the sound
> That saved a wretch like me!
> I once was lost, but now am found,
> Was blind, but now I see.
> 'Twas grace that taught my heart to fear,
> and grace my fears relieved;
> How precious did that grace appear
> the hour I first believed!
> Through many dangers, toils, and snares,
> I have already come;
> 'Tis grace has brought me safe thus far,
> and grace will lead me home.
> The Lord has promised good to me,
> His word my hope secures;

He will my shield and portion be
as long as life endures.
Yes, when this flesh and heart shall fail,
and mortal life shall cease;
I shall possess within the veil
a life of joy and peace.
The earth shall soon dissolve like snow,
the sun forbear to shine;
But God, Who called me here below,
will be forever mine.
When we've been there ten thousand years,
bright, shining as the sun,
We've no less days to sing God's praise
than when we first begun.

PASTOR:

Ye are they which have continued with Me in My temptations. And I appoint unto you a kingdom, as My Father hath appointed unto Me: that ye may eat and drink at My table in My kingdom.

Let us return again to the Throne of grace to seek that mercy that we shall nee for the days that lay ahead as we remember that the LORD Jesus shall return for us and as we realize that His return might be soon.

PASTOR:

And when they had sung an hymn, they went out into the mount of Olives.

The Service will be dismissed by the Congregation singing the hymn *Blessed Assurance*. The chorus will be sung only following the last verse.

Blessed assurance, Jesus is mine!
O what a foretaste of glory divine
Heir of salvation, purchase of God,
born of His Spirit, washed in His blood.
Perfect submission, perfect delight,

visions of rapture now burst on my sight;
Angels descending bring from above,
echoes of mercy, whispers of love.
Perfect submission, all is at rest,
I in my Saviour am happy and blest,
Watching and waiting, looking above,
filled with His goodness, lost in His love.

CHORUS:

This is my story, this is my song.
Praising my Saviour all the day long;
This is my story, this is my song,
Praising my Saviour all day long.

The Congregation is reminded to leave this service quietly and prayerfully, considering what the church has remembered in this service.

---

¹ The Gospel of Luke is the basis for the chronology.

² Matthew 5:23 Therefore if thou bring thy gift to the altar, and there rememberest that thy brother hath ought against thee; 24 Leave there thy gift before the altar, and go thy way; first be reconciled to thy brother, and then come and offer thy gift.

³ This responsive reading was prepared by combining the records of the four Gospels with the account of the Apostle Paul from First Corinthians, chapter eleven, and is presented as a synthesis, which uses the Gospel of Luke as the chronological authority.

Hallelujah! What a Saviour!

Man of Sorrows! what a name
For the Son of God, who came
Ruined sinners to reclaim.
Hallelujah! What a Savior!
Bearing shame and scoffing rude,
In my place condemned He stood;
Sealed my pardon with His blood.
Hallelujah! What a Savior!
Guilty, vile, and helpless we;
Spotless Lamb of God was He;
"Full atonement!" can it be?
Hallelujah! What a Savior!
Lifted up was He to die;
"It is finished!" was His cry;
Now in Heav'n exalted high.
Hallelujah! What a Savior!
When He comes, our glorious King,
All His ransomed home to bring,
Then anew His song we'll sing:
Hallelujah! What a Savior!

Phillip Bliss
In Public Domain

THE APPLICATION OF THE DOCTRINES

16

THE OBEDIENCE OF DUTY

Baptism and Communion are properly identified as church ordinances. As ordinances, they have the force of law.[1] They are the commands of the LORD Jesus as the Head of His church to His followers. Obedience to those commands is not to be the slavish response of fear, but the submission and conformity that rises from the affection of love.

Neither baptism nor Communion has either the magical qualities or the spiritual efficacy that is capable of removing sin from the person receiving the ordinances. The water of baptism is nothing more and nothing less than water. The water used in the act of baptism is not holy in the well, the river, or in the faucet before the baptism or during the baptism. The water never changes and never is altered in substance. The unleavened bread and the fruit of the vine never change and they are never altered in substance.

The water does not become holy water. The bread does not become the actual body of Christ. The grape juice does not become the literal blood of Christ. The concept that the substance of the elements is transformed into something other than what they are is more connected with magicians than with churches. Scripture does not contain any room for such foolish ideas to be superimposed on the ordinances.

Being baptized does not change a person spiritually. Participation in the Communion service does not spiritually alter a person. The person is not affected spiritually, materially, or physically by either baptism or Communion.

Baptism does unite the believer with the local church—the Biblical terminology is *added to the church*—and I would not minimize the importance of that aspect of baptism. Baptism is important because baptism is the public profession of faith by the believer. Communion is important because Communion is the time of remembrance that should revive and renew the love of the believer for the Saviour. In neither observance does the believer do anything more than faithfully obey the command of the LORD. Faithfulness in obedience is commendable, but it does not earn salvation or sin-cleansing. Even so, submission to baptism and participation in Communion are both expected of the believer.

Charles Spurgeon explained this expectation and necessity with his usual clarity.

> The confession of Christ, which is here intended, is still better to be carried out by a dutiful attention to those two ordinances

which are intended by Christ to be the distinctive *badge of believers*. Under the old Mosaic dispensation, ordinances were only for Israelites. Circumcision and the Passover were not for Philistines, nor for Egyptians, but for the seed of Abraham, and for the seed of Abraham and proselytes alone. It is even so under the Christian dispensation. We have no ordinances for aliens; we have no ordinances for strangers and foreigners; they are both intended for the commonwealth of Israel. You will remember how very carefully the ancient believers kept up these ordinances. You will find that the Ethiopian eunuch traveled all the way from the realm of Candace, in order that he might be present at the temple worship, because that was the distinctive worship of the Jew and of the proselyte to the Jewish faith. He would not be away. You remember how carefully and anxiously the heads of the Jewish householders saw to it, that they and all their children were present at the celebration of the Passover; they would not one of them neglect that which was distinctive of themselves as a separated people. Now, baptism is the mark of distinction between the Church and the world. It very beautifully sets forth the death of the baptized person to the world. Professedly, he is no longer of the world; he is buried to it, and he rises again to a new life. No symbol could be more significant. In the immersion of believers there seems to me to be a wondrous setting forth of the burial of the believer to all the world in the burial of Christ Jesus. It is the crossing of the Rubicon. If Caesar crossed the Rubicon, there would never be peace between him and the senate again.

He draws his sword, and he throws away his scabbard. Such is the act of baptism to the believer. It is the crossing of the Rubicon: it is as much as to say, "I cannot come back again to you; I am dead to you; and to prove I am, I am absolutely buried to you; I have nothing more to do with the world. I am Christ's, and Christ's for ever." [sic] Then, the Lord's Supper: how beautifully that ordinance sets forth the distinction of the believer from the world in his life and that by which his life is nourished. He eats the flesh of Christ, and drinks his blood. I marvel at some of you who love my Lord that you should keep away from his table. It is his dying will— "This do ye in remembrance of me." It is so kind of him to institute such an ordinance at all; to let us, who were as the dogs, sit at the children's table and eat bread such as angels never knew. I understand not, my dear brother, my dear sister, what sort of love yours can be if you hear Jesus say, "If ye love me, keep my commandments," and yet you neglect his ordinances. You will say, they are non-essential; and I will reply to you, most true, they are non-essential for your salvation, but they are not non-essential for your comfort; nor are they non-essential for your obedience. It is for a child to do what his parent bids him. If, my loving friend, my dear Redeemer had bidden me do something hurtful to myself, I would do it out of love to him; how much rather, then, when he said to me, "This do in remembrance of me." Both these ordinances bring a cross with them to some degree, especially the first. I was noting when reading yesterday the life of good Andrew Fuller, after he had been baptized, some of the young men in the village were wont to mock him, asking him how he liked being dipped? And such like questions which are common enough now-a-days. I could but notice that the scoff of a hundred years ago is just the scoff of to-day. But, brethren, you are not afraid, I trust, to be pointed at as a baptized believer? You believe that these are his commands. I charge you, therefore, before God and the elect angels, before whom you shall be judged at the last great day, if you with your hearts have believed, with your mouths make the confession which these ordinances imply, and God shall surely give you a sweet reward therein.[2]

The emphasis on the non-efficacy of baptism and Communion does not translate into a denial of the proper necessity of the believer to submit to baptism and to participate in Communion. Faithfulness is commendable, but it is not meritorious. Unfaithfulness will receive correction; and, should the correction fail to produce corrected conduct, chastisement will be applied.

Is there any ordinance of Christ which some of you have never attended to? Have you attended to baptism and the Lord's Supper? I charge you, before the living God, see to it as you value your own peace of mind. "He that knoweth his master's will, and doeth it not, shall be beaten with many stripes." I am not now speaking of the discipline of the law—the Christian is not under that—I am speaking, however, of the discipline of Christ's own house, over which Christ is the Master, and this is the law of Christ's house—if we will not be obedient we shall not abide in the comfortable enjoyment of his love, but we shall be chastened, and scourged, and smitten, until we become willing to yield ourselves up to the Lord's mind. Through thick and thin, through fair and foul, through poverty or wealth, through shame or honor, Christian, cling close to your Master, Be you among those virgin-souls, who—*"Withersoe'er the Lamb doth lead, From his footsteps ne'er depart."*[3]

I encourage my reader to receive the LORD Jesus as Saviour, to follow His command and be baptized, and to participate in the Communion service in the church where his membership is placed.

[1] *Merriam-Webster 11th Collegiate Dictionary* defines ordinance as "an authoritative decree or direction, a law set forth by a governmental authority."

[2] *SwordSearcher. Park Street and Metropolitan Tabernacle Pulpit, Confession with the Mouth.* Charles Haddon Spurgeon.

[3] *SwordSearcher. Park Street and Metropolitan Tabernacle Pulpit, Joshua's Obedience.* Charles Haddon Spurgeon

APPENDICES

Appendix A
USING THE CHURCH COVENANT

Membership in a Baptist church has traditionally been recognized as a covenant relationship. In this era of casual associations, many Baptist churches no longer even mention the Church Covenant. The result is that church membership does not have the significance for these generations that it had held for centuries. The casualness of the connection with their church is reflected in the attendance, the participation, and the lifestyles of contemporary American Baptists.

In past generations, Baptist congregations read the Church Covenant at the service for the organization of the church and at subsequent Communion services. The custom would wisely be resurrected. Church membership is a covenant entered by the members, one with another and with the Head of the church, the LORD Jesus Christ.

The following Church Covenant is based upon the most widely used Church Covenant of the last two centuries in America.

Having been led, as we believe by the Spirit of GOD, to receive the LORD Jesus Christ as our Saviour and on the profession of our faith, having been baptized in the name of the Father, and of the Son, and of the Holy Ghost, we do now in the presence of GOD, angels, and this assembly, most joyfully enter into covenant with one another, as one body in Christ.

We engage therefore, by the aid of the Holy Spirit to walk together in Christian love; to strive for the advancement of this church, in knowledge, holiness, and comfort; to promote her prosperity and spirituality; to sustain her worship, ordinances, discipline and doctrines; to give to her a sacred preeminence over all institutions of human origin; to contribute cheerfully and regularly to the support of the ministry, the expenses of this church, the relief of the poor, and the spread of the gospel through all nations.

We also engage to maintain family and secret devotion; to religiously educate our children; to seek the salvation of our kindred and acquaintance; to walk circumspectly in the world; to be just in our dealings, faithful in our engagements, and exemplary in our deportment; to avoid all tattling, backbiting, and excessive anger; to abstain from the sale and use of intoxicating drinks as a beverage and drugs for non-medical purposes; and to be zealous in our efforts to advance the kingdom of our Saviour.

We further engage to watch over one another in brotherly love; to remember each other in prayer; to aid each other in sickness and distress; to cultivate Christian sympathy in feeling and courtesy in speech; to be slow to take offense, but always ready for reconciliation, and mindful of the rule of our Saviour to secure it without delay.

We, moreover, engage that when we remove from this place we will as soon as possible unite with some other church of like faith and practice, where we can carry out the spirit of this covenant and the principles of the word of GOD.

Amen

Within that Covenant is expressed the duties and the responsibilities of the individual members and of the church as the corporate body. Every member of a Baptist church ought to have his responsibilities brought to his attention on a regular basis.

In former days, almost every Baptist church had a framed copy of the Church Covenant on a front wall of the church. The church that I pastor receives it printed on the back of the weekly information booklet given to the congregation.

It would be appropriate to have the church covenant read at every Remembrance service.

Appendix B
A SINGLE ISSUE COMMENTARY

Through the verbal plenary inspiration of the Holy Spirit, this Epistle was dictated and signed by the Apostle Paul. It was written down by his amanuensis Sosthenes, and was spiritually directed and physically addressed (by both the intent of its special content and the destination of its specific address) "unto the church of God which is at Corinth."

Several conclusions flow quite naturally from these facts; the Epistle is:

1. Divine in origin, inerrant in content, infallible in composition, unchangeable in revelation, and eternal in truth (2 Timothy 3:16; 2 Peter 3:15-18).[1]

2. Neither an allegory or a parable but a very real letter written by a very real person dealing with very real problems existing in a very real church (1:1-2).[2]

3. A document that teaches the identical doctrines, truths, practices and prin-

ciples that the Apostle taught in every church (7:17; 14:33)[3] and which were the customs in every one of the churches of GOD (11:16).[4]

The Epistle declares several important facts concerning the church at Corinth; these include the following:

1. This church at Corinth actually did exist; it was a particular church—the church of GOD which was at Corinth (1:2).[5]

2. This church was located in a certain city; it was the church at Corinth, a local church (1:2).[6]

3. This church was a specific church; it was the church at Corinth that Paul had started (2:6, 10; 3:15).[7]

4. This church was existing at a distinct time; it "lived and moved and had its being" concurrent with the lifetime of Paul (1:2).[8]

The church of GOD at Corinth was not some mystical, invisible, intangible, ethereal, universal church. This church was a visible and very real, particular, specific, definite, distinct, geographically locatable and tangible New Testament church; the identical body that today is considered *a local church*. With precise, clear, and unmistakable phrases, this Epistle describes the church that existed at Corinth in the days of the apostle Paul, and thereby helps to establish the authoritative definition for all New Testament churches— both those churches existing in the days of the New Testament and every genuine New Testament church existing any time since.

Any organization that does not meet the specific strict standards of the New Testament ought not to be recognized as a New Testament church. The organization may be a sincere religious entity holding high and noble values, but it is not a New Testament church. Genuine believers may be members of that organization, but it is not a New Testament church.

The definition of a New Testament church is determined by the New Testament and not by either sincerity or effectiveness. To the extent that any individual *church* comes short of the New Testament delineation that individual *church* is that much less than a New Testament church.

The church to which the Apostle addressed this letter is described in the Epistle at some length. It is revealed as being:

1. a body of believers (12:27, 11:29),[9] which

2. had been called into existence by the Apostle Paul (2:6,10; 3:15)[10] who had received the commission of the church at Antioch to do so (Acts 13:1-3; 15:40),[11] and that

3. had been named "the church of God which was at Corinth" (1:2);[12] and which,

4. was located in a definite city (1:2)[13] of Achaia (the southern part of modern Greece) (16:15),[14] the city of Corinth.

In this city of Corinth, the members of this church assembled in specific ways:

1. as a church (11:22),[15]

2. whole and complete (14:23; 12:13,27),[16]

203

3. gathering together in a church building or meeting place (11:18; 14:19,28,35)[17] which was compared to a house (11:22, see also 1 Timothy 3:15).[18]

This church building or meeting place was identified as:

1. the place where the members of the church regularly gathered together in one place (11:20, 22; 14:23)[19] on the first day of the week (16:2),[20] which was the established time of meeting when the members brought their tithes and offerings to this place and there laid those tithes and offerings in store (16:2);[21]

2. the place where heresies sometimes appeared (11:19; 15:12)[22] and where sin sometimes surfaced (5:1-2)[23] and the place where the members gathered to administer discipline to these unruly members (5:1-13);[24]

3. the place where the members assembled to observe the ordinances of baptism and the LORD'S Table (11:2, 23-34);[25]

4. the place where the members exercised their spiritual gifts (12:26),[26] listened to the preaching and teaching of the word of GOD (14:4,5),[27] shared testimonies (14:16-17),[28] sang hymns, gospel songs and the Psalms, (14:15, 26, see also Colossians 3:16);[29]

5. prayed for each other;[30] and

6. the place to which the members invited the lost to attend to hear the gospel (14:23-25[31]).

Therefore, since the Apostle wrote to this actual, certain, and distinct church, the words *you, your, yourselves, yours,* and *ye* in this Epistle must be understood to refer to the church of GOD which is at Corinth. While certain general applications might be made of this usage of the pronoun in specific instances to other believers, members of other churches, and even those living in other times, the underlying and undeniable fact remains and must be accepted that Paul intended in his employment of these words to refer to the members of this church in Corinth. Sometimes the words encompass collectively the membership of the church as a whole; while at other times, the words speak of the membership in its capacity as the body of members of that church. Paul also uses the words *thee, thou, thy,* and *thine* to refer to the individual members of the church of GOD that is at Corinth.

Grammatically, it is possible in contemporary usage in the English language for the words *you* and *your* to be used as both the singular pronoun or the plural pronoun depending upon the context, but every reader of the Bible needs to understand that this is not the usage of the Authorized Version.

In every instance, the terms *yourselves, yours,* and *ye* are, to be understood, without exception, as plural forms of the second person personal pronoun. The translators of the Authorized Version were consistent in using *thee, thou, thy,* and *thine* exclusively for the singular of the second person personal pronoun.

In the era when the translators were engaged in the work of translation, the common practice in the English language was not to use these different pronouns to make this distinction. In the Epistle Dedicatory, they did not use thee or thou in referencing King James. The pronouns were chosen for use to retain the visible distinction between the singular and plural second plural. It is to our advantage that they did so. We may discern whether the verse addresses one person or a group.

When the terms *we, us, our, ours,* and *ourselves* are used, Paul sometimes has in mind Sosthenes and himself; sometimes, he includes in these terms the church of GOD which is at Corinth, Sosthenes, and himself; other times he refers to the other apostles and himself collectively in the first person plural. The context of a particular use of these particular pronouns must be carefully examined to determine which of these three uses is intended.

In the use of the first person personal plural pronoun as with the second person personal pronoun, general applications to believers in all ages may be considered and may be quite fitting and proper; even so, this application of truth does not change the original and intended purpose in the choice of the words themselves.

The immediate view and the intended audience of the Apostle and of this Epistle is that of the specific church at Corinth. The principles are applicable to all New Testament churches of whatever geographical location and in whatever era of time.

Any particular passage of Scripture must

always be approached with an honest effort to accept, evaluate and understand

(1) the person that was used by the Holy Spirit to utter or to pen the words,

(2) the person or persons to whom the words were directed,

(3) the literal and historical definition of the individual words used,

(4) how those particular words would have been understood by the recipient of the passage, and

(5) how the passage *sits* in relation to its total Biblical context.

The full context should be understood as not only the close verses surrounding the text but also the chapter in which the passage is found, the book, the Testament, indeed the entire Bible as a whole combined with the historical setting of the passage. Uprooting a verse from that total context and transplanting it into another setting is not a legitimate form of Bible study nor can it be considered a justifiable or rational action. Such a maneuver is neither valid nor honest and it is, and must always be, completely unacceptable. Any *understanding* of the Epistle that does not consider these basic principles of hermeneutics will lead to false conclusions and could even provide fuel for dangerous heresies, exactly as such careless, ignorant or malicious study has so often accomplished precisely those results in the past.

To provide assistance in the effort to perceive how the Apostle, writing under the direct and directive inspiration of the Holy Spirit, considered and described this "church of God which was at Corinth," I have placed the phrase <the church of God which is at Corinth> following every use of the words *you, your, yourselves, yours,* and *ye.*

While reading the Epistle with this *addition* may seem to be tedious, the consistency of the repetition of the words in the context compels the heart and mind to accept the identification with a force that is possible in no other method. I encourage you to persevere and to *endure faithfully unto the end.*

The First Epistle of Paul the Apostle to the Church of God, which is at Corinth, commonly called
The First Epistle of Paul the Apostle to the Corinthians

CHAPTER 1

1 Paul, called to be an Apostle of Jesus Christ through the will of God, and Sosthenes our brother, 2 Unto the church of God which is at Corinth, to them that are sanctified in Christ Jesus, called to be saints, with all that in every place call upon the name of Jesus Christ our Lord, both theirs and ours: 3 Grace be unto you <the church of God which is at Corinth>, and peace, from God our Father, and from the Lord Jesus Christ. 4 I thank my God always on your <the church of God which is at Corinth> behalf, for the grace of God which is given you <the church of God which is at Corinth> by Jesus Christ; 5 That in every thing ye <the church of God which is at Corinth> are enriched by him, in all utterance, and in all knowledge; 6 Even as the testimony of Christ was con-

firmed in you <the church of God which is at Corinth>: 7 So that ye <the church of God which is at Corinth> come behind in no gift; waiting for the coming of our Lord Jesus Christ: 8 Who shall also confirm you <the church of God which is at Corinth> unto the end, that ye <the church of God which is at Corinth> may be blameless in the day of our Lord Jesus Christ. 9 God is faithful, by whom ye <the church of God which is at Corinth> were called unto the fellowship of his Son Jesus Christ our Lord. 10 Now I beseech you <the church of God which is at Corinth>, brethren, by the name of our Lord Jesus Christ, that ye <the church of God which is at Corinth> all speak the same thing, and that there be no divisions among you <the church of God which is at Corinth>; but that ye <the church of God which is at Corinth> be perfectly joined together in the same mind and in the same judgment. 11 For it hath been declared unto me of you <the church of God which is at Corinth>, my brethren, by them which are of the house of Chloe, that there are contentions among you <the church of God which is at Corinth>. 12 Now this I say, that every one of you <the church of God which is at Corinth> saith, I am of Paul; and I of Apollos; and I of Cephas; and I of Christ. 13 Is Christ divided? was Paul crucified for you <the church of God which is at Corinth>? or were ye <the church of God which is at Corinth> baptized in the name of Paul? 14 I thank God that I baptized none of you <the church of God which is at Corinth>, but Crispus and Gaius; 15 Lest any should say that I had baptized in mine own name. 16 And I baptized also the household of Stephanas: besides, I know not whether I baptized any other. 17 For Christ sent me not to baptize, but to preach the gospel: not with wisdom of words, lest the cross of Christ should be made of none effect. 18 For the preaching of the cross is to them that perish foolishness; but unto us which are saved it is the power of God. 19 For it is written, I will destroy the wisdom of the wise, and will bring to nothing the understanding of the prudent. 20 Where is the wise? where is the scribe? where is the disputer of this world? hath not God made foolish the wisdom of this world? 21 For after that in the wisdom of God the world by wisdom knew not God, it pleased God by the foolishness of preaching to save them that believe. 22 For the Jews require a sign, and the Greeks seek after wisdom: 23 But we preach Christ crucified, unto the Jews a stumblingblock, and unto the Greeks foolishness; 24 But unto them which are called, both Jews and Greeks, Christ the power of God, and the wisdom of God. 25 Because the foolishness of God is wiser than men; and the weakness of God is stronger than men. 26 For ye <the church of God which is at Corinth> see your <the church of God which is at Corinth> calling, brethren, how that not many wise men after the flesh, not many mighty, not many noble, are called: 27 But God hath chosen the foolish things of the world to confound the wise; and God hath chosen the weak things of the world to confound the things which are mighty; 28 And base things of the world, and things which are despised, hath God chosen, yea, and things which are not, to bring to nought things that are: 29 That no flesh should glory in his presence. 30 But of him are ye <the church of God which is at Corinth> in Christ Jesus, who of God is made unto us wisdom, and righteousness, and sanctification, and redemption: 31 That, according as it is written, He that glorieth, let him glory in the Lord.

CHAPTER 2

1 And I, brethren, when I came to you <the church of God which is at Corinth>, came not with excellency of speech or of wisdom, declaring unto you <the church of God which is at Corinth> the testimony of God. 2 For I determined not to know any thing among you <the church of God which is at Corinth>, save Jesus Christ, and him crucified. 3 And I was with you <the church of God which is at Corinth> in weakness, and in fear, and in much trembling. 4 And my speech and my preaching was not with enticing words of man's wisdom, but in demonstration of the Spirit and of power: 5 That your <the church of God which is at Corinth> faith should not stand in the wisdom of men, but in the power of God. 6 Howbeit we speak wisdom among them that are perfect: yet not the wisdom of this world, nor of the princes of this world, that come to nought: 7 But we speak the wisdom of God in a mystery, even the hidden wisdom, which God ordained before the world unto our glory: 8 Which none of the princes of this world knew: for had they known

it, they would not have crucified the Lord of glory. 9 But as it is written, Eye hath not seen, nor ear heard, neither have entered into the heart of man, the things which God hath prepared for them that love him. 10 But God hath revealed them unto us by his Spirit: for the Spirit searcheth all things, yea, the deep things of God. 11 For what man knoweth the things of a man, save the spirit of man which is in him? even so the things of God knoweth no man, but the Spirit of God. 12 Now we have received, not the spirit of the world, but the spirit which is of God; that we might know the things that are freely given to us of God. 13 Which things also we speak, not in the words which man's wisdom teacheth, but which the Holy Ghost teacheth; comparing spiritual things with spiritual. 14 But the natural man receiveth not the things of the Spirit of God: for they are foolishness unto him: neither can he know them, because they are spiritually discerned. 15 But he that is spiritual judgeth all things, yet he himself is judged of no man. 16 For who hath known the mind of the Lord, that he may instruct him? But we have the mind of Christ.

CHAPTER 3

1 And I, brethren, could not speak unto you <the church of God which is at Corinth> as unto spiritual, but as unto carnal, even as unto babes in Christ. 2 I have fed you <the church of God which is at Corinth> with milk, and not with meat: for hitherto ye <the church of God which is at Corinth> were not able to bear it,

neither yet now are ye <the church of God which is at Corinth> able. 3 For ye <the church of God which is at Corinth> are yet carnal: for whereas there is among you <the church of God which is at Corinth> envying, and strife, and divisions, are ye <the church of God which is at Corinth> not carnal, and walk as men? 4 For while one saith, I am of Paul; and another, I am of Apollos; are ye <the church of God which is at Corinth> not carnal? 5 Who then is Paul, and who is Apollos, but ministers by whom ye <the church of God which is at Corinth> believed, even as the Lord gave to every man? 6 I have planted, Apollos watered; but God gave the increase. 7 So then neither is he that planteth any thing, neither he that watereth; but God that giveth the increase. 8 Now he that planteth and he that watereth are one: and every man shall receive his own reward according to his own labour. 9 For we are labourers together with God: ye <the church of God which is at Corinth> are God's husbandry, ye <the church of God which is at Corinth> are God's building. 10 According to the grace of God which is given unto me, as a wise masterbuilder, I have laid the foundation, and another buildeth thereon. But let every man take heed how he buildeth thereupon. 11 For other foundation can no man lay than that is laid, which is Jesus Christ. 12 Now if any man build upon this foundation gold, silver, precious stones, wood, hay, stubble; 13 Every man's work shall be made manifest: for the day shall declare it, because it shall be revealed by fire; and the fire shall

213

try every man's work of what sort it is. 14 If any man's work abide which he hath built thereupon, he shall receive a reward. 15 If any man's work shall be burned, he shall suffer loss: but he himself shall be saved; yet so as by fire. 16 Know ye <the church of God which is at Corinth> not that ye <the church of God which is at Corinth> are the temple of God, and that the Spirit of God dwelleth in you <the church of God which is at Corinth>? 17 If any man defile the temple of God, him shall God destroy; for the temple of God is holy, which temple ye <the church of God which is at Corinth> are. 18 Let no man deceive himself. If any man among you <the church of God which is at Corinth> seemeth to be wise in this world, let him become a fool, that he may be wise. 19 For the wisdom of this world is foolishness with God. For it is written, He taketh the wise in their own craftiness. 20 And again, The Lord knoweth the thoughts of the wise, that they are vain. 21 Therefore let no man glory in men. For all things are yours <the church of God which is at Corinth>; 22 Whether Paul, or Apollos, or Cephas, or the world, or life, or death, or things present, or things to come; all are yours <the church of God which is at Corinth>; 23 And ye <the church of God which is at Corinth> are Christ's; and Christ is God's.

CHAPTER 4

1 Let a man so account of us, as of the ministers of Christ, and stewards of the mysteries of God. 2 Moreover it is required in stewards, that a man be found faithful.

3 But with me it is a very small thing that I should be judged of you <the church of God which is at Corinth>, or of man's judgment: yea, I judge not mine own self. 4 For I know nothing by myself; yet am I not hereby justified: but he that judgeth me is the Lord. 5 Therefore judge nothing before the time, until the Lord come, who both will bring to light the hidden things of darkness, and will make manifest the counsels of the hearts: and then shall every man have praise of God. 6 And these things, brethren, I have in a figure transferred to myself and to Apollos for your <the church of God which is at Corinth> sakes; that ye <the church of God which is at Corinth> might learn in us not to think of men above that which is written, that no one of you <the church of God which is at Corinth> be puffed up for one against another. 7 For who maketh thee to differ from another? and what hast thou that thou didst not receive? now if thou didst receive it, why dost thou glory, as if thou hadst not received it? 8 Now ye <the church of God which is at Corinth> are full, now ye <the church of God which is at Corinth> are rich, ye <the church of God which is at Corinth> have reigned as kings without us: and I would to God ye <the church of God which is at Corinth> did reign, that we also might reign with you <the church of God which is at Corinth>. 9 For I think that God hath set forth us the apostles last, as it were appointed to death: for we are made a spectacle unto the world, and to angels, and to men. 10 We are fools for Christ's sake, but ye <the church of God which is at Cor-

inth> are wise in Christ; we are weak, but ye <the church of God which is at Corinth> are strong; ye <the church of God which is at Corinth> are honourable, but we are despised. 11 Even unto this present hour we both hunger, and thirst, and are naked, and are buffeted, and have no certain dwellingplace; 12 And labour, working with our own hands: being reviled, we bless; being persecuted, we suffer it: 13 Being defamed, we entreat: we are made as the filth of the world, and are the offscouring of all things unto this day. 14 I write not these things to shame you <the church of God which is at Corinth>, but as my beloved sons I warn you <the church of God which is at Corinth>. 15 For though ye <the church of God which is at Corinth> have ten thousand instructors in Christ, yet have ye <the church of God which is at Corinth> not many fathers: for in Christ Jesus I have begotten you <the church of God which is at Corinth> through the gospel. 16 Wherefore I beseech you <the church of God which is at Corinth>, be ye <the church of God which is at Corinth> followers of me. 17 For this cause have I sent unto you <the church of God which is at Corinth> Timotheus, who is my beloved son, and faithful in the Lord, who shall bring you <the church of God which is at Corinth> into remembrance of my ways which be in Christ, as I teach every where in every church. 18 Now some are puffed up, as though I would not come to you <the church of God which is at Corinth>. 19 But I will come to you <the church of God which is at Corinth> shortly, if the Lord will, and will know, not the speech of them which are puffed up, but the power. 20 For the kingdom of God is not in word, but in power. 21 What will Ye <the church of God which is at Corinth>? shall I come unto you <the church of God which is at Corinth> with a rod, or in love, and in the spirit of meekness?

CHAPTER 5

1 It is reported commonly that there is fornication among you <the church of God which is at Corinth>, and such fornication as is not so much as named among the Gentiles, that one should have his father's wife. 2 And ye <the church of God which is at Corinth> are puffed up, and have not rather mourned, that he that hath done this deed might be taken away from among you <the church of God which is at Corinth>. 3 For I verily, as absent in body, but present in spirit, have judged already, as though I were present, concerning him that hath so done this deed, 4 In the name of our Lord Jesus Christ, when ye <the church of God which is at Corinth> are gathered together, and my spirit, with the power of our Lord Jesus Christ, 5 To deliver such an one unto Satan for the destruction of the flesh, that the spirit may be saved in the day of the Lord Jesus. 6 Your glorying is not good. Know ye <the church of God which is at Corinth> not that a little leaven leaveneth the whole lump? 7 Purge out therefore the old leaven, that ye <the church of God which is at Corinth> may be a new lump, as ye <the church of God which is at Corinth> are unleavened. For

even Christ our passover is sacrificed for us: 8 Therefore let us keep the feast, not with old leaven, neither with the leaven of malice and wickedness; but with the unleavened bread of sincerity and truth. 9 I wrote unto you <the church of God which is at Corinth> in an epistle not to company with fornicators: 10 Yet not altogether with the fornicators of this world, or with the covetous, or extortioners, or with idolaters; for then must ye <the church of God which is at Corinth> needs go out of the world. 11 But now I have written unto you <the church of God which is at Corinth> not to keep company, if any man that is called a brother be a fornicator, or covetous, or an idolater, or a railer, or a drunkard, or an extortioner; with such an one no not to eat. 12 For what have I to do to judge them also that are without? do not ye <the church of God which is at Corinth> judge them that are within? 13 But them that are without God judgeth. Therefore put away from among yourselves <the church of God which is at Corinth> that wicked person.

CHAPTER 6

1 Dare any of you <the church of God which is at Corinth>, having a matter against another, go to law before the unjust, and not before the saints? 2 Do ye <the church of God which is at Corinth> not know that the saints shall judge the world? and if the world shall be judged by you <the church of God which is at Corinth>, are ye <the church of God which is at Corinth> unworthy to judge the smallest matters? 3 Know ye <the church of

218

God which is at Corinth> not that we
shall judge angels? how much more things
that pertain to this life? 4 If then ye <the
church of God which is at Corinth> have
judgments of things pertaining to this life,
set them to judge who are least esteemed
in the church. 5 I speak to your <the
church of God which is at Corinth>
shame. Is it so, that there is not a wise
man among you <the church of God
which is at Corinth>? no, not one that
shall be able to judge between his brethren? 6 But brother goeth to law with
brother, and that before the unbelievers. 7
Now therefore there is utterly a fault
among you <the church of God which is
at Corinth>, because ye <the church of
God which is at Corinth> go to law one
with another. Why do ye <the church of
God which is at Corinth> not rather take
wrong? why do ye <the church of God
which is at Corinth> not rather suffer
yourselves <the church of God which is
at Corinth> to be defrauded? 8 Nay, ye
<the church of God which is at Corinth>
do wrong, and defraud, and that your
<the church of God which is at Corinth>
brethren. 9 Know ye <the church of God
which is at Corinth> not that the unright-
eous shall not inherit the kingdom of God?
Be not deceived: neither fornicators, nor
idolaters, nor adulterers, nor effeminate,
nor abusers of themselves with mankind,
10 Nor thieves, nor covetous, nor drunk-
ards, nor revilers, nor extortioners, shall
inherit the kingdom of God. 11 And such
were some of you <the church of God
which is at Corinth>: but ye <the church
of God which is at Corinth> are washed,

but ye <the church of God which is at Corinth> are sanctified, but ye <the church of God which is at Corinth> are justified in the name of the Lord Jesus, and by the Spirit of our God. 12 All things are lawful unto me, but all things are not expedient: all things are lawful for me, but I will not be brought under the power of any. 13 Meats for the belly, and the belly for meats: but God shall destroy both it and them. Now the body is not for fornication, but for the Lord; and the Lord for the body. 14 And God hath both raised up the Lord, and will also raise up us by his own power. 15 Know ye <the church of God which is at Corinth> not that your <the church of God which is at Corinth> bodies are the members of Christ? shall I then take the members of Christ, and make them the members of an harlot? God forbid. 16 What? know ye <the church of God which is at Corinth> not that he which is joined to an harlot is one body? for two, saith he, shall be one flesh. 17 But he that is joined unto the Lord is one spirit. 18 Flee fornication. Every sin that a man doeth is without the body; but he that committeth fornication sinneth against his own body. 19 What? know ye <the church of God which is at Corinth> not that your <the church of God which is at Corinth> body is the temple of the Holy Ghost which is in you <the church of God which is at Corinth>, which ye <the church of God which is at Corinth> have of God, and ye <the church of God which is at Corinth> are not your <the church of God which is at Corinth> own? 20 For ye <the church of God which is at

Corinth> are bought with a price: therefore glorify God in your <the church of God which is at Corinth> body, and in your <the church of God which is at Corinth> spirit, which are God's.

CHAPTER 7

1 Now concerning the things whereof ye <the church of God which is at Corinth> wrote unto me: It is good for a man not to touch a woman. 2 Nevertheless, to avoid fornication, let every man have his own wife, and let every woman have her own husband. 3 Let the husband render unto the wife due benevolence: and likewise also the wife unto the husband. 4 The wife hath not power of her own body, but the husband: and likewise also the husband hath not power of his own body, but the wife. 5 Defraud ye <the church of God which is at Corinth> not one the other, except it be with consent for a time, that ye <the church of God which is at Corinth> may give yourselves <the church of God which is at Corinth> to fasting and prayer; and come together again, that Satan tempt you <the church of God which is at Corinth> not for your <the church of God which is at Corinth> incontinency. 6 But I speak this by permission, and not of commandment. 7 For I would that all men were even as I myself. But every man hath his proper gift of God, one after this manner, and another after that. 8 I say therefore to the unmarried and widows, It is good for them if they abide even as I. 9 But if they cannot contain, let them marry: for it is better to marry than to burn. 10 And unto the married I command, yet

not I, but the Lord, Let not the wife depart from her husband: 11 But and if she depart, let her remain unmarried, or be reconciled to her husband: and let not the husband put away his wife. 12 But to the rest speak I, not the Lord: If any brother hath a wife that believeth not, and she be pleased to dwell with him, let him not put her away. 13 And the woman which hath an husband that believeth not, and if he be pleased to dwell with her, let her not leave him. 14 For the unbelieving husband is sanctified by the wife, and the unbelieving wife is sanctified by the husband: else were your <the church of God which is at Corinth> children unclean; but now are they holy. 15 But if the unbelieving depart, let him depart. A brother or a sister is not under bondage in such cases: but God hath called us to peace. 16 For what knowest thou, O wife, whether thou shalt save thy husband? or how knowest thou, O man, whether thou shalt save thy wife? 17 But as God hath distributed to every man, as the Lord hath called every one, so let him walk. And so ordain I in all churches. 18 Is any man called being circumcised? let him not become uncircumcised. Is any called in uncircumcision? let him not be circumcised. 19 Circumcision is nothing, and uncircumcision is nothing, but the keeping of the commandments of God. 20 Let every man abide in the same calling wherein he was called. 21 Art thou called being a servant? care not for it: but if thou mayest be made free, use it rather. 22 For he that is called in the Lord, being a servant, is the Lord's freeman: likewise also he

that is called, being free, is Christ's servant. 23 Ye <the church of God which is at
Corinth> are bought with a price; be not
ye <the church of God which is at Cor-
inth> the servants of men. 24 Brethren,
let every man, wherein he is called, therein abide with God. 25 Now concerning vir-
gins I have no commandment of the Lord:
yet I give my judgment, as one that hath
obtained mercy of the Lord to be faithful.
26 I suppose therefore that this is good for
the present distress, I say, that it is good
for a man so to be. 27 Art thou bound unto a wife? seek not to be loosed. Art thou
loosed from a wife? seek not a wife. 28 But
and if thou marry, thou hast not sinned;
and if a virgin marry, she hath not sinned.
Nevertheless such shall have trouble in
the flesh: but I spare you <the church of
God which is at Corinth>. 29 But this I
say, brethren, the time is short: it
remaineth, that both they that have wives
be as though they had none; 30 And they
that weep, as though they wept not; and
they that rejoice, as though they rejoiced
not; and they that buy, as though they
possessed not; 31 And they that use this
world, as not abusing it: for the fashion of
this world passeth away. 32 But I would
have you <the church of God which is at
Corinth> without carefulness. He that is
unmarried careth for the things that be-
long to the Lord, how he may please the
Lord: 33 But he that is married careth for
the things that are of the world, how he
may please his wife. 34 There is difference
also between a wife and a virgin. The unmarried woman careth for the things of
the Lord, that she may be holy both in

body and in spirit: but she that is married careth for the things of the world, how she may please her husband. 35 And this I speak for your <the church of God which is at Corinth> own profit; not that I may cast a snare upon you <the church of God which is at Corinth>, but for that which is comely, and that ye <the church of God which is at Corinth> may attend upon the Lord without distraction. 36 But if any man think that he behaveth himself uncomely toward his virgin, if she pass the flower of her age, and need so require, let him do what he will, he sinneth not: let them marry. 37 Nevertheless he that standeth stedfast in his heart, having no necessity, but hath power over his own will, and hath so decreed in his heart that he will keep his virgin, doeth well. 38 So then he that giveth her in marriage doeth well; but he that giveth her not in marriage doeth better. 39 The wife is bound by the law as long as her husband liveth; but if her husband be dead, she is at liberty to be married to whom she will; only in the Lord. 40 But she is happier if she so abide, after my judgment: and I think also that I have the Spirit of God.

CHAPTER 8

1 Now as touching things offered unto idols, we know that we all have knowledge. Knowledge puffeth up, but charity edifieth. 2 And if any man think that he knoweth any thing, he knoweth nothing yet as he ought to know. 3 But if any man love God, the same is known of him. 4 As concerning therefore the eating of those things that are offered in sacrifice

unto idols, we know that an idol is nothing in the world, and that there is none other God but one. 5 For though there be that are called gods, whether in heaven or in earth, (as there be gods many, and lords many,) 6 But to us there is but one God, the Father, of whom are all things, and we in him; and one Lord Jesus Christ, by whom are all things, and we by him. 7 Howbeit there is not in every man that knowledge: for some with conscience of the idol unto this hour eat it as a thing offered unto an idol; and their conscience being weak is defiled. 8 But meat commendeth us not to God: for neither, if we eat, are we the better; neither, if we eat not, are we the worse. 9 But take heed lest by any means this liberty of yours <the church of God which is at Corinth> become a stumblingblock to them that are weak. 10 For if any man see thee which hast knowledge sit at meat in the idol's temple, shall not the conscience of him which is weak be emboldened to eat those things which are offered to idols; 11 And through thy knowledge shall the weak brother perish, for whom Christ died? 12 But when ye <the church of God which is at Corinth> sin so against the brethren, and wound their weak conscience, ye <the church of God which is at Corinth> sin against Christ. 13 Wherefore, if meat make my brother to offend, I will eat no flesh while the world standeth, lest I make my brother to offend.

CHAPTER 9

1 Am I not an Apostle? am I not free? have I not seen Jesus Christ our Lord? are not

ye <the church of God which is at Cor-inth> my work in the Lord? 2 If I be not an Apostle unto others, yet doubtless I am to you <the church of God which is at Corinth>: for the seal of mine apostleship are ye <the church of God which is at Corinth> in the Lord. 3 Mine answer to them that do examine me is this, 4 Have we not power to eat and to drink? 5 Have we not power to lead about a sister, a wife, as well as other apostles, and as the brethren of the Lord, and Cephas? 6 Or I only and Barnabas, have not we power to forbear working? 7 Who goeth a warfare any time at his own charges? who planteth a vineyard, and eateth not of the fruit thereof? or who feedeth a flock, and eateth not of the milk of the flock? 8 Say I these things as a man? or saith not the law the same also? 9 For it is written in the law of Moses, Thou shalt not muzzle the mouth of the ox that treadeth out the corn. Doth God take care for oxen? 10 Or saith he it altogether for our sakes? For our sakes, no doubt, this is written: that he that ploweth should plow in hope; and that he that thresheth in hope should be partaker of his hope. 11 If we have sown unto you <the church of God which is at Corinth> spiritual things, is it a great thing if we shall reap your <the church of God which is at Corinth> carnal things? 12 If others be partakers of this power over you <the church of God which is at Corinth>, are not we rather? Nevertheless we have not used this power; but suffer all things, lest we should hinder the gospel of Christ. 13 Do ye <the church of God which is at Corinth> not know that they

226

which minister about holy things live of the things of the temple? and they which wait at the altar are partakers with the altar? 14 Even so hath the Lord ordained that they which preach the gospel should live of the gospel. 15 But I have used none of these things: neither have I written these things, that it should be so done unto me: for it were better for me to die, than that any man should make my glorying void. 16 For though I preach the gospel, I have nothing to glory of: for necessity is laid upon me; yea, woe is unto me, if I preach not the gospel! 17 For if I do this thing willingly, I have a reward: but if against my will, a dispensation of the gospel is committed unto me. 18 What is my reward then? Verily that, when I preach the gospel, I may make the gospel of Christ without charge, that I abuse not my power in the gospel. 19 For though I be free from all men, yet have I made myself servant unto all, that I might gain the more. 20 And unto the Jews I became as a Jew, that I might gain the Jews; to them that are under the law, as under the law, that I might gain them that are under the law; 21 To them that are without law, as without law, (being not without law to God, but under the law to Christ,) that I might gain them that are without law. 22 To the weak became I as weak, that I might gain the weak: I am made all things to all men, that I might by all means save some. 23 And this I do for the gospel's sake, that I might be partaker thereof with you <the church of God which is at Corinth>. 24 Know ye <the church of God which is at Corinth> not that they which run in a race run all, but one receiveth the prize? So run, that ye <the church of God which is at Corinth> may obtain. 25 And every man that striveth for the mastery is temperate in all things. Now they do it to obtain a corruptible crown; but we an incorruptible. 26 I therefore so run, not as uncertainly; so fight I, not as one that beateth the air: 27 But I keep under my body, and bring it into subjection: lest that by any means, when I have preached to others, I myself should be a castaway.

CHAPTER 10

1 Moreover, brethren, I would not that ye <the church of God which is at Corinth> should be ignorant, how that all our fathers were under the cloud, and all passed through the sea; 2 And were all baptized unto Moses in the cloud and in the sea; 3 And did all eat the same spiritual meat; 4 And did all drink the same spiritual drink: for they drank of that spiritual Rock that followed them: and that Rock was Christ. 5 But with many of them God was not well pleased: for they were overthrown in the wilderness. 6 Now these things were our examples, to the intent we should not lust after evil things, as they also lusted. 7 Neither be ye <the church of God which is at Corinth> idolaters, as were some of them; as it is written, The people sat down to eat and drink, and rose up to play. 8 Neither let us commit fornication, as some of them committed, and fell in one day three and twenty thousand. 9 Neither let us tempt Christ, as some of them also tempted, and were destroyed of serpents. 10 Neither murmur ye <the church of God which is

at Corinth>, as some of them also murmured, and were destroyed of the destroyer. 11 Now all these things happened unto them for ensamples: and they are written for our admonition, upon whom the ends of the world are come. 12 Wherefore let him that thinketh he standeth take heed lest he fall. 13 There hath no temptation taken you <the church of God which is at Corinth> but such as is common to man: but God is faithful, who will not suffer you <the church of God which is at Corinth> to be tempted above that ye <the church of God which is at Corinth> are able; but will with the temptation also make a way to escape, that ye <the church of God which is at Corinth> may be able to bear it. 14 Wherefore, my dearly beloved, flee from idolatry. 15 I speak as to wise men; judge ye <the church of God which is at Corinth> what I say. 16 The cup of blessing which we bless, is it not the communion of the blood of Christ? The bread which we break, is it not the communion of the body of Christ? 17 For we being many are one bread, and one body: for we are all partakers of that one bread. 18 Behold Israel after the flesh: are not they which eat of the sacrifices partakers of the altar? 19 What say I then? that the idol is any thing, or that which is offered in sacrifice to idols is any thing? 20 But I say, that the things which the Gentiles sacrifice, they sacrifice to devils, and not to God: and I would not that ye <the church of God which is at Corinth> should have fellowship with devils. 21 Ye <the church of God which is at Corinth> cannot drink the cup of the Lord, and the cup of devils:

ye <the church of God which is at Cor-inth> cannot be partakers of the Lord's table, and of the table of devils. 22 Do we provoke the Lord to jealousy? are we stronger than he? 23 All things are lawful for me, but all things are not expedient: all things are lawful for me, but all things edify not. 24 Let no man seek his own, but every man another's wealth. 25 Whatsoev-er is sold in the shambles, that eat, asking no question for conscience sake: 26 For the earth is the Lord's, and the fulness thereof. 27 If any of them that believe not bid you <the church of God which is at Corinth> to a feast, and ye <the church of God which is at Corinth> be disposed to go; whatsoever is set before you <the church of God which is at Corinth>, eat, asking no question for conscience sake. 28 But if any man say unto you <the church of God which is at Corinth>, This is offered in sacrifice unto idols, eat not for his sake that showed it, and for con-science sake: for the earth is the Lord's, and the fulness thereof: 29 Conscience, I say, not thine own, but of the other: for why is my liberty judged of another man's conscience? 30 For if I by grace be a par-taker, why am I evil spoken of for that for which I give thanks? 31 Whether therefore ye <the church of God which is at Cor-inth> eat, or drink, or whatsoever ye <the church of God which is at Corinth> do, do all to the glory of God. 32 Give none of-fence, neither to the Jews, nor to the Gen-tiles, nor to the church of God: 33 Even as I please all men in all things, not seeking mine own profit, but the profit of many, that they may be saved.

CHAPTER 11

1 Be ye <the church of God which is at Corinth> followers of me, even as I also am of Christ. 2 Now I praise you <the church of God which is at Corinth>, brethren, that ye <the church of God which is at Corinth> remember me in all things, and keep the ordinances, as I delivered them to you <the church of God which is at Corinth>. 3 But I would have you <the church of God which is at Corinth> know, that the head of every man is Christ; and the head of the woman is the man; and the head of Christ is God. 4 Every man praying or prophesying, having his head covered, dishonoureth his head. 5 But every woman that prayeth or prophesieth with her head uncovered dishonoureth her head: for that is even all one as if she were shaven. 6 For if the woman be not covered, let her also be shorn: but if it be a shame for a woman to be shorn or shaven, let her be covered. 7 For a man indeed ought not to cover his head, forasmuch as he is the image and glory of God: but the woman is the glory of the man. 8 For the man is not of the woman; but the woman of the man. 9 Neither was the man created for the woman; but the woman for the man. 10 For this cause ought the woman to have power on her head because of the angels. 11 Nevertheless neither is the man without the woman, neither the woman without the man, in the Lord. 12 For as the woman is of the man, even so is the man also by the woman; but all things of God. 13 Judge in yourselves: is it comely that a woman pray

unto God uncovered? 14 Doth not even nature itself teach you <the church of God which is at Corinth>, that, if a man have long hair, it is a shame unto him? 15 But if a woman have long hair, it is a glory to her: for her hair is given her for a covering. 16 But if any man seem to be contentious, we have no such custom, neither the churches of God. 17 Now in this that I declare unto you <the church of God which is at Corinth> I praise you <the church of God which is at Corinth> not, that ye <the church of God which is at Corinth> come together not for the better, but for the worse. 18 For first of all, when ye <the church of God which is at Corinth> come together in the church, I hear that there be divisions among you <the church of God which is at Corinth>; and I partly believe it. 19 For there must be also heresies among you <the church of God which is at Corinth>, that they which are approved may be made manifest among you <the church of God which is at Corinth>. 20 When ye <the church of God which is at Corinth> come together therefore into one place, this is not to eat the Lord's supper. 21 For in eating every one taketh before other his own supper: and one is hungry, and another is drunken. 22 What? have ye <the church of God which is at Corinth> not houses to eat and to drink in? or despise ye <the church of God which is at Corinth> the church of God, and shame them that have not? What shall I say to you <the church of God which is at Corinth>? shall I praise you <the church of God which is at Corinth> in this? I praise you <the church of

God which is at Corinth> not. 23 For I have received of the Lord that which also I delivered unto you <the church of God which is at Corinth>, That the Lord Jesus the same night in which he was betrayed took bread: 24 And when he had given thanks, he brake it, and said, Take, eat: this is my body, which is broken for you [Notice that this *you* is spoken to the disciples in the upper room.]: this do in remembrance of me. 25 After the same manner also he took the cup, when he had supped, saying, This cup is the new testament in my blood: this do ye [Notice that this *ye* is spoken to the disciples in the upper room.], as oft as ye [Notice that this *ye* is spoken to the disciples in the upper room] drink it, in remembrance of me. 26 For as often as ye [This *ye* was not spoken by the LORD Jesus in the upper room, but is directed by Paul to the church of God which is at Corinth.] eat this bread, and drink this cup, ye <the church of God which is at Corinth> do show the Lord's death till he come. 27 Wherefore whosoever shall eat this bread, and drink this cup of the Lord, unworthily, shall be guilty of the body and blood of the Lord. 28 But let a man examine himself, and so let him eat of that bread, and drink of that cup. 29 For he that eateth and drinketh unworthily, eateth and drinketh damnation to himself, not discerning the Lord's body. 30 For this cause many are weak and sickly among you <the church of God which is at Corinth>, and many sleep. 31 For if we would judge ourselves, we should not be judged. 32 But when we are judged, we are chastened

233

of the Lord, that we should not be condemned with the world. 33 Wherefore, my
brethren, when ye <the church of God
which is at Corinth> come together to eat,
tarry one for another. 34 And if any man
hunger, let him eat at home; that ye <the
church of God which is at Corinth> come
not together unto condemnation. And the
rest will I set in order when I come.

CHAPTER 12

1 Now concerning spiritual gifts, brethren,
I would not have you <the church of God
which is at Corinth> ignorant. 2 Ye <the
church of God which is at Corinth> know
that ye <the church of God which is at
Corinth> were Gentiles, carried away unto
these dumb idols, even as ye <the church
of God which is at Corinth> were led. 3
Wherefore I give you <the church of God
which is at Corinth> to understand, that
no man speaking by the Spirit of God
calleth Jesus accursed: and that no man
can say that Jesus is the Lord, but by the
Holy Ghost. 4 Now there are diversities of
gifts, but the same Spirit. 5 And there are
differences of administrations, but the
same Lord. 6 And there are diversities of
operations, but it is the same God which
worketh all in all. 7 But the manifestation
of the Spirit is given to every man to profit
withal. 8 For to one is given by the Spirit
the word of wisdom; to another the word
of knowledge by the same Spirit; 9 To another faith by the same Spirit; to another
the gifts of healing by the same Spirit; 10
To another the working of miracles; to another prophecy; to another discerning of
spirits; to another divers kinds of tongues;

to another the interpretation of tongues: 11 But all these worketh that one and the selfsame Spirit, dividing to every man severally as he will. 12 For as the body is one, and hath many members, and all the members of that one body, being many, are one body: so also is Christ. 13 For by one Spirit are we all baptized into one body, whether we be Jews or Gentiles, whether we be bond or free; and have been all made to drink into one Spirit. 14 For the body is not one member, but many. 15 If the foot shall say, Because I am not the hand, I am not of the body; is it therefore not of the body? 16 And if the ear shall say, Because I am not the eye, I am not of the body; is it therefore not of the body? 17 If the whole body were an eye, where were the hearing? If the whole were hearing, where were the smelling? 18 But now hath God set the members every one of them in the body, as it hath pleased him. 19 And if they were all one member, where were the body? 20 But now are they many members, yet but one body. 21 And the eye cannot say unto the hand, I have no need of thee: nor again the head to the feet, I have no need of you <the church of God which is at Corinth>. 22 Nay, much more those members of the body, which seem to be more feeble, are necessary: 23 And those members of the body, which we think to be less honourable, upon these we bestow more abundant honour; and our uncomely parts have more abundant comeliness. 24 For our comely parts have no need: but God hath tempered the body together, having given more abundant honour to that part which lacked: 25 That there should be no schism in the body; but that the members should have the same care one for another. 26 And whether one member suffer, all the members suffer with it; or one member be honoured, all the members rejoice with it. 27 Now ye <the church of God which is at Corinth> are the body of Christ, and members in particular. 28 And God hath set some in the church, first apostles, secondarily prophets, thirdly teachers, after that miracles, then gifts of healings, helps, governments, diversities of tongues. 29 Are all apostles? are all prophets? are all teachers? are all workers of miracles? 30 Have all the gifts of healing? do all speak with tongues? do all interpret? 31 But covet earnestly the best gifts: and yet show I unto you <the church of God which is at Corinth> a more excellent way.

CHAPTER 13

1 Though I speak with the tongues of men and of angels, and have not charity, I am become as sounding brass, or a tinkling cymbal. 2 And though I have the gift of prophecy, and understand all mysteries, and all knowledge; and though I have all faith, so that I could remove mountains, and have not charity, I am nothing. 3 And though I bestow all my goods to feed the poor, and though I give my body to be burned, and have not charity, it profiteth me nothing. 4 Charity suffereth long, and is kind; charity envieth not; charity vaunteth not itself, is not puffed up, 5 Doth not behave itself unseemly, seeketh not her own, is not easily provoked,

thinketh no evil; 6 Rejoiceth not in iniqui-ty, but rejoiceth in the truth; 7 Beareth all things, believeth all things, hopeth all things, endureth all things. 8 Charity nev-er faileth: but whether there be prophe-cies, they shall fail; whether there be tongues, they shall cease; whether there be knowledge, it shall vanish away. 9 For we know in part, and we prophesy in part. 10 But when that which is perfect is come, then that which is in part shall be done away. 11 When I was a child, I spake as a child, I understood as a child, I thought as a child: but when I became a man, I put away childish things. 12 For now we see through a glass, darkly; but then face to face: now I know in part; but then shall I know even as also I am known. 13 And now abideth faith, hope, charity, these three; but the greatest of these is charity.

CHAPTER 14

1 Follow after charity, and desire spiritual gifts, but rather that ye <the church of God which is at Corinth> may prophesy. 2 For he that speaketh in an unknown tongue speaketh not unto men, but unto God: for no man understandeth him; howbeit in the spirit he speaketh myster-ies. 3 But he that prophesieth speaketh unto men to edification, and exhortation, and comfort. 4 He that speaketh in an unknown tongue edifieth himself; but he that prophesieth edifieth the church. 5 I would that ye <the church of God which is at Corinth> all spake with tongues, but rather that ye <the church of God which is at Corinth> prophesied: for greater is

he that prophesieth than he that speaketh with tongues, except he interpret, that the church may receive edifying. 6 Now, brethren, if I come unto you <the church of God which is at Corinth> speaking with tongues, what shall I profit you <the church of God which is at Corinth>, except I shall speak to you <the church of God which is at Corinth> either by revelation, or by knowledge, or by prophesying, or by doctrine? 7 And even things without life giving sound, whether pipe or harp, except they give a distinction in the sounds, how shall it be known what is piped or harped? 8 For if the trumpet give an uncertain sound, who shall prepare himself to the battle? 9 So likewise ye <the church of God which is at Corinth>, except ye <the church of God which is at Corinth> utter by the tongue words easy to be understood, how shall it be known what is spoken? for ye <the church of God which is at Corinth> shall speak into the air. 10 There are, it may be, so many kinds of voices in the world, and none of them is without signification. 11 Therefore if I know not the meaning of the voice, I shall be unto him that speaketh a barbarian, and he that speaketh shall be a barbarian unto me. 12 Even so ye <the church of God which is at Corinth>, forasmuch as ye <the church of God which is at Corinth> are zealous of spiritual gifts, seek that ye <the church of God which is at Corinth> may excel to the edifying of the church. 13 Wherefore let him that speaketh in an unknown tongue pray that he may interpret. 14 For if I pray in an unknown tongue, my spirit prayeth, but my understanding is unfruitful. 15 What is it then? I will pray with the spirit, and I will pray with the understanding also: I will sing with the spirit, and I will sing with the understanding also. 16 Else when thou shalt bless with the spirit, how shall he that occupieth the room of the unlearned say Amen at thy giving of thanks, seeing he understandeth not what thou sayest? 17 For thou verily givest thanks well, but the other is not edified. 18 I thank my God, I speak with tongues more than ye <the church of God which is at Corinth> all: 19 Yet in the church I had rather speak five words with my understanding, that by my voice I might teach others also, than ten thousand words in an unknown tongue. 20 Brethren, be not children in understanding: howbeit in malice be ye <the church of God which is at Corinth> children, but in understanding be men. 21 In the law it is written, With men of other tongues and other lips will I speak unto this people; and yet for all that will they not hear me, saith the Lord. 22 Wherefore tongues are for a sign, not to them that believe, but to them that believe not: but prophesying serveth not for them that believe not, but for them which believe. 23 If therefore the whole church be come together into one place, and all speak with tongues, and there come in those that are unlearned, or unbelievers, will they not say that ye <the church of God which is at Corinth> are mad? 24 But if all prophesy, and there come in one that believeth not, or one unlearned, he is convinced of all, he is judged of all: 25 And thus are the secrets of his heart made manifest; and so falling down on his face he will worship God, and report that God is in you <the church of God which is at Corinth> of a truth. 26 How is it then, brethren? when ye <the church of God which is at Corinth> come together, every one of you <the church of God which is at Corinth> hath a psalm, hath a doctrine, hath a tongue, hath a revelation, hath an interpretation. Let all things be done unto edifying. 27 If any man speak in an unknown tongue, let it be by two, or at the most by three, and that by course; and let one interpret. 28 But if there be no interpreter, let him keep silence in the church; and let him speak to himself, and to God. 29 Let the prophets speak two or three, and let the other judge. 30 If any thing be revealed to another that sitteth by, let the first hold his peace. 31 For ye <the church of God which is at Corinth> may all prophesy one by one, that all may learn, and all may be comforted. 32 And the spirits of the prophets are subject to the prophets. 33 For God is not the author of confusion, but of peace, as in all churches of the saints. 34 Let your <the church of God which is at Corinth> women keep silence in the churches: for it is not permitted unto them to speak; but they are commanded to be under obedience, as also saith the law. 35 And if they will learn any thing, let them ask their husbands at home: for it is a shame for women to speak in the church. 36 What? came the word of God out from you <the church of God which is at Corinth>? or came it unto you <the church of God which is at Cor-

inth> only? 37 If any man think himself to be a prophet, or spiritual, let him acknowledge that the things that I write unto you <the church of God which is at Corinth> are the commandments of the Lord. 38 But if any man be ignorant, let him be ignorant. 39 Wherefore, brethren, covet to prophesy, and forbid not to speak with tongues. 40 Let all things be done decently and in order.

CHAPTER 15

1 Moreover, brethren, I declare unto you <the church of God which is at Corinth> the gospel which I preached unto you <the church of God which is at Corinth>, which also ye <the church of God which is at Corinth> have received, and wherein ye <the church of God which is at Corinth> stand; 2 By which also ye <the church of God which is at Corinth> are saved, if ye <the church of God which is at Corinth> keep in memory what I preached unto you <the church of God which is at Corinth>, unless ye <the church of God which is at Corinth> have believed in vain. 3 For I delivered unto you <the church of God which is at Corinth> first of all that which I also received, how that Christ died for our sins according to the scriptures; 4 And that he was buried, and that he rose again the third day according to the scriptures: 5 And that he was seen of Cephas, then of the twelve: 6 After that, he was seen of above five hundred brethren at once; of whom the greater part remain unto this present, but some are fallen asleep. 7 After that, he was seen of James; then of all the apostles. 8 And last of all

he was seen of me also, as of one born out of due time. 9 For I am the least of the apostles, that am not meet to be called an apostle, because I persecuted the church of God. 10 But by the grace of God I am what I am: and his grace which was bestowed upon me was not in vain; but I laboured more abundantly than they all: yet not I, but the grace of God which was with me. 11 Therefore whether it were I or they, so we preach, and so ye <the church of God which is at Corinth> believed. 12 Now if Christ be preached that he rose from the dead, how say some among you <the church of God which is at Corinth> that there is no resurrection of the dead? 13 But if there be no resurrection of the dead, then is Christ not risen: 14 And if Christ be not risen, then is our preaching vain, and your <the church of God which is at Corinth> faith is also vain. 15 Yea, and we are found false witnesses of God; because we have testified of God that he raised up Christ: whom he raised not up, if so be that the dead rise not. 16 For if the dead rise not, then is not Christ raised: 17 And if Christ be not raised, your <the church of God which is at Corinth> faith is vain; ye <the church of God which is at Corinth> are yet in your <the church of God which is at Corinth> sins. 18 Then they also which are fallen asleep in Christ are perished. 19 If in this life only we have hope in Christ, we are of all men most miserable. 20 But now is Christ risen from the dead, and become the firstfruits of them that slept. 21 For since by man came death, by man came also the resurrection of the dead. 22 For as in

Adam all die, even so in Christ shall all be made alive. 23 But every man in his own order: Christ the firstfruits; afterward they that are Christ's at his coming. 24 Then cometh the end, when he shall have delivered up the kingdom to God, even the Father; when he shall have put down all rule and all authority and power. 25 For he must reign, till he hath put all enemies under his feet. 26 The last enemy that shall be destroyed is death. 27 For he hath put all things under his feet. But when he saith all things are put under him, it is manifest that he is excepted, which did put all things under him. 28 And when all things shall be subdued unto him, then shall the Son also himself be subject unto him that put all things under him, that God may be all in all. 29 Else what shall they do which are baptized for the dead, if the dead rise not at all? why are they then baptized for the dead? 30 And why stand we in jeopardy every hour? 31 I protest by your <the church of God which is at Corinth> rejoicing which I have in Christ Jesus our Lord, I die daily. 32 If after the manner of men I have fought with beasts at Ephesus, what advantageth it me, if the dead rise not? let us eat and drink; for to morrow we die. 33 Be not deceived: evil communications corrupt good manners. 34 Awake to righteousness, and sin not; for some have not the knowledge of God: I speak this to your <the church of God which is at Corinth> shame. 35 But some man will say, How are the dead raised up? and with what body do they come? 36 Thou fool, that which thou sowest is not quickened, except it die: 37 And that which thou sowest, thou sowest not that body that shall be, but bare grain, it may chance of wheat, or of some other grain: 38 But God giveth it a body as it hath pleased him, and to every seed his own body. 39 All flesh is not the same flesh: but there is one kind of flesh of men, another flesh of beasts, another of fishes, and another of birds. 40 There are also celestial bodies, and bodies terrestrial: but the glory of the celestial is one, and the glory of the terrestrial is another. 41 There is one glory of the sun, and another glory of the moon, and another glory of the stars: for one star differeth from another star in glory. 42 So also is the resurrection of the dead. It is sown in corruption; it is raised in incorruption: 43 It is sown in dishonour; it is raised in glory: it is sown in weakness; it is raised in power: 44 It is sown a natural body; it is raised a spiritual body. There is a natural body, and there is a spiritual body. 45 And so it is written, The first man Adam was made a living soul; the last Adam was made a quickening spirit. 46 Howbeit that was not first which is spiritual, but that which is natural; and afterward that which is spiritual. 47 The first man is of the earth, earthy: the second man is the Lord from heaven. 48 As is the earthy, such are they also that are earthy: and as is the heavenly, such are they also that are heavenly. 49 And as we have borne the image of the earthy, we shall also bear the image of the heavenly. 50 Now this I say, brethren, that flesh and blood cannot inherit the kingdom of God; neither doth corruption inherit incorruption. 51 Behold, I show you <the church of God which is at Corinth> a mystery; We shall not all sleep, but we shall all be changed, 52 In a moment, in the twinkling of an eye, at the last trump: for the trumpet shall sound, and the dead shall be raised incorruptible, and we shall be changed. 53 For this corruptible must put on incorruption, and this mortal must put on immortality. 54 So when this corruptible shall have put on incorruption, and this mortal shall have put on immortality, then shall be brought to pass the saying that is written, Death is swallowed up in victory. 55 O death, where is thy sting? O grave, where is thy victory? 56 The sting of death is sin; and the strength of sin is the law. 57 But thanks be to God, which giveth us the victory through our Lord Jesus Christ. 58 Therefore, my beloved brethren, be ye <the church of God which is at Corinth> stedfast, unmoveable, always abounding in the work of the Lord, forasmuch as ye <the church of God which is at Corinth> know that your <the church of God which is at Corinth> labour is not in vain in the Lord.

CHAPTER 16

1 Now concerning the collection for the saints, as I have given order to the churches of Galatia, even so do ye <the church of God which is at Corinth>. 2 Upon the first day of the week let every one of you <the church of God which is at Corinth> lay by him in store, as God hath prospered him, that there be no gatherings when I come. 3 And when I come, whomsoever ye <the church of God which

is at Corinth> shall approve by your <the church of God which is at Corinth> letters, them will I send to bring your <the church of God which is at Corinth> liberality unto Jerusalem. 4 And if it be meet that I go also, they shall go with me. 5 Now I will come unto you <the church of God which is at Corinth>, when I shall pass through Macedonia: for I do pass through Macedonia. 6 And it may be that I will abide, yea, and winter with you <the church of God which is at Corinth>, that ye <the church of God which is at Corinth> may bring me on my journey whithersoever I go. 7 For I will not see you <the church of God which is at Corinth> now by the way; but I trust to tarry a while with you <the church of God which is at Corinth>, if the Lord permit. 8 But I will tarry at Ephesus until Pentecost. 9 For a great door and effectual is opened unto me, and there are many adversaries. 10 Now if Timotheus come, see that he may be with you <the church of God which is at Corinth> without fear: for he worketh the work of the Lord, as I also do. 11 Let no man therefore despise him: but conduct him forth in peace, that he may come unto me: for I look for him with the brethren. 12 As touching our brother Apollos, I greatly desired him to come unto you <the church of God which is at Corinth> with the brethren: but his will was not at all to come at this time; but he will come when he shall have convenient time. 13 Watch ye <the church of God which is at Corinth>, stand fast in the faith, quit you <the church of God which is at Corinth> like men, be strong. 14 Let all your <the

church of God which is at Corinth> things be done with charity. 15 I beseech you <the church of God which is at Corinth>, brethren, (ye know the house of Stephanas, that it is the firstfruits of Achaia, and that they have addicted themselves to the ministry of the saints,) 16 That ye <the church of God which is at Corinth> submit yourselves <the church of God which is at Corinth> unto such, and to every one that helpeth with us, and laboureth. 17 I am glad of the coming of Stephanas and Fortunatus and Achaicus: for that which was lacking on your <the church of God which is at Corinth> part they have supplied. 18 For they have refreshed my spirit and yours <the church of God which is at Corinth>: therefore acknowledge ye <the church of God which is at Corinth> them that are such. 19 The churches of Asia salute you <the church of God which is at Corinth>. Aquila and Priscilla salute you <the church of God which is at Corinth> much in the Lord, with the church that is in their house. 20 All the brethren greet you <the church of God which is at Corinth>. Greet ye <the church of God which is at Corinth> one another with an holy kiss. 21 The salutation of me Paul with mine own hand. 22 If any man love not the Lord Jesus Christ, let him be Anathema Maranatha. 23 The grace of our Lord Jesus Christ be with you <the church of God which is at Corinth>. 24 My love be with you <the church of God which is at Corinth> all in Christ Jesus. Amen.

¹ 2 Timothy 3:16 All scripture *is* given by inspiration of God, and *is* profitable for doctrine, for reproof, for correction, for instruction in righteousness:

2 Peter 3:15 And account *that* the longsuffering of our Lord *is* salvation; even as our beloved brother Paul also according to the wisdom given unto him hath written unto you; 16 As also in all *his* epistles, speaking in them of these things; in which are some things hard to be understood, which they that are unlearned and unstable wrest, as *they do* also the other scriptures, unto their own destruction. 17 Ye therefore, beloved, seeing ye know *these things* before, beware lest ye also, being led away with the error of the wicked, fall from your own stedfastness. 18 But grow in grace, and *in* the knowledge of our Lord and Saviour Jesus Christ. To him *be* glory both now and for ever. Amen.

² 1 Corinthians 1:1 Paul, called *to be* an apostle of Jesus Christ through the will of God, and Sosthenes *our* brother, 2 Unto the church of God which is at Corinth, to them that are sanctified in Christ Jesus, called *to be* saints, with all that in every place call upon the name of Jesus Christ our Lord, both theirs and ours:

³ 1 Corinthians 7:17 But as God hath distributed to every man, as the Lord hath called every one, so let him walk. And so ordain I in all churches.

1 Corinthians 14:33 For God is not *the author* of confusion, but of peace, as in all churches of the saints.

⁴ 1 Corinthians 11:16 But if any man seem to be contentious, we have no such custom, neither the churches of God.

⁵ 1 Corinthians 1:2 Unto the church of God which is at Corinth, to them that are sanctified in Christ Jesus, called *to be* saints, with all that in every place call upon the name of Jesus Christ our Lord, both theirs and ours:

⁶ Ibid.

⁷ 1 Corinthians 2:6 Howbeit we speak wisdom among them that are perfect: yet not the wisdom of this world, nor of the princes of this world, that come to nought: ... 10 But God hath revealed *them* unto us by his Spirit: for the Spirit searcheth all things, yea, the deep things of God. ... 3:15 If any man's work shall be

burned, he shall suffer loss: but he himself shall be saved; yet so as by fire.

[8] 1 Corinthians 1:2 Unto the church of God which is at Corinth, to them that are sanctified in Christ Jesus, called *to be* saints, with all that in every place call upon the name of Jesus Christ our Lord, both theirs and ours:

[9] 1 Corinthians 12:27 Now ye are the body of Christ, and members in particular.
1 Corinthians 11:29 For he that eateth and drinketh unworthily, eateth and drinketh damnation to himself, not discerning the Lord's body.

[10] 1 Corinthians 2:6 Howbeit we speak wisdom among them that are perfect: yet not the wisdom of this world, nor of the princes of this world, that come to nought: ... 2:10 But God hath revealed *them* unto us by his Spirit: for the Spirit searcheth all things, yea, the deep things of God. ... 3:15 If any man's work shall be burned, he shall suffer loss: but he himself shall be saved; yet so as by fire.

[11] Acts 13:1 Now there were in the church that was at Antioch certain prophets and teachers; as Barnabas, and Simeon that was called Niger, and Lucius of Cyrene, and Manaen, which had been brought up with Herod the tetrarch, and Saul. 2 As they ministered to the Lord, and fasted, the Holy Ghost said, Separate me Barnabas and Saul for the work whereunto I have called them. 3 And when they had fasted and prayed, and laid *their* hands on them, they sent *them* away. ... 15:40 And Paul chose Silas, and departed, being recommended by the brethren unto the grace of God.

[12] 1 Corinthians 1:2 Unto the church of God which is at Corinth, to them that are sanctified in Christ Jesus, called *to be* saints, with all that in every place call upon the name of Jesus Christ our Lord, both theirs and ours:

[13] Ibid.

[14] 1 Corinthians 16:15 I beseech you, brethren, (ye know the house of Stephanas, that it is the firstfruits of Achaia, and *that* they have addicted themselves to the ministry of the saints,)

[15] 1 Corinthians 11:22 What? have ye not houses to eat and to drink in? or despise ye the church of God,

and shame them that have not? What shall I say to you? shall I praise you in this? I praise *you* not.

¹⁶ 1 Corinthians 14:23 If therefore the whole church be come together into one place, and all speak with tongues, and there come in *those that are* unlearned, or unbelievers, will they not say that ye are mad?
1 Corinthians 12:13 For by one Spirit are we all baptized into one body, whether *we be* Jews or Gentiles, whether *we be* bond or free; and have been all made to drink into one Spirit. ... 27 Now ye are the body of Christ, and members in particular.

¹⁷ 1 Corinthians 11:18 For first of all, when ye come together in the church, I hear that there be divisions among you; and I partly believe it. ... 14:19 Yet in the church I had rather speak five words with my under-standing, that *by my voice* I might teach others also, than ten thousand words in an *unknown* tongue. ... 14:28 But if there be no interpreter, let him keep silence in the church; and let him speak to himself, and to God. ... 14:35 And if they will learn any thing, let them ask their husbands at home: for it is a shame for women to speak in the church.

¹⁸ 1 Corinthians 11:22 What? have ye not houses to eat and to drink in? or despise ye the church of God, and shame them that have not? What shall I say to you? shall I praise you in this? I praise *you* not.
1 Timothy 3:15 But if I tarry long, that thou mayest know how thou oughtest to behave thyself in the house of God, which is the church of the living God, the pillar and ground of the truth.

¹⁹ 1 Corinthians 11:20 When ye come together therefore into one place, *this* is not to eat the Lord's supper. ... 22 What? have ye not houses to eat and to drink in? or despise ye the church of God, and shame them that have not? What shall I say to you? shall I praise you in this? I praise *you* not. ... 14:23 If therefore the whole church be come together into one place, and all speak with tongues, and there come in *those that are* unlearned, or unbelievers, will they not say that ye are mad?

²⁰ 1 Corinthians 16:2 Upon the first *day* of the week let every one of you lay by him in store, as *God* hath prospered him, that there be no gatherings when I come.

21 Ibid.

22 1 Corinthians 11:19 For there must be also heresies among you, that they which are approved may be
made manifest among you. ... 15:12 Now if Christ be
preached that he rose from the dead, how say some
among you that there is no resurrection of the dead?

23 1 Corinthians 5:1 It is reported commonly *that
there is* fornication among you, and such fornication as
is not so much as named among the Gentiles, that one
should have his father's wife. 2 And ye are puffed up,
and have not rather mourned, that he that hath done
this deed might be taken away from among you.

24 1 Corinthians 5:1 It is reported commonly *that
there is* fornication among you, and such fornication as
is not so much as named among the Gentiles, that one
should have his father's wife. 2 And ye are puffed up,
and have not rather mourned, that he that hath done
this deed might be taken away from among you. 3 For I
verily, as absent in body, but present in spirit, have
judged already, as though I were present, *concerning*
him that hath so done this deed, 4 In the name of our
Lord Jesus Christ, when ye are gathered together, and
my spirit, with the power of our Lord Jesus Christ, 5 To
deliver such an one unto Satan for the destruction of
the flesh, that the spirit may be saved in the day of the
Lord Jesus. 6 Your glorying *is* not good. Know ye not
that a little leaven leaveneth the whole lump? 7 Purge
out therefore the old leaven, that ye may be a new
lump, as ye are unleavened. For even Christ our
passover is sacrificed for us: 8 Therefore let us keep the
feast, not with old leaven, neither with the leaven of
malice and wickedness; but with the unleavened *bread*
of sincerity and truth. 9 I wrote unto you in an epistle
not to company with fornicators: 10 Yet not altogether
with the fornicators of this world, or with the covetous,
or extortioners, or with idolaters; for then must ye
needs go out of the world. 11 But now I have written
unto you not to keep company, if any man that is
called a brother be a fornicator, or covetous, or an
idolater, or a railer, or a drunkard, or an extortioner;
with such an one no not to eat. 12 For what have I to
do to judge them also that are without? do not ye judge
them that are within? 13 But them that are without

God judgeth. Therefore put away from among your-selves that wicked person.

25 1 Corinthians 11:2 Now I praise you, brethren, that ye remember me in all things, and keep the ordinances, as I delivered *them* to you. ... 23 For I have received of the Lord that which also I delivered unto you, That the Lord Jesus the *same* night in which he was betrayed took bread: 24 And when he had given thanks, he brake *it*, and said, Take, eat: this is my body, which is broken for you: this do in remembrance of me. 25 After the same manner also *he took* the cup, when he had supped, saying, This cup is the new testament in my blood: this do ye, as oft as ye drink *it*, in remembrance of me. 26 For as often as ye eat this bread, and drink this cup, ye do shew the Lord's death till he come. 27 Wherefore whosoever shall eat this bread, and drink *this* cup of the Lord, unworthily, shall be guilty of the body and blood of the Lord. 28 But let a man examine himself, and so let him eat of *that* bread, and drink of *that* cup. 29 For he that eateth and drinketh unworthily, eateth and drinketh damnation to himself, not discerning the Lord's body. 30 For this cause many *are* weak and sickly among you, and many sleep. 31 For if we would judge ourselves, we should not be judged. 32 But when we are judged, we are chastened of the Lord, that we should not be con-demned with the world. 33 Wherefore, my brethren, when ye come together to eat, tarry one for another. 34 And if any man hunger, let him eat at home; that ye come not together unto condemnation. And the rest will I set in order when I come.

26 1 Corinthians 12:26 And whether one member suffer, all the members suffer with it; or one member be honoured, all the members rejoice with it.

27 1 Corinthians 14:4 He that speaketh in an *un-known* tongue edifieth himself; but he that prophesieth edifieth the church. 5 I would that ye all spake with tongues, but rather that ye prophesied: for greater *is* he that prophesieth than he that speaketh with tongues, except he interpret, that the church may receive edifying.

28 1 Corinthians 14:16 Else when thou shalt bless with the spirit, how shall he that occupieth the room of the unlearned say Amen at thy giving of thanks, seeing

he understandeth not what thou sayest? 17 For thou verily givest thanks well, but the other is not edified.

[29] 1 Corinthians 14:15 What is it then? I will pray with the spirit, and I will pray with the understanding also: I will sing with the spirit, and I will sing with the understanding also. ... 26 How is it then, brethren? when ye come together, every one of you hath a psalm, hath a doctrine, hath a tongue, hath a revelation, hath an interpretation. Let all things be done unto edifying. Colossians 3:16 Let the word of Christ dwell in you richly in all wisdom; teaching and admonishing one another in psalms and hymns and spiritual songs, singing with grace in your hearts to the Lord.

[30] 1 Corinthians 11:33 Wherefore, my brethren, when ye come together to eat, tarry one for another. 2 Corinthians 1:11 Ye also helping together by prayer for us, that for the gift *bestowed* upon us by the means of many persons thanks may be given by many on our behalf. ... 9:14 And by their prayer for you, which long after you for the exceeding grace of God in you.

[31] 1 Corinthians 14:23 If therefore the whole church be come together into one place, and all speak with tongues, and there come in *those that are* unlearned, or unbelievers, will they not say that ye are mad? 24 But if all prophesy, and there come in one that believeth not, or *one* unlearned, he is convinced of all, he is judged of all: 25 And thus are the secrets of his heart made manifest; and so falling down on *his* face he will worship God, and report that God is in you of a truth.

Appendix C
DEFINING THE CHURCH AND BAPTISM

T he following statements are taken from *The Constitution and The Articles of Faith of the Heritage Baptist Church of Pensacola.* The doctrines expressed in that document were substantially based upon the New Hampshire Confession of Faith of 1833. We believe that these statements express clearly those teachings of the Scriptures that this church affirms and that her Baptist forefathers historically believed and practiced concerning the definition of the New Testament Church and the church ordinance of baptism.

THIS WE BELIEVE OF A GOSPEL CHURCH

We believe that a New Testament Church is a congregation of baptized believers,[a] associated by covenant in the faith and in the fellowship of the Gospel,[b] observing the ordinances of Christ,[c] governed by His laws,[d] and exercising the gifts, rights, and privileges invested in them by His word;ᵉ that her only scriptural and ordained officers are bishops or elders or pastors and deacons,ᶠ whose qualifications, claims, and duties are defined in the Epistles to Timothy and Titus.

ᵃ 1 Corinthians 1:1-13; Matthew 18:17; Acts 5:11; Acts 8:1; Acts 11:26; 1 Corinthians 4:17; 1 Corinthians 14:23; 3 John 9; 1 Timothy 3:5.

ᵇ Acts 2:41,42; 1 Corinthians 8:5; Acts 2:47; 1 Corinthians 5:12,13.

ᶜ 1 Corinthians 11:2; 2 Thessalonians 3:6; Romans 16:17:20; 1 Corinthians 11:23-33; Matthew 18:15-20; 1 Corinthians 5:6; 2 Corinthians 2:7.

ᵈ Matthew 28:20; John 14:15; John 15:12; 1 John 4:21; John 14:21; 1 Thessalonians 4:2; 2 John 6; Galatians 6:2; All of the Epistles.

ᵉ Ephesians 4:7; 1 Corinthians 14:12; Philippians 1:27; 1 Corinthians 12:14.

ᶠ Philippians 1:1; Acts 14:23; Acts 15:22; 1 Timothy 3; Titus 1.

THIS WE BELIEVE OF BAPTISM AND THE LORD'S SUPPER

We believe that Christian baptism is the immersion in water of a believerᵃ in the name of the Father, and of the Son, and of the Holy Ghost,ᵇ to show forth in a solemn and beautiful emblem our faith in the crucified, buried, and risen Saviour representing the effect of our faith in our death to sin and the resurrection to a new life;ᶜ that baptism is a prerequisite to the privileges of a church relation and to the LORD'S Supper,ᵈ in which the members

of the church, by the sacred use of the unleavened bread and the fruit of the vine, are to
commemorate together the dying love of
Christ,[e] preceded always by solemn self-examination.[f]

a Acts 8:36-39; Matthew 3:5,6; John 4:1,2;
Matthew 28:19; Mark 16:16; Acts
2:38; Acts 8:12; Acts 16:32-34; Acts
18:8.

b Matthew 28:19; Acts 10:47,48; Galatians
3:27,28.

c Romans 6:4; Colossians 2:12; 1 Peter
3:20,21; Acts 22:16.

d Acts 2:41,42; Matthew 28:19,20; The
Book of the Acts and the Epistles.

e 1 Corinthians 11:26; Matthew 26:26-29;
Mark 14:22-25; Luke 22:14-20.

f 1 Corinthians 11:17-32; 1 Corinthians
10:3-32; John 6:26-71.

Appendix D

THE NEW TESTAMENT REFERENCES FOR THE RELEVANT GREEK WORDS

All dictionaries agree that the English words *baptize, baptism* and *Baptist"* are transliterations of the relevant Greek words and are not translations of those words. No reputable theological work disputes this fact.

The English word *baptize* is the Greek word βαπτιζω transliterated.

Matthew 3:6 And were baptized of him in Jordan, confessing their sins.

Matthew 3:11 I indeed baptize you with water unto repentance: but he that cometh after me is mightier than I, whose shoes I am not worthy to bear: he shall baptize you with the Holy Ghost, and with fire:

Matthew 3:13 Then cometh Jesus from Galilee to Jordan unto John, to be baptized of him.

Matthew 3:14 But John forbad him, saying, I have need to be baptized of thee, and comest thou to me?

Matthew 3:16 And Jesus, when he was baptized, went up straightway out of the water: and, lo, the heavens were opened unto him, and he saw the Spirit of God descending like a dove, and lighting upon him:

Matthew 20:22 But Jesus answered and said, Ye know not what ye ask. Are ye able to drink of the cup that I shall drink of, and to be baptized with the baptism that I am baptized with? They say unto him, We are able.

Matthew 20:23 And he saith unto them, Ye shall drink indeed of my cup, and be baptized with the baptism that I am baptized with: but to sit on my right hand, and on my left, is not mine to give, but it shall be given to them for whom it is prepared of my Father.

Mark 1:4 John did baptize in the wilderness, and preach the baptism of repentance for the remission of sins.

Mark 1:5 And there went out unto him all the land of Judaea, and they of Jerusalem, and were all baptized of him in the river of Jordan, confessing their sins.

Mark 1:8 I indeed have baptized you with water: but he shall baptize you with the Holy Ghost.

Mark 1:9 And it came to pass in those days, that Jesus came from Nazareth of Galilee, and was baptized of John in Jordan.

Mark 10:38 But Jesus said unto them, Ye know not what ye ask: can ye drink of the cup that I drink of? and be baptized with the baptism that I am baptized with?

Mark 10:39 And they said unto him, We can. And Jesus said unto them, Ye shall indeed drink of the cup that I drink of; and with the baptism that I am baptized withal shall ye be baptized:

Mark 16:16 He that believeth and is baptized shall be saved; but he that believeth not shall be damned.

Luke 3:7 Then said he to the multitude that came forth to be baptized of him, O generation of vipers, who hath warned you to flee from the wrath to come?

Luke 3:12 Then came also publicans to be baptized, and said unto him, Master, what shall we do?

Luke 3:16 John answered, saying unto them all, I indeed baptize you with water; but one mightier than I cometh, the latchet of whose shoes I am not worthy to unloose: he shall baptize you with the Holy Ghost and with fire:

Luke 3:21 Now when all the people were baptized, it came to pass, that Jesus also being baptized, and praying, the heaven was opened,

Luke 7:29 And all the people that heard him, and the publicans, justified God, being baptized with the baptism of John.

Luke 7:30 But the Pharisees and lawyers rejected the counsel of God against themselves, being not baptized of him.

Luke 12:50 But I have a baptism to be baptized with; and how am I straitened till it be accomplished!

John 1:25 And they asked him, and said unto him, Why baptizest thou then, if thou be not that Christ, nor Elias, neither that prophet?

John 1:26 John answered them, saying, I

baptize with water: but there standeth one among you, whom ye know not;

John 1:33 And I knew him not: but he that sent me to baptize with water, the same said unto me, Upon whom thou shalt see the Spirit descending, and remaining on him, the same is he which baptizeth with the Holy Ghost.

John 3:22 After these things came Jesus and his disciples into the land of Judaea; and there he tarried with them, and baptized.

John 3:23 And John also was baptizing in Aenon near to Salim, because there was much water there: and they came, and were baptized.

John 3:26 And they came unto John, and said unto him, Rabbi, he that was with thee beyond Jordan, to whom thou barest witness, behold, the same baptizeth, and all men come to him.

John 4:1 When therefore the Lord knew how the Pharisees had heard that Jesus made and baptized more disciples than John,

John 4:2 (Though Jesus himself baptized not, but his disciples,)

John 10:40 And went away again beyond Jordan into the place where John at first baptized; and there he abode.

Acts 1:5 For John truly baptized with water; but ye shall be baptized with the Holy Ghost not many days hence.

Acts 2:38 Then Peter said unto them, Repent, and be baptized every one of you in the name of Jesus Christ for the remission of sins, and ye shall receive the gift of the Holy Ghost.

Acts 2:41 Then they that gladly received

his word were baptized: and the same day there were added unto them about three thousand souls.

Acts 8:12 But when they believed Philip preaching the things concerning the kingdom of God, and the name of Jesus Christ, they were baptized, both men and women.

Acts 8:13 Then Simon himself believed also: and when he was baptized, he continued with Philip, and wondered, beholding the miracles and signs which were done.

Acts 8:16 (For as yet he was fallen upon none of them: only they were baptized in the name of the Lord Jesus.)

Acts 8:36 And as they went on their way, they came unto a certain water: and the eunuch said, See, here is water; what doth hinder me to be baptized?

Acts 8:38 And he commanded the chariot to stand still: and they went down both into the water, both Philip and the eunuch; and he baptized him.

Acts 9:18 And immediately there fell from his eyes as it had been scales: and he received sight forthwith, and arose, and was baptized.

Acts 10:47 Can any man forbid water, that these should not be baptized, which have received the Holy Ghost as well as we?

Acts 10:48 And he commanded them to be baptized in the name of the Lord. Then prayed they him to tarry certain days.

Acts 11:16 Then remembered I the word of the Lord, how that he said, John indeed baptized with water; but ye shall be baptized with the Holy Ghost.

Acts 16:15 And when she was baptized, and her household, she besought us, saying, If ye have judged me to be faithful to the Lord, come into my house, and abide there. And she constrained us.

Acts 16:33 And he took them the same hour of the night, and washed their stripes; and was baptized, he and all his, straightway.

Acts 18:8 And Crispus, the chief ruler of the synagogue, believed on the Lord with all his house; and many of the Corinthians hearing believed, and were baptized.

Acts 19:3 And he said unto them, Unto what then were ye baptized? And they said, Unto John's baptism.

Acts 19:4 Then said Paul, John verily baptized with the baptism of repentance, saying unto the people, that they should believe on him which should come after him, that is, on Christ Jesus.

Acts 19:5 When they heard this, they were baptized in the name of the Lord Jesus.

Acts 22:16 And now why tarriest thou? arise, and be baptized, and wash away thy sins, calling on the name of the Lord.

Romans 6:3 Know ye not, that so many of us as were baptized into Jesus Christ were baptized into his death?

1 Corinthians 1:13 Is Christ divided? was Paul crucified for you? or were ye baptized in the name of Paul?

1 Corinthians 1:14 I thank God that I baptized none of you, but Crispus and Gaius;

1 Corinthians 1:15 Lest any should say that I had baptized in mine own name.

1 Corinthians 1:16 And I baptized also the household of Stephanas: besides, I know

not whether I baptized any other.

1 Corinthians 1:17 For Christ sent me not to baptize, but to preach the gospel: not with wisdom of words, lest the cross of Christ should be made of none effect.

1 Corinthians 10:2 And were all baptized unto Moses in the cloud and in the sea;

1 Corinthians 12:13 For by one Spirit are we all baptized into one body, whether we be Jews or Gentiles, whether we be bond or free; and have been all made to drink into one Spirit.

1 Corinthians 15:29 Else what shall they do which are baptized for the dead, if the dead rise not at all? why are they then baptized for the dead?

Galatians 3:27 For as many of you as have been baptized into Christ have put on Christ.

The English word *baptism* is the Greek word βαπτισμα transliterated.

Matthew 3:7 But when he saw many of the Pharisees and Sadducees come to his baptism, he said unto them, O generation of vipers, who hath warned you to flee from the wrath to come?

Matthew 20:22 But Jesus answered and said, Ye know not what ye ask. Are ye able to drink of the cup that I shall drink of, and to be baptized with the baptism that I am baptized with? They say unto him, We are able.

Matthew 20:23 And he saith unto them, Ye shall drink indeed of my cup, and be baptized with the baptism that I am baptized with: but to sit on my right hand, and on my left, is not mine to give, but it shall be given to them for whom it is prepared of my Father.

Matthew 21:25 The baptism of John, whence was it? from heaven, or of men? And they reasoned with themselves, saying, If we shall say, From heaven; he will say unto us, Why did ye not then believe him?

Mark 1:4 John did baptize in the wilderness, and preach the baptism of repentance for the remission of sins.

Mark 10:38 But Jesus said unto them, Ye know not what ye ask: can ye drink of the cup that I drink of? and be baptized with the baptism that I am baptized with?

Mark 10:39 And they said unto him, We can. And Jesus said unto them, Ye shall indeed drink of the cup that I drink of; and with the baptism that I am baptized withal shall ye be baptized:

Mark 11:30 The baptism of John, was it from heaven, or of men? answer me.

Luke 3:3 And he came into all the country about Jordan, preaching the baptism of repentance for the remission of sins;

Luke 7:29 And all the people that heard him, and the publicans, justified God, being baptized with the baptism of John.

Luke 12:50 But I have a baptism to be baptized with; and how am I straitened till it be accomplished!

Luke 20:4 The baptism of John, was it from heaven, or of men?

Acts 1:22 Beginning from the baptism of John, unto that same day that he was taken up from us, must one be ordained to be a witness with us of his resurrection.

Acts 10:37 That word, I say, ye know, which was published throughout all Judaea, and began from Galilee, after the baptism which John preached;

Acts 13:24 When John had first preached before his coming the baptism of repentance to all the people of Israel.

Acts 18:25 This man was instructed in the way of the Lord; and being fervent in the spirit, he spake and taught diligently the things of the Lord, knowing only the baptism of John.

Acts 19:3 And he said unto them, Unto what then were ye baptized? And they said, Unto John's baptism.

Acts 19:4 Then said Paul, John verily baptized with the baptism of repentance, saying unto the people, that they should believe on him which should come after him, that is, on Christ Jesus.

Romans 6:4 Therefore we are buried with him by baptism into death: that like as Christ was raised up from the dead by the glory of the Father, even so we also should walk in newness of life.

Ephesians 4:5 One Lord, one faith, one baptism,

Colossians 2:12 Buried with him in baptism, wherein also ye are risen with him through the faith of the operation of God, who hath raised him from the dead.

Hebrews 6:2 Of the doctrine of baptisms, and of laying on of hands, and of resurrection of the dead, and of eternal judgment.

1 Peter 3:21 The like figure whereunto even baptism doth also now save us (not the putting away of the filth of the flesh, but the answer of a good conscience toward God,) by the resurrection of Jesus Christ:

The English word *Baptist* is the Greek word βαπτιστης transliterated.

Matthew 3:1 In those days came John the Baptist, preaching in the wilderness of Judaea,

Matthew 11:11 Verily I say unto you, Among them that are born of women there hath not risen a greater than John the Baptist: notwithstanding he that is least in the kingdom of heaven is greater than he.

Matthew 11:12 And from the days of John the Baptist until now the kingdom of heaven suffereth violence, and the violent take it by force.

Matthew 14:2 And said unto his servants, This is John the Baptist; he is risen from the dead; and therefore mighty works do show forth themselves in him.

Matthew 14:8 And she, being before instructed of her mother, said, Give me here John Baptist's head in a charger.

Matthew 16:14 And they said, Some say that thou art John the Baptist: some, Elias; and others, Jeremias, or one of the prophets.

Matthew 17:13 Then the disciples understood that he spake unto them of John the Baptist.

Mark 6:14 And king Herod heard of him; (for his name was spread abroad:) and he said, That John the Baptist was risen from the dead, and therefore mighty works do show forth themselves in him.

Mark 6:24 And she went forth, and said unto her mother, What shall I ask? And she said, The head of John the Baptist.

Mark 6:25 And she came in straightway

with haste unto the king, and asked, saying, I will that thou give me by and by in a charger the head of John the Baptist.

Mark 8:28 And they answered, John the Baptist: but some say, Elias; and others, One of the prophets.

Luke 7:20 When the men were come unto him, they said, John Baptist hath sent us unto thee, saying, Art thou he that should come? or look we for another?

Luke 7:28 For I say unto you, Among those that are born of women there is not a greater prophet than John the Baptist: but he that is least in the kingdom of God is greater than he.

Luke 7:33 For John the Baptist came neither eating bread nor drinking wine; and ye say, He hath a devil.

Luke 9:19 They answering said, John the Baptist; but some say, Elias; and others say, that one of the old prophets is risen again.

Appendix E

A SAMPLING OF UNSCRIPTURAL TEACHINGS CONCERNING BAPTISM

The following comments are quotations taken from statements of doctrinal belief written or distributed by the person or group identified. No suggestion should be inferred that every member of one of these identified religious groups believe all that is recorded here. Not all of those who identify with any particular cause understand all that the cause represents or believes. This is true even among those who call themselves Baptists. Such conduct is not a virtue; but it is reality. Obviously not all of the erroneous teachings concerning baptism that are propagated by various Christian groups are included in this section.

JOHN WESLEY

John Wesley, the founder of Methodism, wrote and the Methodist Church teaches as follows:

It is certain that our church supposes that

all who are baptized in their infancy are at
the same time born again. ... If infants are
guilty of original sin they cannot be saved
in the ordinary way, unless this be
washed away by baptism.

Into what do we Methodists baptize
adults?

By baptism we, who are by nature children of wrath, are made the children of
God. ... In all ages the outward baptism is
a means of the inward. ... By water then,
as a means—the water of baptism—we are
regenerated or born again.[1]

In his *Notes on the New Testament*, Wesley
wrote the following commentary concerning
the individually cited verses:

Matthew 28:19 Go ye therefore, and teach
all nations, baptizing them in the name of
the Father, and of the Son, and of the Holy Ghost:

This includes the whole design of Christ's
commission. Baptizing and teaching are
the two great branches of that general design. And these were to be determined by
the circumstances of things: which made
it necessary in baptizing adult Jews or
heathens, to teach them before they were
baptized; in disciplining their children, to
baptize them before they were taught; as
the Jewish children, in all ages, were first
circumcised, and after taught to do all
God had commanded them.

John 3:5 Jesus answered, Verily, verily, I
say unto thee, Except a man be born of
water and of the Spirit, he cannot enter
into the kingdom of God.

Except he experience the great inward
change by the Spirit, and be baptized
(whatever baptism can be had), as the

outward sign and means of it. [The paren-
thesis in the original—JLM.]

Acts 22:16 And now why tarriest thou?
arise, and be baptized, and wash away thy
sins, calling on the name of the Lord.

Baptism, administered to real penitents, is
both a means and a seal of pardon. Nor
did God ordinarily in the primitive Church
bestow this on any, unless through this
means.

Romans 6:3 Know ye not, that so many of
us as were baptized into Jesus Christ
were baptized into his death?

In baptism we, through faith, are ingrafted
into Christ; and we draw new spiritual life
from this new root, through His Spirit, who
fashions us like unto Him, and particularly
with regard to His death and resurrection.

1 Corinthians 12:13 For by one Spirit are
we all baptized into one body, whether we
be Jews or Gentiles, whether we be bond
or free; and have been all made to drink
into one Spirit.

For by that one Spirit, which we received
in baptism, we are all united in one body.

Galatians 3:27 For as many of you as have
been baptized into Christ have put on
Christ.

For as many of you as have testified of
your faith by being baptized in the name
of Christ, have put on Christ—have received Him as your righteousness, and are
therefore sons of God through Him.

1 Peter 3:21 The like figure whereunto
even baptism doth also now save us (not
the putting away of the filth of the flesh,
but the answer of a good conscience toward God,) by the resurrection of Jesus
Christ:

273

The thing typified by the ark, even baptism, now saveth us—that is, through the water of baptism we are saved from the sin which overwhelms the world as a flood; not, indeed, the bare outward sign, but he inward grace; a Divine consciousness that both our persons and our actions are accepted through Him who died and arose again for us.

JOSEPH SMITH

Joseph Smith, the founding prophet of the Latter Day Saints (Mormons) in all of its branches and permutations, taught and all Latter Day Saints, Reorganized and otherwise, still teach as follows:

Nature of Baptism—In the theology of the Church of Jesus Christ of Latter-day Saints, water baptism ranks as the third principle and the first essential ordinance of the Gospel. Baptism is the getaway leading into the fold of Christ, the portal to the Church, the established rite of naturalization in the kingdom of God. The candidate for admission into the Church, having obtained the professed faith in the LORD Jesus Christ and having sincerely repented of his sins, is properly required to give evidence of his spiritual sanctification by some outward ordinance, prescribed by authority as the sign or symbol of his new profession. The initiatory [sic] ordinance is baptism by water, to be followed by the higher baptism of the Holy Spirit; and, as a result of this act of obedience, remission of sins is granted.[2]

The Establishment of Baptism dated from the time of the earliest history of the race. When the Lord manifested Himself to Adam after the expulsion from the Garden of

274

Eden, He promised the patriarch of the race: `If thou wilt turn unto me, and hearken unto my voice, and believe, and repent of all they transgressions, and be baptized, even in water, in the name of my Only Begotten Son, who is full of grace and truth, which is Jesus Christ, the only name which shall be given under heaven, whereby salvation shall come unto the children of men, ye shall receive the gift of the Holy Ghost, asking all things in his name, and whatsoever ye shall ask, it shall be given you. ... And it came to pass, when the Lord had spoken with Adam, our father, that Adam cried unto the Lord, and he was caught away by the Spirit of the Lord, and was carried down into the water, and was laid under the water, and was brought forth out of the water. And thus he was baptized, and the Spirit of God descended upon him, and thus he was born of the Spirit, and became quickened in the inner man. [3]

No one has reason to hope for salvation except by complying with the laws of God, of which baptism is an essential part.[4]

Baptism required of All—The universality of the law of baptism has been already dwelt with. Compliance with the ordinance has been shown to be an essential to salvation, and this condition applies to all mankind. Nowhere in scripture is a distinction made in this regard between the living and dead. The dead are those who have lived in mortality upon the earth: the living are mortals who yet shall pass through the ordained change that we call death. All are children of the same Father, all to be judged and rewarded or punished by the same unerring justice, with the same interpositions sic of benignant mercy.[5]

275

Work of the Living for the Dead—The redemption of the dead will be affected in
accordance with the law of God, which is
written in justice and framed in mercy. It
is alike impossible for any spirit, in the
flesh or disembodied, to obtain promise of
eternal glory except on condition of obedience to the laws and ordinances of the
Gospel. And, as baptism is essential to the
salvation of the living, it is likewise indis-
pensable to the dead.

Herein is shown the necessity of vicarious
work—the living ministering in behalf of
the dead; the children doing for their pro-
genitors what is beyond the power of the
latter to do for themselves.[6]

MARY BAKER EDDY

Mary Baker Eddy the founder of Christian
Science, who taught of death:

DEATH. An illusion, the lie of life in matter, the unreal and untrue; the opposite of
Life.

Matter has no life, hence it has no real
existence. Mind is immortal. The flesh,
warring against Spirit; that which frets
itself free from one belief of life where Life
is not yields to eternal life. Any material
evidence of death is false, for it contradicts
the spiritual facts of being.

Eddy also said of baptism:

BAPTISM. Purification by Spirit; submergence in Spirit.[7]

Explaining this, or rather attempting to
explain this metaphysical approach to baptism, Christian Science offers the following
statement: "Because matter is unreal, baptism
and Eucharist are not physically performed
and are spiritually understood. Mary Baker

Eddy puts it this way: 'Our baptism is purification from all error. Our Eucharist is spiritual communion with the one God. Our bread, 'which cometh down from heaven,' is Truth. Our cup is the cross. Our wine the inspiration of Love, the draught the Master drank and commended to his followers.'" (*Science and Health*, p. 35.)

The following is to be found on the website of the Mother Church.

> AS MOTHER CHURCH EMPLOYEES have traveled the world meeting with members, one interesting thing they've learned is that in some countries people may be asked to provide evidence of baptism in order to participate in certain public activities, such as voting or school attendance. Since baptism has an important and specific meaning to the teachings of Christian Science, it caused us to think about what such a statement might look like. While your branch church may find a different approach, here's one example we hope might help our readers to think of baptism in a fresh way. — Nathan A. Talbot, Clerk of The Mother Church.

> PEOPLE PRACTICE BAPTISM in many ways. The outward symbol of immersion in water tells of an inward desire for purification. Christian Scientists emphasize the meaning behind a Christian symbol more than the outward practice of a symbolic act. They practice baptism daily by studying the Word of God and living their lives in a way that give evidence they are being bathed in Spirit and thus cleansed of sin.[8]

MARTIN LUTHER

Dr. Martin Luther, one of the primary Reformers and the founder of the Lutheran denomination, wrote

What does Baptism give or profit?

It gives forgiveness of sins, delivers from death and the devil, and gives eternal salvation to all who believe this, as the words and promises of God declare.

How can water do such great things?

It is not the water indeed that does them, but the word of God which is in and with the water, and faith, which trusts such word of God with water. For without the word of God the water is simple water and no Baptism. But with the word of God it is Baptism, that is, a gracious water of life and a washing of regeneration in the Holy Ghost.[9]

What great things, then, does Baptism give or work?

A. It works forgiveness of sins;

B. It delivers from death and the devil;

C. It gives eternal salvation.[10]

In the *Large Catechism*, Martin Luther wrote in *Part Fourth: Baptism,* under number six:

Baptism is no human trifle, but instituted by God Himself, moreover, that it is most solemnly and strictly commanded that we must be baptized or we cannot be saved, lest any one regard it as a trifling matter, like putting on a new red coat. For it is of the greatest importance that we esteem Baptism excellent, glorious, and exalted, for which we contend and fight chiefly, because the world is now so full of sects clamoring that Baptism is an external thing, and that external things are of no benefit. But let it be ever so much an external thing, here stand God's Word and command which institute, establish, and confirm Baptism. But what God institutes and commands cannot be a vain, but must be a most precious thing, though in appearance it were of less value than a straw.

Under number fourteen in the same *Part Fourth*, he wrote:

From this now learn a proper understanding of the subject, and how to answer the question what Baptism is, namely thus, that it is not mere ordinary water, but water comprehended in God's Word and command, and sanctified thereby, so that it is nothing else than a divine water; not that the water in itself is nobler than other water, but that God's Word and command are added.

Continuing under numbers twenty-four through twenty-nine, he wrote:

Therefore state it most simply thus, that the power, work, profit, fruit, and end of Baptism is this, namely, to save. For no one is baptized in order that he may become a prince, but, as the words declare, that he be saved. But to be saved, we know, is nothing else than to be delivered from sin, death, and the devil, and to enter into the kingdom of Christ, and to live with Him forever. Here you see again how highly and precious we should esteem Baptism, because in it we obtain such an unspeakable treasure, which also indicates sufficiently that it cannot be ordinary mere water. For mere water could not do such a thing, but the Word does it, and (as said above) the fact that the name of

God is comprehended therein. But where the name of God is, there must be also life and salvation, that it may indeed be called a divine, blessed, fruitful, and gracious water; for by the Word such power is imparted to Baptism that it is a laver of regeneration, as St. Paul also calls it, Titus 3, 5. But as our would-be wise, new spirits assert that faith alone saves, **[We may understand those Baptists that Luther so detested to be these *new spirits* who assert that faith alone saves. —JLM]** and that works and external things avail nothing, we answer: It is true, indeed, that nothing in us is of any avail but faith, as we shall hear still further. But these blind guides **[the Baptists—JLM]** are unwilling to see this, namely, that faith must have something which it believes, that is, of which it takes hold, and upon which it stands and rests. Thus faith clings to the water, and believes that it is Baptism, in which there is pure salvation and life; not through the water (as we have sufficiently stated), but through the fact that it s embodied in the Word and institution of God, and the name of God inheres in it. Now, if I believe this, what else is it than believing in God as in Him who has given and planted His Word into this ordinance, and proposes to us this external thing wherein we may apprehend such a treasure?

THE CHURCH OF CHRIST

Several years ago, Ray Hawk, at that time an evangelist serving the Belleview Church of Christ of Pensacola, challenged me to a debate on the issue of whether baptism is essential to salvation. The only problem was that he conveniently forgot to invite me to participate in the debate.

He took several statements from my radio sermons and rebutted them in printed form in such a way as to convey the impression that we had met and debated. He fabricated an entire debate and printed a manufactured transcript. That was deceitful and dishonest. It was also cowardly. The two of us never did meet face-to-face.

The following material expressing his views comes from his fabricated debate and subsequent letters exchanged between us after I discovered his deception.

> Yes, the body of Christ IS THE CHURCH! (capitalization in the original) It is just that simple. To be in the body is to be in the church. To be in the church is to be in the body of Christ. One enters the church by water baptism, Acts 2:38-41. But, to enter the church is to enter the body of Christ! Salvation is found IN (capitalization in original) the body/church of Christ! Therefore, since water baptism is the entrance into the church/body, and salvation is a blessing found IN (capitalization in original) that body/church, water baptism is essential to our salvation, I Peter 3:21, Acts 22:16.
>
> I believe what the Bible does. We are immersed in water to be immersed into Christ and into his (lack of capitalization in original) death, Rom. 6:3, 4. Christ shed his (lack of capitalization in original) blood in his (lack of capitalization in original) death. When we get into his (lack of capitalization in original) death by baptism, we come in contact with his (lack of capitalization in original) blood. BLOOD (capitalization in original) is WHAT (capi-

talization in original) washes our sins, Matt. 26:28. WATER BAPTISM (capitalization in original) is WHEN (capitalization in original) our sins are washed away, Acts 2:38.

Though Hawk presented his comments in a fraudulent way, those statements are accurate in offering a legitimate presentation of the belief of the followers of Thomas Campbell, Alexander Campbell, and Barton Stone, the Disciples of Christ, the Church of Christ, the church of Christ, (two separate groups) the Christian Church, and the others that grew out of the Restoration Movement.

THE ROMAN CATHOLIC CHURCH

Pope Paul VI, with the title of Vicar of Christ, issued on June 30, 1968, the *Profession of the Faith of the Catholic Church* in which he stated

> We believe in one Baptism instituted by Our [sic] LORD Jesus Christ for the remission of sins.

> Baptism should be administered even to little children who have not yet been able to be guilty of any personal sin, in order that, though born deprived of supernatural grace, they may be reborn "of water and the Holy Spirit" to the divine life in Christ Jesus.

The New Saint Joseph Baltimore Catechism #2 (imprimatur: Francis Cardinal Spellman, Archbishop of New York) presents the following as the doctrine that is to be unquestioningly accepted by "all the faithful."

> 315. What is Baptism?

> > Baptism is the sacrament that gives our souls the new life of sanctifying

grace by which we become children of God and heirs of heaven.

316. What sins does Baptism take away?

Baptism takes away original sin; and also actual sin and all the punishment due to them, if the person baptized be guilty of any actual sins and truly sorry for them.

318. Who can administer Baptism?

The priest is the usual minister of Baptism, but if there is danger that someone will die without baptism, anyone else may and should baptize.

321. How can those be saved who through no fault of their own have not received the sacrament of Baptism?

Those who through no fault of their own have not received the sacrament of Baptism can be saved through what is called baptism of blood or baptism of desire.

However, only Baptism of water actually makes a person a member of the Church. It might be compared to a ladder up which one climbs into the Bark of Peter, as the Church is often called.

Baptism of blood or desire makes a member of the Church in desire. These are the two lifelines trailing from the sides of the Church to save those who are outside the Church through no fault of their own.

The New Saint Joseph Baltimore Catechism #2 (imprimatur: Francis Cardinal Spellman, Archbishop of New York) further states

148. ... Baptism washes away all sins. If a person were to die right after Baptism, he

would go straight to heaven.

The New Saint Joseph First Communion Catechism (imprimatur: Francis Cardinal Spellman) contains the following doctrinal statements.

41. What did Baptism do for you?

Baptism washed away original sin from my soul and made it rich in the grace of God.

Baptism is birth.

By it we are born of God.

He sends His Son into our soul.

God becomes our Father too.

Mary becomes our Mother.

The Holy Spirit pours grace into us.

Baptism washes us from original sin.

It drives away the devil.

He can no longer hurt us unless we let him.

THE PRESBYTERIAN CHURCH

The Westminster Shorter Catechism, authorized by the General Assembly of the Presbyterian Church in the USA (1894) and still the valid doctrinal statement for many Presbyterians contains the following statements.

88. What are the outward and ordinary means whereby Christ communicateth to us the benefits of redemption?

The outward and ordinary means whereby Christ communicateth to us the benefits of redemption are His ordinances, especially the Word, Sacraments, and prayer; all which are made effectual to the elect for salvation.

91. How do the Sacraments become effec-

tual means of salvation?

> The Sacraments become effectual means of salvation, not from any virtue in them, or in him that doth administer them; but only by the blessing of Christ, and the working of His Spirit in them that by faith receive them.

92. What is a Sacrament?

> A Sacrament is a holy ordinance instituted by Christ; wherein, by sensible sign, Christ and the benefits of the new covenant are represented, sealed, and applied to believers.

93. Which are the Sacraments of the New Testament?

> The Sacraments of the New Testament are Baptism, and the Lord's Supper.

94. What is Baptism?

> Baptism is a Sacrament, wherein the washing with water, in the name of the Father, and of the Son, and of the Holy Ghost, doth signify and seal our engrafting into Christ, and partaking of the benefits of the covenant of grace, and our engagement to be the Lord's.

95. To whom is Baptism to be administered?

> Baptism is not to be administered to any that are out of the visible Church, till they profess their faith in Christ, and obedience to Him, but the infants of such as are members of the visible Church, are to be baptized.

[1] *Wesley's Works*, volume 6, section 4
[2] Pearl of Great Price, Book of Moses, page 120
[3] Pearl of Great Price, Book of Moses, Pages 121-122
[4] Pearl of Great Price, Book of Moses, page 134
[5] Pearl of Great Price, Book of Moses, page 145
[6] Pearl of Great Price, Book of Moses, page 149, 150
[7] Science and Health with Key to the Scriptures; Mary Baker Eddy, pages 584, 581
[8] http://christianscience.com/member-resources/for-churches/branch-churches-and-societies/information-and-resources/statement-of-baptism
[9] Luther's Small Catechism, page 16-17
[10] Luther's Small Catechism, page 174

Appendix F
3000 BAPTISMS IN ONE DAY

In the early days of my ministry, I had the experience of meeting an individual that felt he could reject the Bible entirely, because of what he believed was the ridiculous claim of baptizing three thousand individuals in one day. Sporadically, this canard is revived to cast dust into the air.

While I accept what is written in the Scriptures as truth and need no evidence beyond the recorded words, the issue is considered and answered as follows.

QUESTION:

Was it actually possible to immerse three thousand individuals on one day?

ANSWER:

The place to look for the answer is in the questioned text.

The first principle of biblical interpretation is, and must always remain, that the words of the text must be accepted to be inspired, inerrant, and infallible. Any confusion is on our part and not on that of the Scripture. With that premise, we approach the text.

Acts 2:1 And when the day of Pentecost was fully come, they were all with one accord in one place. 2 And suddenly there came a sound from heaven as of a rushing mighty wind, and it filled all the house where they were sitting. 3 And there appeared unto them cloven tongues like as of fire, and it sat upon each of them. 4 And they were all filled with the Holy Ghost, and began to speak with other tongues, as the Spirit gave them utterance. 5 And there were dwelling at Jerusalem Jews, devout men, out of every nation under heaven. 6 Now when this was noised abroad, the multitude came together, and were confounded, because that every man heard them speak in his own language. 7 And they were all amazed and marvelled, saying one to another, Behold, are not all these which speak Galilaeans? 8 And how hear we every man in our own tongue, wherein we were born? 9 Parthians, and Medes, and Elamites, and the dwellers in Mesopotamia, and in Judaea, and Cappadocia, in Pontus, and Asia, 10 Phrygia, and Pamphylia, in Egypt, and in the parts of Libya about Cyrene, and strangers of Rome, Jews and proselytes, 11 Cretes and Arabians, we do hear them speak in our tongues the wonderful works of God. 12 And they were all amazed, and were in doubt, saying one to another, What meaneth this? 13 Others mocking said, These men are full of new wine. 14 But Peter, standing up with the eleven, lifted up his voice, and said unto them, Ye men of Judaea, and all ye that dwell at Jerusalem, be this known unto you, and hearken to my words: 15 For these are not drunken, as ye suppose, seeing it is but the third hour of the day. 16 But this is that which was spoken by the prophet Joel; 17 And it shall come to pass in the last days, saith God, I will pour out of my Spirit upon all flesh: and your sons and your daughters shall prophesy, and your young men shall see visions, and your old men shall dream dreams: 18 And on my servants and on my handmaidens I will pour out in those days of my Spirit; and they shall prophesy: 19 And I will show wonders in heaven above, and signs in the earth beneath; blood, and fire, and vapour of smoke: 20 The sun shall be turned into darkness, and the moon into blood, before that great and notable day of the Lord come: 21 And it shall come to pass, that whosoever shall call on the name of the Lord shall be saved. 22 Ye men of Israel, hear these words; Jesus of Nazareth, a man approved of God among you by miracles and wonders and signs, which God did by him in the midst of you, as ye yourselves also know: 23 Him, being delivered by the determinate counsel and foreknowledge of God, ye have taken, and by wicked hands have crucified and slain: 24 Whom God hath raised up, having loosed the pains of death: because it was not possible that he should be holden of it. 25 For David speaketh concerning him, I foresaw the Lord always before my face, for he is on my right hand, that I should not be moved: 26 Therefore did my heart rejoice, and my tongue was glad; moreover also my flesh shall rest in hope: 27 Because thou wilt not leave my soul in hell, neither wilt thou suffer thine Holy One to see corruption. 28 Thou hast made known to me the ways of life; thou shalt make me full of joy with thy countenance. 29 Men and brethren, let me freely speak unto you of the patriarch David, that he is both dead and buried, and his sepulchre is with us unto this day. 30 Therefore being a prophet, and knowing that God had sworn with an oath to him, that of the fruit of his loins, according to the flesh, he would raise up Christ to sit on his throne; 31 He seeing this before spake of the resurrection of Christ, that his soul was not left in hell, neither his flesh did see corruption. 32 This Jesus hath God raised up, whereof we all are witnesses. 33 Therefore being by the right hand of God exalted, and having received of the Father the promise of the Holy Ghost, he hath shed forth this, which ye now see and hear. 34 For David is not ascended into the heavens: but he saith himself, The Lord said unto my Lord, Sit thou on my right hand, 35 Until I make thy foes thy footstool. 36 Therefore let all the house of Israel know assuredly, that God hath made that same Jesus, whom ye have crucified, both Lord and Christ. 37 Now when they heard this, they were pricked in their heart, and said unto Peter and to the rest of the apostles, Men and brethren, what shall we do? 38 Then Peter said unto them, Repent, and be baptized every one of you in the name of Jesus Christ for the remission of sins, and ye shall receive the gift of the Holy Ghost. 39 For the promise is unto you, and to your children, and to all that are afar off, even as many as the Lord our God shall call. 40 And with many other words did he testify and exhort, saying, Save yourselves from this untoward generation. 41 **Then they that gladly received his word were baptized: and the same day there were added unto them about three thousand souls.** 42 And they continued stedfastly in the apostles' doctrine and fellowship, and in breaking of bread, and in prayers. 43 And fear came upon every soul: and many wonders and signs were done by the apostles. 44 And all that believed were together, and had all things common; 45 And sold their possessions and goods, and parted them to all men, as every man had need. 46 And they, continuing daily with one accord in the temple, and breaking bread from house to house, did eat their meat with gladness and singleness of heart, 47 Praising God, and having favour with all the people. And the Lord **added to the church** daily such as should be saved.

Through the wording of this passage would seem to be unmistakable and the apparent conclusions undeniable, nonetheless, the passage has been used to produce conflict and heresy. For instance, the thirty-eighth verse has been promoted as teaching that salvation is *by baptism*—that doctrine is false and is answered elsewhere in this paper.

Other questions have been raised regarding the text, in particular, the possibility that three thousand individual believers could be immersed in one day. It is suggested that the apostles could not physically accomplish the task and that, even if they could have done so, Jerusalem did not have sufficient water available to do so.

These supposed impossibilities are used to promote affusion (pouring or sprinkling) rather than immersion or to teach a *baptism in the Spirit* instead of *baptism with water.* The fact that Peter clearly separates *the gift of the Spirit* from the act of baptism is simply disregarded by these individuals.

Notice the events and the order in which these occurred:

1. Peter preached the Gospel. (verses 14-36)
2. Among those that heard the preaching were individuals that came under conviction through that preaching and asked what they could do about their sin of rejecting Christ. (verse 37)
3. Peter told them to repent and to be baptized. (verses 38-40)
4. Those who believed were then baptized. (verse 41) The baptism followed their belief and was the public profession of that belief.
5. Those baptized believers were added by their baptism to an entity identified as *them,* which is the church at Jerusalem. (verse 41-47)

All these activities occurred the same day. That these events took place exactly as stated in the text is unquestionable as to the record of the biblical fact; exactly how these baptisms might have been accomplished is not stated.

FIRST OBJECTION

It is alleged that even if they were physically able to accomplish the task, the twelve apostles would not have sufficient time to perform individual immersions on three thousand believers in the limited amount of time that would be left in the day. This contention is chiefly promoted by the advocates of the modes of pouring and sprinkling as evidence that immersion was either not the mode of baptism or, at least, not the primary method of baptism.

Response

To deny that the immersions were accomplished is to challenge the integrity of the Scriptures. Both the language definition and the Biblical usage for the Greek word transliterated as *baptize* have been documented in previous chapters. However, I add one more testimony, that of *the* voice that to the strongest Protestant advocates for sprinkling and pouring ought to provide them no comfort whatsoever. Since his words from this source settle all other issues of doctrine for the majority of Protestants, one wonders why these are ignored.

> "Whether the person baptized is to be wholly immersed, and that whether once or thrice, or whether he is only to be sprinkled with water, is not of the least consequence: churches should be at liberty to adopt either, according to the diversity of climates, although it is evident that the term *baptize* means to immerse, and that this was the form used by the primitive church."

To save my reader the journey to the endnotes, those are the words of John Calvin, as found in *Institutes of the Christian Religion, Book Four,* Chapter 15, Section 19, page 1045.

If Christians or churches have *the liberty*

to adopt (or adapt) the command concerning baptism according to climates (another translation of *Institutes* reads *cultures*), who is to determine those commands that are inviolable? This expressed attitude of Calvin explains his advocacy of his other doctrines; those collectively assigned the title of Calvinism. When a given word of Scripture may be adjusted and altered in definition to suit geography or climate then the word of GOD becomes malleable and is no longer immutable. This latitudinarian approach to the interpretation of the words of Scripture is more cultic than orthodox.

The assertion of the authority to set aside the Biblical record of the practice of John the Baptist, Jesus of Nazareth, Peter of Capernaum, Philip of Jerusalem, Saul of Tarsus, and every church in the New Testament is megalomaniacal.[1] The desire for that authority is not Biblical in origin. The spirit that instigates that desire is not the Holy Spirit. Eve was the first of humanity to succumb to the concept of the words of GOD having meaning other than the definition of the words. Any individual, whether human or spirit that manipulates the word of GOD has a self-serving motive.

The willingness to ignore the examples of Scripture and the capacity to substitute different terms for the words given by the Holy Ghost to holy men of old by individuals that claim affinity to Scripture and to the GOD that gave the Scripture is the combination that produces the aberrant doctrines of the cults. No believer ought to yield to that temptation.

In chapter six of Lewis Carroll's *Through*

the *Looking Glass*,[2] the character Humpty Dumpty vocalizes the spirit that underlies this concept of the exploitation of the words of scripture for convenience and expediency.

> 'When I use a word,' Humpty Dumpty said, in rather a scornful tone, 'it means just what I choose it to mean—neither more nor less.'
>
> 'The question is,' said Alice, 'whether you can make words mean so many different things.'
>
> 'The question is,' said Humpty Dumpty, 'which is to be master—that's all.'

I have written of Humpty Dumpty theologians. These are men and women who refuse to allow the words of Scripture to be the master; they usurp that position to themselves. These advocates of accommodation to times, places, and circumstances accuse the person that holds to the authority of the word of GOD of bibliolatry—worshippers of the words rather than worship of GOD.

In the mold of Humpty Dumpty, these individuals have decided that their intellect or the wisdom of their authoritative spiritual teacher is sufficient to impose their definitions upon the words of GOD. That arrogance leads to idolatry, even if it is titled scholarship.

The Greek word transliterated for us as *baptize* has the basic understanding of *to immerse*. To impose upon the word *baptism* a definition designed for agreement with a preconceived philosophy is poor scholarship and unwarranted tampering with the text.

The verse is unmistakable in its assertion: "Then they that gladly received his word were baptized: and the same day there were added unto them about three thousand souls." There is no ambiguity. They heard; they believed; they were baptized; they were added. The hearing, the receiving, the baptizing, and the adding all transpired on the same day.

We may speculate as to *how* those baptisms were accomplished and our speculation may or may not be accurate; however, the fact is never to be questioned. We will either accept the Scripture or reject the Scripture.

The Apostle Peter begins his response around 9 A.M. (verse 15). While I concede that the passage might not present the entire message that Peter preached and does not offer any portions of the messages that others of the Twelve preached,[3] the Twelve still could have started to baptize the believers before the late morning passed, continuing at least until sundown.

The date was forty days after the resurrection or some six weeks following Passover.[4] Sunset in Jerusalem for early May is approximately 7:20 and for mid June about 7:50.[5] Depending upon the beginning of the baptisms, the day would have provided several hours of daylight (as much as over ten hours) within which to baptize.

However, to make ample allowances for preparation and to be conservative, we will use only seven hours. Dividing the three thousand individuals by seven hours would require about four hundred and thirty baptisms per hour.

If we suppose that only the twelve apostles actually performed these three thousand baptisms, each apostle would need to average baptizing thirty-five or thirty-six individuals during each of the five hours. While this might not be impossible with good coordination, it assuredly would be exhausting. Were each candidate to be prepared and ready to step into place, it is possible in theory that it might be done; *but it would not seem to be practical.*

However, that is not our only option to consider. The church could authorize any individual to baptize since the authority to baptize resides in the church and not with any given individual. Therefore, the seventy[6] who also had been *appointed* by the LORD Jesus could have been used to baptize. Since the number one hundred twenty appears to have included only the male members,[7] all of the men could have been authorized to baptize.[8] If the seventy assisted the twelve, then each *baptizer* needed to baptize only thirty-six individuals within the seven hours. If the one hundred twenty were involved, then the number drops to only twenty-five. Whether the eighty-two or the one hundred and twenty baptized, scarcely more than an hour would have been required.

The alleged impossibility of immersing three thousand individuals in the span of one afternoon is simply not a valid objection. More than one church in modern times has laid claim to baptizing in excess of three thousand individuals in one day.[9]

SECOND OBJECTION

It is firmly stated that there was insufficient water available in Jerusalem for the disciples to perform 3000 baptisms by immersion.

RESPONSE

There are those who do object to baptism by immersion by suggesting that Jerusalem had insufficient water for such massive baptisms. Since the text affirms the event, no validation of waters sources is required.

However, the archaeological record reveals that Jerusalem had several pools in the First Century.[10] Among these, the pool of Siloam or the pool of Bethesda (both are spring fed) would certainly have been available. The quantity of water required was present and accessible. This objection is also without any merit.

SUMMATION

The biblically attested truth and the historically assured fact is that on one day three thousand individuals actually were immersed in baptism. Scripture plainly states that these individuals were baptized by being buried in the waters of baptism and raised to walk in newness of life as a picture of personal identification with the LORD Jesus Christ and as an act of public identification with the followers of the LORD Jesus Christ. That these immersions took place under and upon the authority of a New Testament Church is in keeping with the revealed pattern of Scripture. All contrary suggestions are rejected as being unscriptural.

---

[1] Merriam-Webster 11th Collegiate Dictionary: delusional mental disorder that is marked by feelings of personal omnipotence and grandeur.

[2] One of the many reasons for which I do not recommend the writings of Lewis Carroll.

[3] That others beside Peter spoke that day is evident in the text. Acts 2:4 And **they** were all filled with the Holy Ghost, and began to speak with other tongues, as the Spirit gave them utterance. ... 7 And **they** were all amazed and marvelled, saying one to another, Behold, are not all **these** which speak Galilaeans? ... 13 Others mocking said, **These** men are full of new wine. ... 15 For **these** are not drunken, as ye suppose, seeing it is *but* the third hour of the day.

[4] The dates for the Passover in the potential years for the Crucifixion are obtainable.

Year	Full moon	Time	Julian Day	Passover Abib 15
26	April 20 Abib 14	2 p.m.	Saturday	April 20
27	April 9 Abib 14	6 p.m.	Wednesday	April 9
28	March 29 Abib 14	5 a.m.	Monday	March 29
29	April 17 Abib 14	5 a.m.	Sunday	April 17
30	April 6 Abib 14	10 p.m.	Thursday	April 6
31	March 27 Abib 14	1 p.m.	Tuesday	March 27
32	April 14 Abib 14	11 a.m.	Monday	April 14
33	April 3 Abib 14	5 p.m.	Friday	April 3
34	March 23 Abib 14	5 p.m.	Tuesday	March 23

This is derived from information provided by the Naval Oceanography Portal [http://www.usno.navy.mil/USNO/astronomical-applications/data-services/spring-phenom].

This is a service of the United States Naval Meteorology and Oceanography Command (NMOC). The website "provides critical information from the ocean depths to the most distant reaches of space, meeting needs in the military, scientific, and civilian communities."

[5] Sunrise and sunset in Jerusalem. http://www.timeanddate.com/worldclock/astronomy.html?n=110

[6] Luke 10:1 After these things the Lord appointed other seventy also, and sent them two and two before his face into every city and place, whither he himself would come. 2 Therefore said he unto them, The harvest truly *is* great, but the labourers *are* few: pray ye therefore the Lord of the harvest, that he would send forth labourers into his harvest. 3 Go your ways: behold, I send you forth as lambs among wolves. 4 Carry neither purse, nor scrip, nor shoes: and salute no man by the way. 5 And into whatsoever house ye enter, first say, Peace *be* to this house. 6 And if the son of peace be there, your peace shall rest upon it: if not, it shall turn to you again. 7 And in the same house remain, eating and drinking such things as they give: for the labourer is worthy of his hire. Go not from house to house. 8 And into whatsoever city ye enter, and they receive you, eat such things as are set before you: 9 And heal the sick that are therein, and say unto them, The kingdom of God is come nigh unto you. 10 But into whatsoever city ye enter, and they receive you not, go your ways out into the streets of the same, and say, 11 Even the very dust of your city, which cleaveth on us, we do wipe off against you: notwithstanding be ye sure of this, that the kingdom of God is come nigh unto you. 12 But I say unto you, that it shall be more tolerable in that day for Sodom, than for that city. 13 Woe unto thee, Chorazin! woe unto thee, Bethsaida! for if the mighty works had been done in Tyre and Sidon, which have been done in you, they had a great while ago repented, sitting in sackcloth and ashes. 14 But it shall be more tolerable for Tyre and Sidon at the judgment, than for you. 15 And thou, Capernaum, which art exalted to heaven, shalt be thrust down to hell. 16 He that heareth you heareth me; and he that despiseth you despiseth me; and he that despiseth me despiseth him that sent me. 17 And the seventy

returned again with joy, saying, Lord, even the devils are subject unto us through thy name.

⁷ Acts 1:15 And in those days Peter stood up in the midst of the disciples, and said, (the number of names together were about an hundred and twenty,) 16 Men *and* brethren, this scripture must needs have been fulfilled, which the Holy Ghost by the mouth of David spake before concerning Judas, which was guide to them that took Jesus.

Acts 2:41 Then they that gladly received his word were baptized: and the same day there were added *unto them* about three thousand souls.

Acts 4:4 Howbeit many of them which heard the word believed; and the number of the men was about five thousand.

⁸ Before anyone faults me for chauvinism, I simply cite the record of Scripture that every baptism in the New Testament was performed by a male.

⁹ The inclusion of any church among these claims does not indicate my endorsement of the organization, the claim, or the source; these are included only to show the possibility of massive baptisms within a relatively limited time. First Baptist Church of Hammond Indiana reported six thousand baptisms in a twenty-four hour period in 1999. Saddleback Church, Lake Forest, California, planned to baptize three thousand on Saturday, March 28, 2009. Others have written of great numbers of baptisms by immersion on a given day. A simple internet search produced the following claims.

Claim 1: 402 baptisms by immersion in 90 minutes
http://perrynoble.com/blog/a-historical-weekend-yeah-god

Claim 2: Pastor Rick Warren, Saddleback Church, has reported that he baptized 800 in one day. "Warren said he was inspired to start the fast after performing 800 baptisms in one day and realizing most people he baptized were overweight."
http://abcnews.go.com/Health/daniel-diet-straight-bible/story?id=21029387

Claim 3: "It was difficult to find enough pastors to baptize all these new converts. Ordained Adventist ministers who didn't work for the local conference were called in to help. Fifty pastors stood in a line in waist-

deep water about 200 feet off-shore at a shallow South Pacific beach. Then lines of baptismal candidates dressed in white walked out toward them. About 5,000 people stood in the water together. Just as it was difficult to know how many were at the meetings, it was difficult to know how many were actually baptized. Pastors who reported so far say they baptized 100 people each. That suggests a figure of 5,000 when all reports are in."
http://news.adventist.org/all-news/news/go/2012-09-04/in-papua-new-guinea-thousands-of-new-adventists-baptized-in-one-day/
Claim 4: Twenty thousand people baptized in one day (video)
https://www.youtube.com/watch?v=J-8SkViTEqQ

[10] A web site devoted to Roman Aqueducts provides the following information on ten identified First Century pools in Jerusalem.
http://www.romanaqueducts.info/aquasite/jerusalempools/

Pools of Jerusalem	Capacity (m3)
1. Siloam Pools	Unknown
2. Solomon's Pools	228.000
3. Temple Mount cisterns	40.000
4. Hezekiah's Pool	30.000
5. Serpents / Sultan's Pool	50.000
6. Mamilla Pool	30.000
7. Bethesda Pools	90.000
8. Israel Pool	110.000
9. Struthion	4.500
10. Birket sitti Miriam	6.000

Previously, unknown ancient wells and reservoirs are discovered periodically in Jerusalem that date to the times of the New Testament.
http://www.jpost.com/Jewish-World/Jewish-News/Massive-reservoir-discovered-beneath-Western-Wall

ABOUT THE AUTHOR

Dr. Jerald Manley is married to Julie Hudson; 2014 will be their 50th Anniversary. They have three children and four grandchildren. He has been preaching since 1958 and pastoring since 1962. He has been in his present pastorate since 1975. He has a B.A. from Bob Jones University, a M.DIV. from Louisiana Baptist Theological Seminary, and the Doctor of Divinity from Pensacola Christian College.

He is the founder and editor of *The Baptist Heritage*. He has written *Confusion at Calvary, When Sorrows Come, The Imaginative Christianity of C. S. Lewis, Resource of Weights and Measures for the Authorized Version, The Song of songs, which is Solomon's, What the Dead Man Wrote, Between the Valleys, Avoid My Mistakes, The Wilted TULIP*, etc.

Made in the USA
Lexington, KY
31 May 2018